IMAGES
of America

AROUND MANSFIELD

I0901126

On the Cover: On June 15, 1917, area men between the ages of 21 and 31 came to the Mansfield Park to register for the World War I draft. Mansfield was an embarkation point for these servicemen. Many residents assembled to pay honor to the draftees by presenting a program focusing on patriotic songs, music, and speeches. (Courtesy of the Mansfield Area Historical Society.)

IMAGES
of America

AROUND MANSFIELD

Mansfield Area Historical Society

Vicki Blankenship
Eric Dodson
Ann Duckworth
Linda Duquesne
Kathy Short

ARCADIA
PUBLISHING

Copyright © 2013 by Mansfield Area Historical Society
ISBN 978-0-7385-9077-6

Published by Arcadia Publishing
Charleston, South Carolina

Printed in the United States of America

Library of Congress Control Number: 2012947057

For all general information, please contact Arcadia Publishing:
Telephone 843-853-2070
Fax 843-853-0044
E-mail sales@arcadiapublishing.com
For customer service and orders:
Toll-Free 1-888-313-2665

Visit us on the Internet at www.arcadiapublishing.com

This book is dedicated to those whose strength and tenacity led to the formation of the town of Mansfield, "Gem of the Ozarks."

Contents

ACKNOWLEDGMENTS

This book would not have been possible without the cooperation of many Mansfield area residents who donated their time and their photographs. Special thanks to the following individuals and organizations for supporting the Mansfield Area Historical Society in its efforts to document and record the local history around Mansfield:

Darrel Adamson, Bill Anderson, Marsha Appleby, Bank of Mansfield, Elaine Barlett, David Barnett, Sherry Beasley, Floyd Blankenship, Jerry and Shirley Bogart, Teresa Cantrell, Willie Cantrell, Gloria Bogart Carter, Cleo Chambers, David Climer, Donna Climer, Jean Coday, Joe Coday, Doyle and Mona Cox, Jean Coy, George Davis, Leah Davis, Sharon Davis, Kay Dennis, Ken Dennis, Larry Dennis, Peggy Dennis, Eddie and Mary Margaret Dodson, Cecil and Evelyn Duquesne, Glen and Mary Eggleston, Alice Findley, Dale and Kathleen Freeman, Bob Goss, Greg Goss, Lola Gray, Jan Hale, Darlene Hatcher, James and Sue Jones, Faye Keith, John and Nina Lemons, John and Teresa Letsinger, Jim Light, George and Jan Manville, the Carl Mays family, Dale McGaw, Murl and Marjorie Pierson, Bill and Janet Newton, Roy and Shirlee Nichols, Katie Peak, the Mary Riley collection, Mike and Connie Roberts, J.D. Ross, Betty Schipper, Lecia Short, Marge Short, Randy Short, Daisy Shull, the Volney and Ilenia Smith collection, Virginia Steury, Dean and Winona Tarbutton, Darren Taylor, Virginia Taylor, Robert Towe, Elva Tripp, Paul and Mary Tripp, Bill and Ann Turner, Sam Wampler, the Wilder Home Association, and Roger Wood.

All pictures of the Wilder family were provided courtesy of the Wilder Home Association.

All pictures of the Mays family were provided courtesy of the Carl Mays family.

All other pictures were donated to the Mansfield Area Historical Society for use in this book.

INTRODUCTION

Early settlers of the Mansfield area came primarily for the fertile farmland and abundant water resources, like the Gasconade River and Bryant Creek. Bounty land was awarded to soldiers of past wars, including the War of 1812. In the 1840s, the US government proclaimed local land for sale. Settlers from Tennessee and Kentucky, who excelled in hunting, trapping, and foraging, flooded the area for farmland.

Native Americans from the Cherokee and Choctaw tribes dropped off the Trail of Tears as it passed through Wright County. They assimilated themselves into the culture but were forced to hide their heritage for fear of losing their lands and their freedom. The term *Black Dutch* became a means of disguising their true roots. Area genealogists nowadays encounter problems when researching Native American ancestry.

The first church in the area was Pleasant Valley Cumberland Presbyterian Church, founded in 1841. As more settlers arrived, churches of different denominations formed to meet spiritual needs of individuals. The hardships and suffering endured by many pioneers could only be alleviated by a strong faith in God. Churches, especially those that also served as schools, became the center of community life. Eventually, many one-room schoolhouses were built in rural communities to accommodate the population growth. As a result, social activities, such as pie suppers, quilting bees, and music parties, became commonplace and centered around the schools as well as the churches.

When the Civil War began, both the Union and Confederacy claimed Missouri as theirs; it became the epitome of a border state. Families and friends found themselves on different sides of the issues and ultimately faced each other on the battlefield. Residents were terrorized by bushwhackers who used guerilla warfare to commit atrocities against families and soldiers.

The Kansas City, Fort Scott & Memphis Railroad established a watering stop in Mansfield, which led to the area becoming an actual town in 1882, founded by two railroad executives: F.M. Mansfield and George Nettleton. Successful businesses opened, mainly due to the accessibility of the railroad and the means to receive and ship items. Other industries, such as mining, contributed to the region's growth. Lead and zinc mines covered over 500 acres north of Mansfield. Mining began in the mid-1880s and continued sporadically until the 1930s. Another major business was logging. Logging was not for the faint of heart. Rugged individuals were needed to fell the large trees and hew them into railroad ties. Loads of lumber were shipped to metropolitan areas needing building supplies.

Pioneers homesteaded the land and survived off their crops, using their produce for both personal consumption and as barter for goods. The economy continued to provide jobs for the steady flow of migrant workers. Small hamlets, such as Olathe, Cedar Gap, Macomb, Odin, and London, sprang up to accommodate rural residents, as the roads to Mansfield would not be paved for years to come. These communities consisted primarily of a general store, a blacksmith shop, a cannery, a church, a post office, and a school. With the introduction of the automobile, the Good Roads organization became instrumental in upgrading and maintaining permanent roads. Country people began to travel to Mansfield and other towns, ultimately eliminating the need for the rural establishments.

During this time, the railroad experienced several train wrecks in the Macomb area. The 1947 wreck that killed engineer Byrd Duncan and fireman Lewis Sanders was the only one that incurred fatalities. In the 1930s a freight train derailed, spilling a carload of vinegar and creating a pond that reeked for 20 years. In the 1940s, a train carrying 200 passengers derailed, and another wreck involved a head-on collision of two passenger trains carrying Major League Baseball players. One of the most memorable train incidents occurred in 1899 when robbers blew up a baggage car and stole $364.

As the 20th century advanced, both beef and dairy farms were established. During this time, Wright County was the number-one dairy-producing region in the state of Missouri, and the area became known as the "Denmark of the Ozarks."

In 1894, the arrival of Almanzo, Laura, and Rose Wilder was barely noticed. The family purchased 40 acres of rocky, hilly land one mile east of Mansfield, which Laura named Rocky Ridge. The family operated their farm in the same way other settlers did, selling firewood from their trees, raising chickens and selling eggs, and growing orchards to sell produce. However, things were soon to change. In 1911, Laura began writing for newspapers and magazines. Her articles were primarily aimed at farmwives, like herself.

As an adult, daughter Rose Wilder left Mansfield, developing her own writing career. She wrote for the *Kansas City Post* and eventually became a war correspondent during World War I. Rose also wrote the books *Free Land* and *Let the Hurricane Roar.* She persuaded her mother to write about her childhood experiences. These novels, the "Little House" books, took the nation by storm, and Mansfield became known as the place where Laura Ingalls Wilder lived and wrote. Thousands of people every year travel to Mansfield to tour the museum and the two Wilder homes: the one at Rocky Ridge and the Rock House that Rose built for her parents.

Another individual who brought attention to Mansfield was Carl Mays, a major league pitcher from 1915 to 1929, who grew up in the Prairie Hollow community. Mays's childhood, like that of most other area children, was sometimes tough. After his father died, Mays assumed the responsibility of supplying food for the family. He developed his throwing accuracy by killing rabbits and squirrels with rocks in order to put meat on the table. After making it in the major leagues, Mays built a home outside Mansfield for his mother, Callie Louisa Mays. The locals dubbed it Mays Mansion. On trips to Mansfield, Carl Mays often brought waders filled with baseballs to give to the children. Using a mattress tied between two trees as a backstop, he taught area youngsters the art of pitching. He also gave old New York Yankee uniforms to the town team, the Mansfield Grays. Mays never forgot his roots, even though life took him across the country.

Mansfield poet Lon Dennis describes the Mansfield we know:

"What Makes Mansfield Grow?"

There's a bustling little city
Down among the Ozark hills;
In the land of balmy sunshine
Smiling valleys, sparkling rills.
Mansfield, gem of all the Ozarks,
Is a city all should know.
Blue grass pastures, fields of clover;
These are what make Mansfield grow.

All around are fields and vineyards
Where fine fruits and berries grow,
And in fertile fields and meadows
Farmers reap just what they sow.
And at morning, noon, and evening
You can hear the cows' soft low;
Fruits and berries, cows and chickens;
These are what make Mansfield grow.

People courteous, kind and friendly
In our little town are found;
And the signs of push and progress
Can be seen on every hand.
Shops and factories, stores and hotels,
All found in a row;
Hustling people, schools and churches;
These are what make Mansfield grow.

Clear, pure air, and balmy sunshine
Make a climate hard to beat,
Wells and springs and sparkling branches
Furnish water cold and sweet.
Highways running all directions
Lead you where you want to go;
Health, contentment, push, and progress;
These are what make Mansfield grow.

One

In These Hills

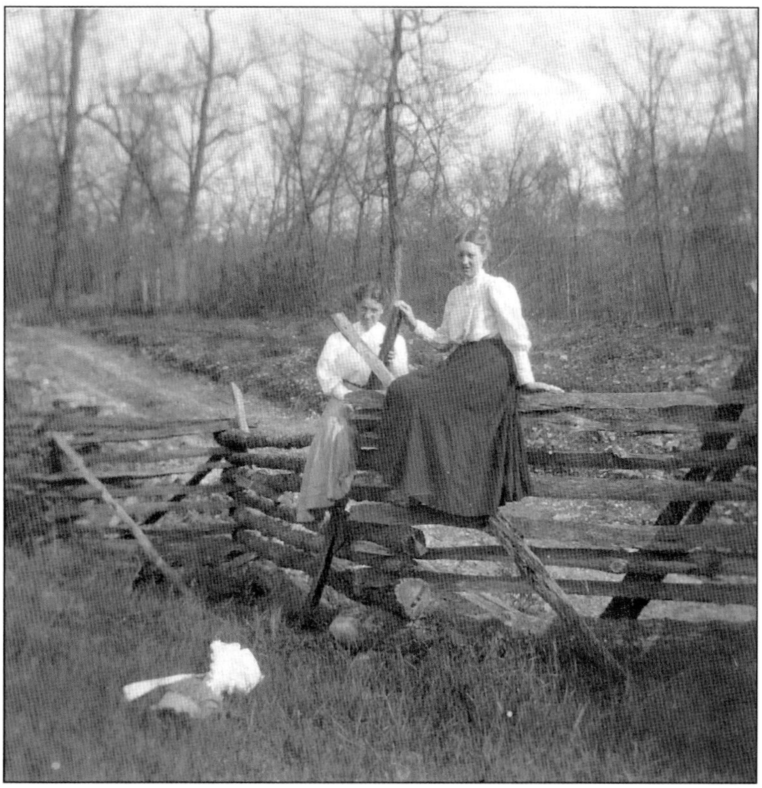

For generations, the Ozark hills have attracted pioneering families like the Wilders and the Mays. The rugged hills, thick timber, abundant water, and native plants were appealing to those eager to settle here and live off the land. This magical allure influenced families who were crossing the country in search of a better life to linger here.

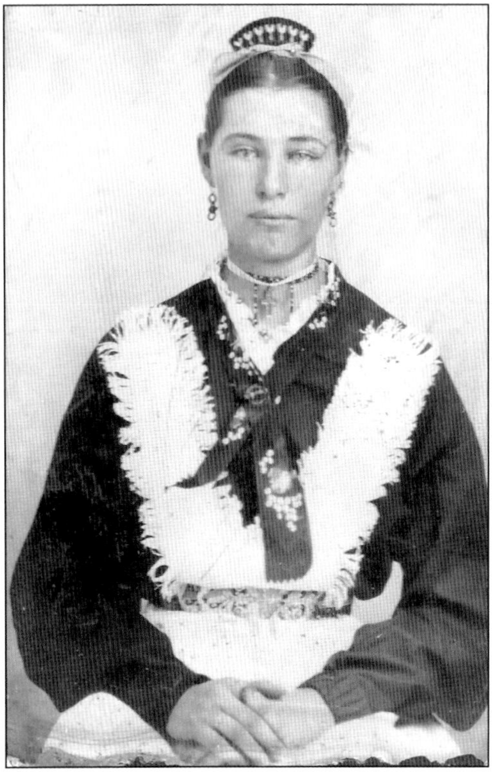

Native Americans, some of whom dropped off the Trail of Tears that wound through Wright County, were forced to hide their heritage for fear of losing their freedom and their land. Family lore recounts that Julia Ann Rippee, left, was of Native American ancestry. Referred to as "Black Dutch," she was most likely a Choctaw princess. Below are, from left to right, Louisa McIntosh Findley, Hazel and Bertha Stout, Amanda McIntosh Drake, and an unidentified child on the Findley Century Farm. Allegedly, Blueford McIntosh and wife Martha Papago, a Native American midwife, were raising daughters Penelope, Amanda, and Louisa in Arkansas. When she delivered babies, Martha had to leave the girls home alone. Blueford came home one day to find the girls cold, hungry, and frightened by a panther that had tried to claw through the floorboards. In his anger, he moved the girls to Mansfield and left Martha behind. Afterwards, Blueford discouraged any discussion concerning their Native American heritage.

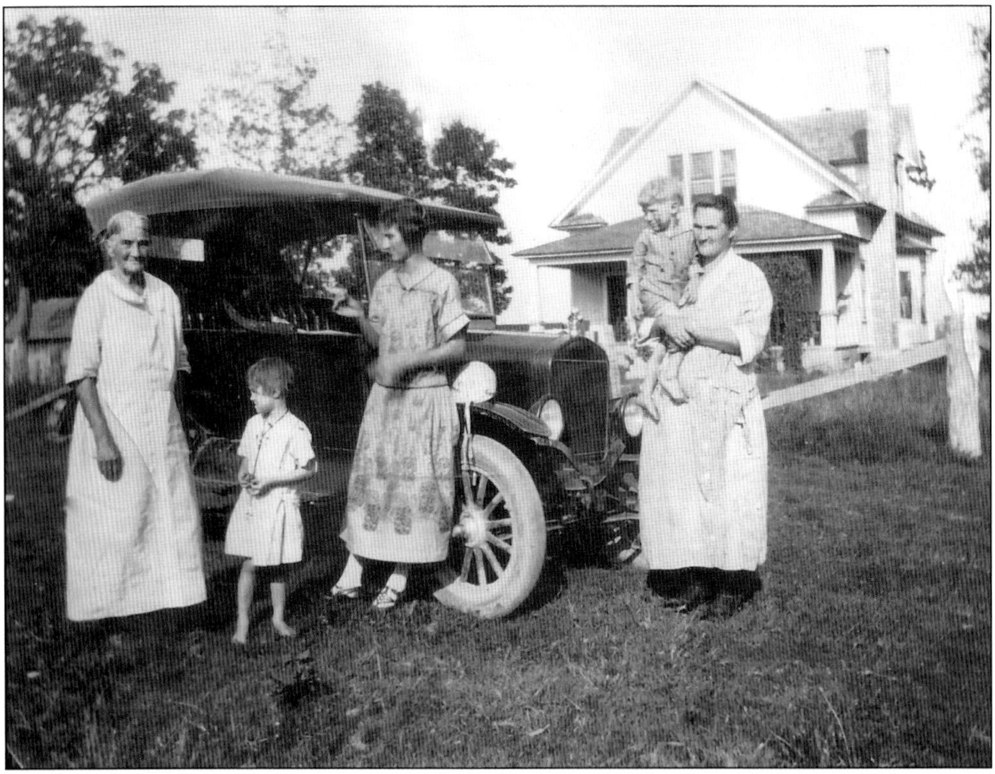

Residents of Wright County were torn apart by the effects of the Civil War. Because families were divided by loyalty, it was difficult to distinguish who was a friend and who was the enemy. These Union veterans of the Civil War are, from left to right, (first row) John Hensley, Bill Dennis, and Andy Taylor; (second row) John Rippee, Andy Newton, John Wesley Gilley, unidentified, and Loss Brazeal.

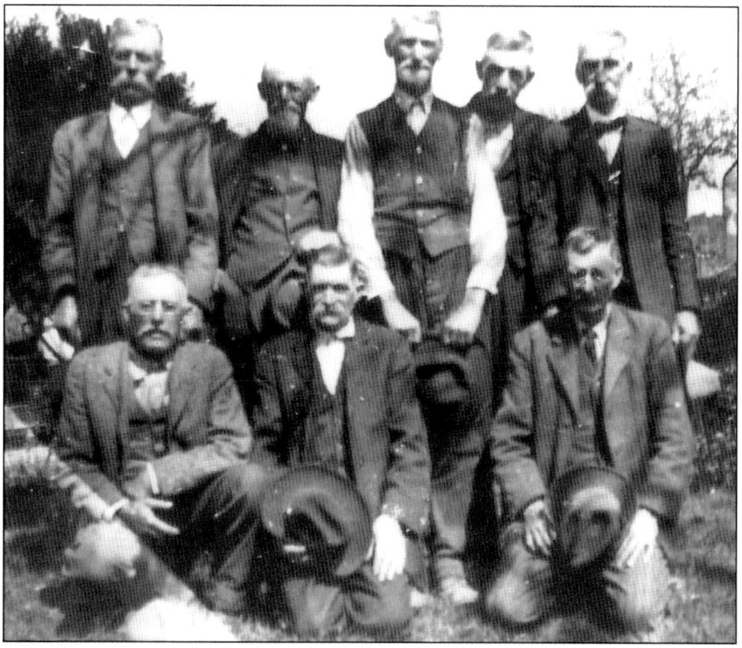

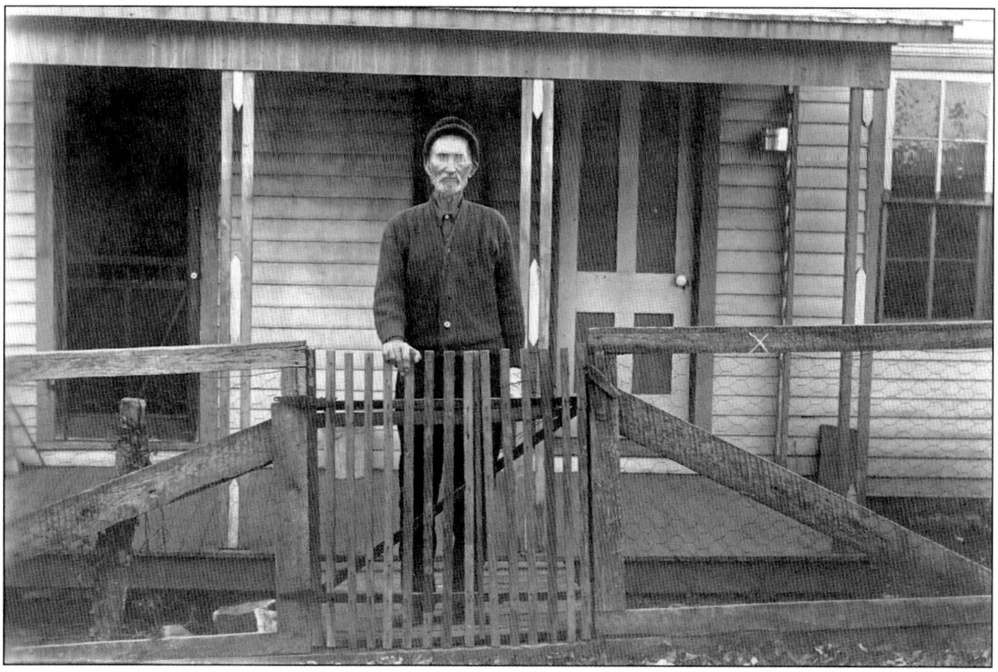

Moses Franklin Rippee, a Civil War veteran, served in both Company L and Company B of the 1st Missouri Cavalry. Many families, including the Rippees, had both northern and southern sympathizers. Prisoners were often forced to sign an allegiance to the opposing army, requiring them to fight alongside their enemy. Inwardly, these "galvanized soldiers" remained steadfast to their convictions, despite their outward actions. This would lend new meaning to the term "brother against brother."

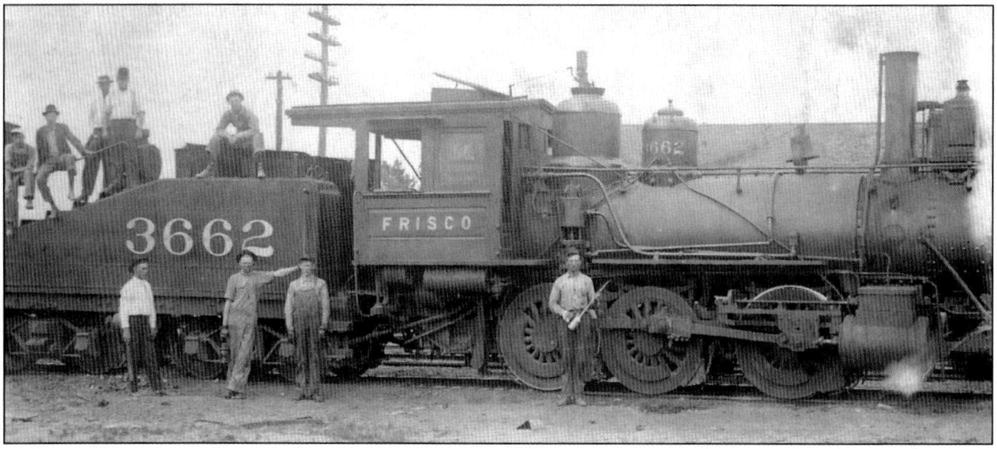

By 1881, the Kansas City, Fort Scott & Gulf Railroad reached the western side of Wright County. The railroad was working to complete the connection between Springfield, Missouri, and Memphis, Tennessee. Due to extremely steep and hilly terrain, watering stations were needed to fill the boiler of the steam locomotive every eight to ten miles. Each stop was also used for any necessary mechanical care, such as oiling and greasing.

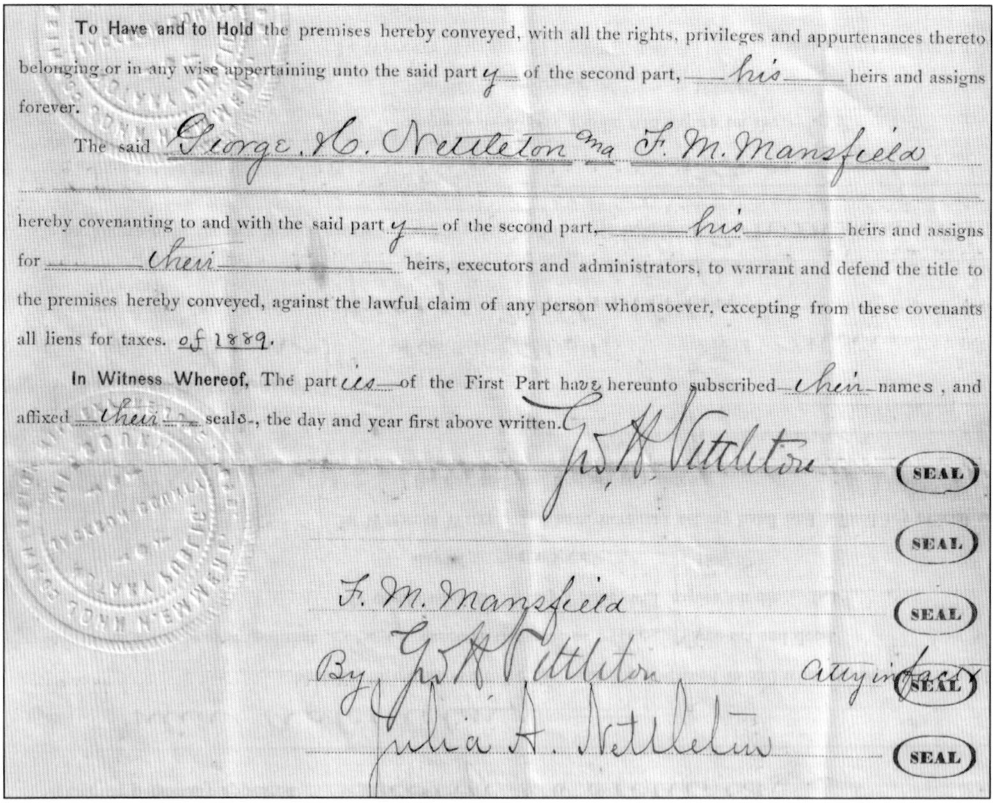

To Have and to Hold the premises hereby conveyed, with all the rights, privileges and appurtenances thereto belonging or in any wise appertaining unto the said part*y* of the second part, *his* heirs and assigns forever.

The said *George H. Nettleton and F. M. Mansfield*

hereby covenanting to and with the said part*y* of the second part, *his* heirs and assigns for *their* heirs, executors and administrators, to warrant and defend the title to the premises hereby conveyed, against the lawful claim of any person whomsoever, excepting from these covenants all liens for taxes. *of 1889.*

In Witness Whereof, The part*ies* of the First Part hav*e* hereunto subscribed *their* names, and affixed *their* seals, the day and year first above written.

Geo H. Nettleton (SEAL)

(SEAL)

F. M. Mansfield (SEAL)

By Geo H Nettleton atty in fact (SEAL)

Julia A. Nettleton (SEAL)

Also in 1881, George Nettleton and F.M. Mansfield, a Hartville attorney, approached farmers Johnnie Williams, David Moore, and Henry Smith about purchasing some of their land. Following the sales, it was learned that the railroad would soon build a watering station nearby. Nettleton and Mansfield hired Thomas Montgomery to survey and lay off the land for the townsite of Mansfield. Interestingly enough, both Nettleton and Mansfield were prominent railroad employees.

As the Memphis Line was being constructed, railroad officials began to realize the benefits of laying this line through the heart of the Ozarks. The line followed a ridge, which was a natural divide, stretching 28 miles across the county. Railroad ties were obtained from the forests along the right-of-way. Teams of oxen, horses, and mules dragged the ties into place. Steam engines provided the power for making the cuts and fills.

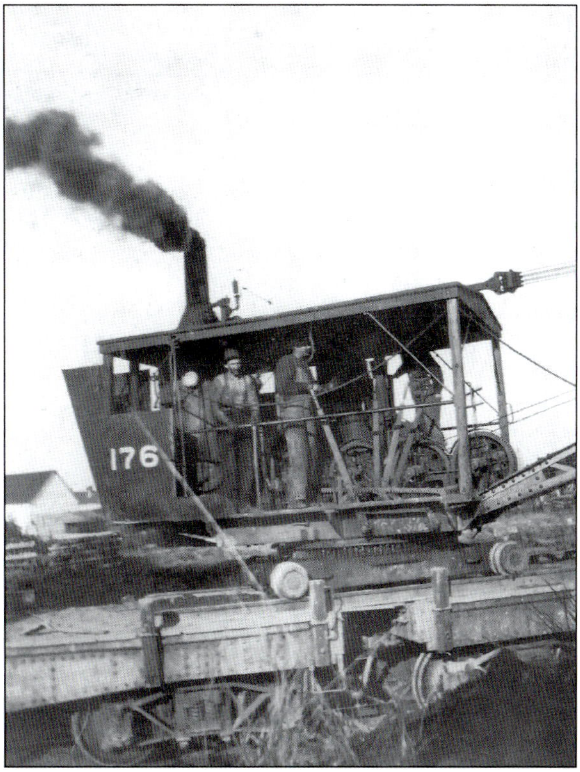

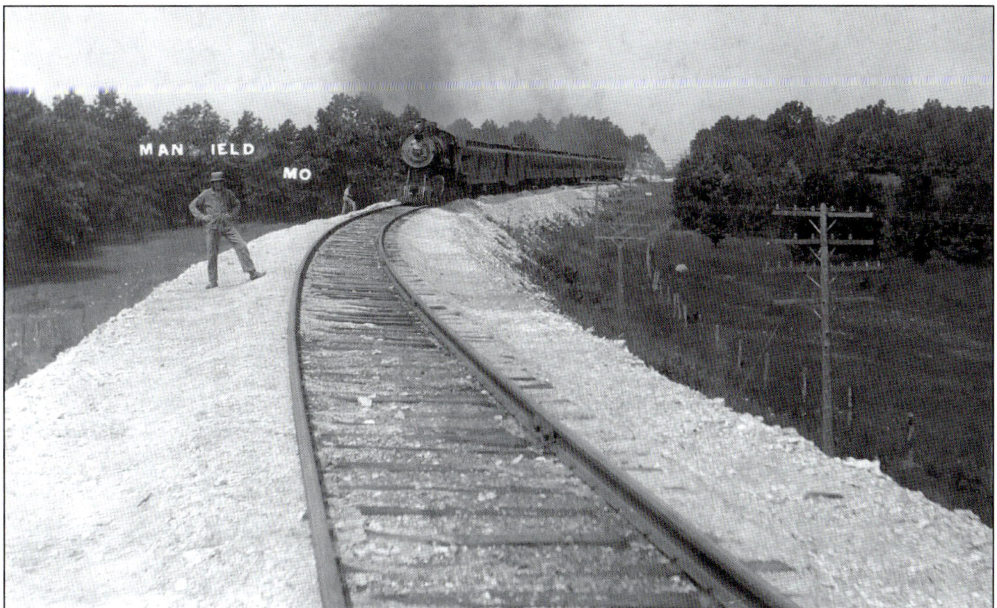

When railroad officials decided to construct the line between Memphis and Springfield, they started with two crews. One crew began in the east, and the other in the west. Workers cleared the right-of-way and graded the bed for the tracks by moving rocks and dirt with picks and shovels. Members of the original crews often stayed and became section hands, maintaining the roadbed.

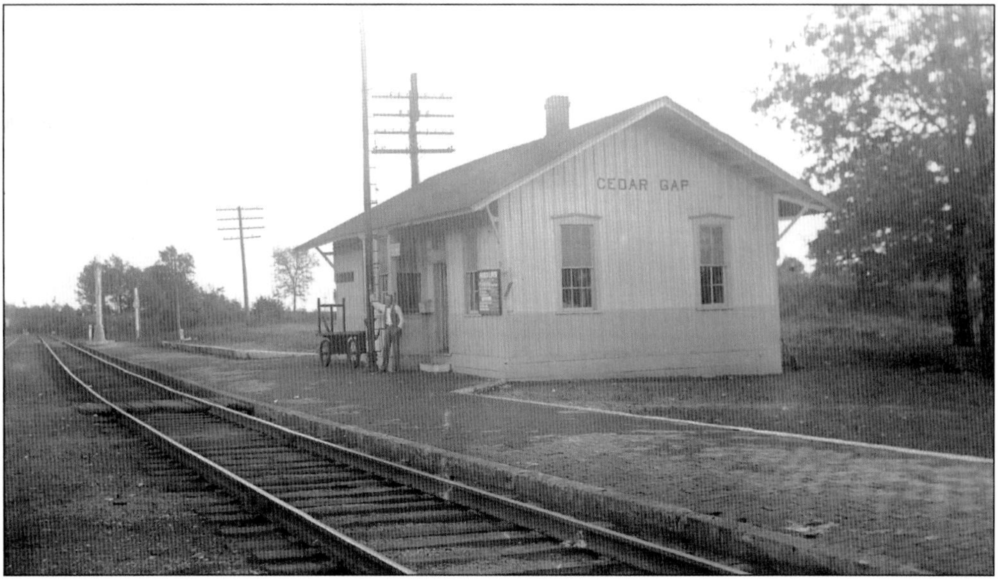

In addition to pumps and watering tanks along the rail route, small lakes were created in Wright County. Old-timers said, "The railroad went to the top of the hill and found the first flat spot and built a lake." Cedar Gap Lake, named after the grove of cedars found there, provided water so that trains could pull Lead Hill into Mansfield. Cedar Gap Depot was established in 1882.

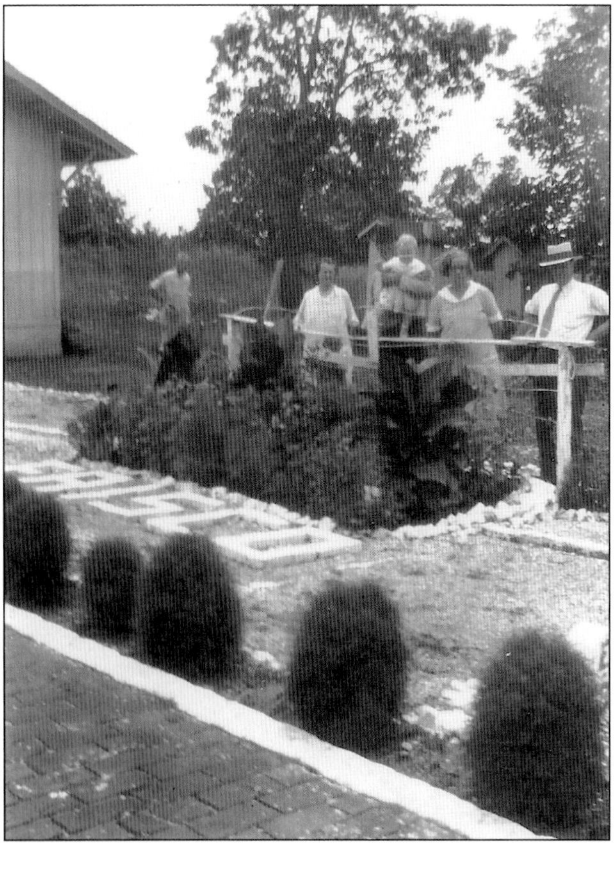

In the early 1930s, the Frisco Railroad held a contest to beautify the stops along its line. The people of Cedar Gap wanted anyone who stopped there to appreciate the beauty of their depot. The brick pathway was edged with shrubs, flowers, and a rock garden with the word *Frisco* spelled out in white stones. Passengers could use one of the two outhouses while the boiler was refilled with water.

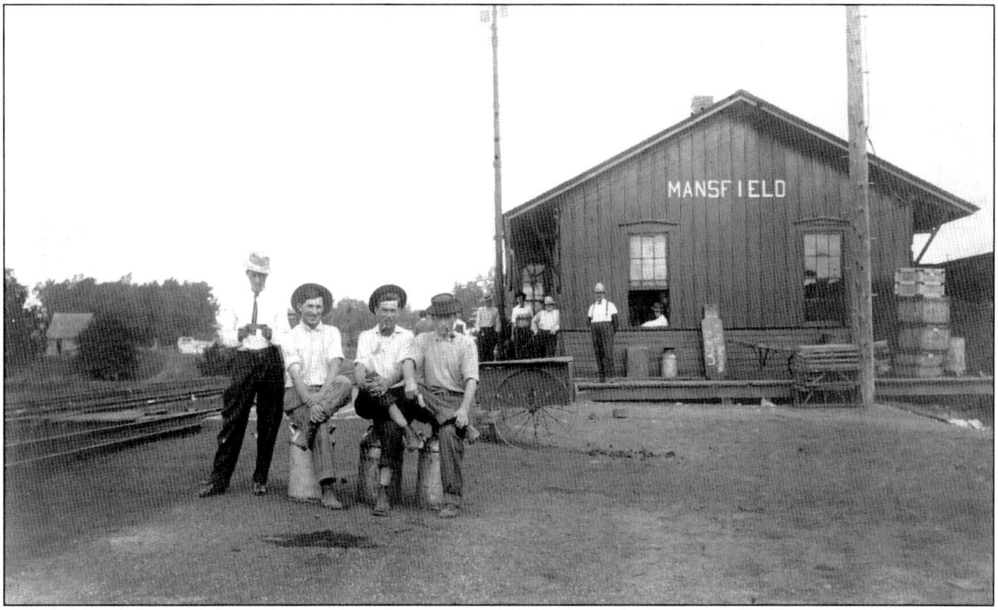

With the founding of Mansfield in 1882, a depot was established. Inside were the agent's office, the telegraph operator's room, the freight room, and the passenger waiting room. Early depot agents and managers included Chester Hawk, Mr. Jeffrys, Frank Parker, William Richey, George Burney, R.D. Harris, Jess Brazeal, and Leonard Johnson. Originally, scheduled trips were made east one day and returned west the next day.

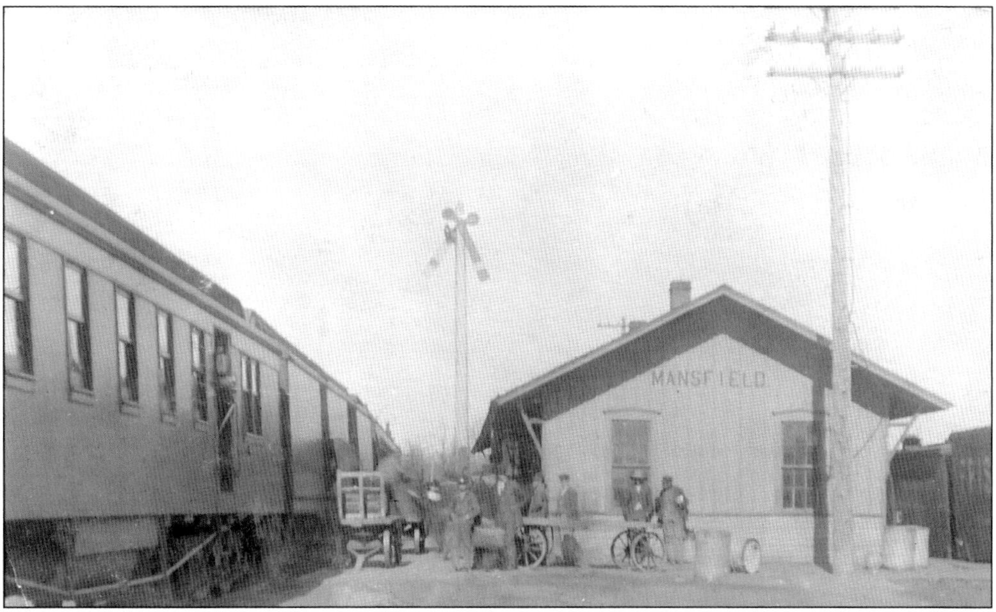

Mansfield became a distribution point for freight, raw materials, and mail. People from towns south to the Arkansas line and north to Grovespring came to conduct business there. In early years, livestock shipments averaged 70 cars per year. In the 1900s, the railroad became an important factor for locals shipping fruit and hardwood timber. Local citizens enjoyed the holiday excursions to Arkansas, for which the railroad charged only a dollar.

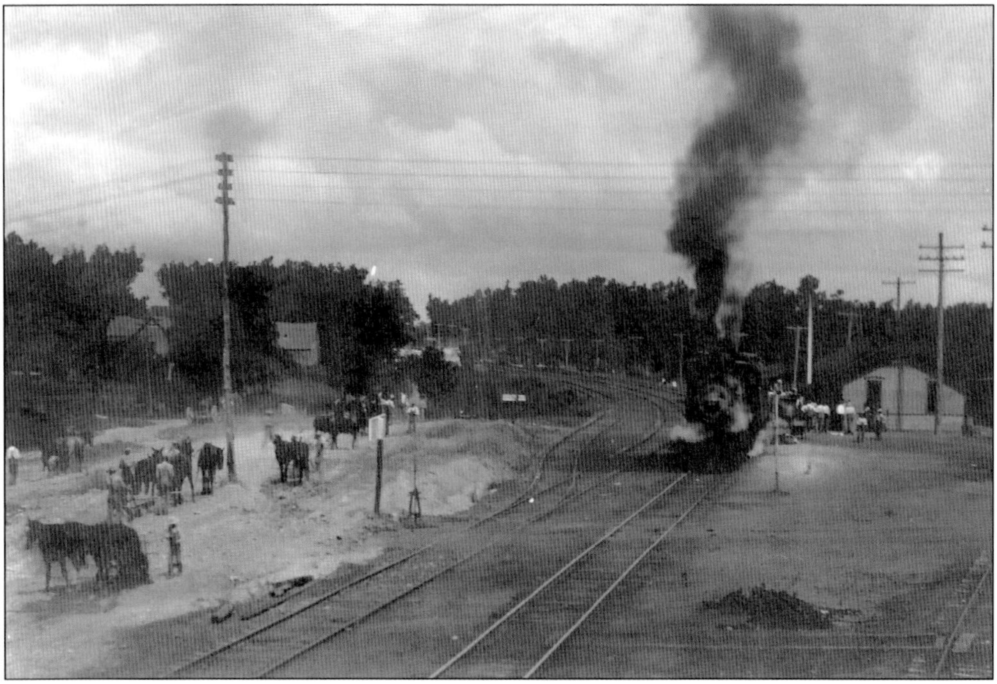

In 1907, local citizens of both Mansfield and Ava lobbied for construction of a connecting railroad. The movement was promoted by J.B. Quigley of St. Louis. The railroad bed began in Mansfield, heading south, and was built using plows and scrapers drawn by mules and horses. Due to the steep terrain, the roadbed was built around the sides of the hills to reduce the number of precipitous grades.

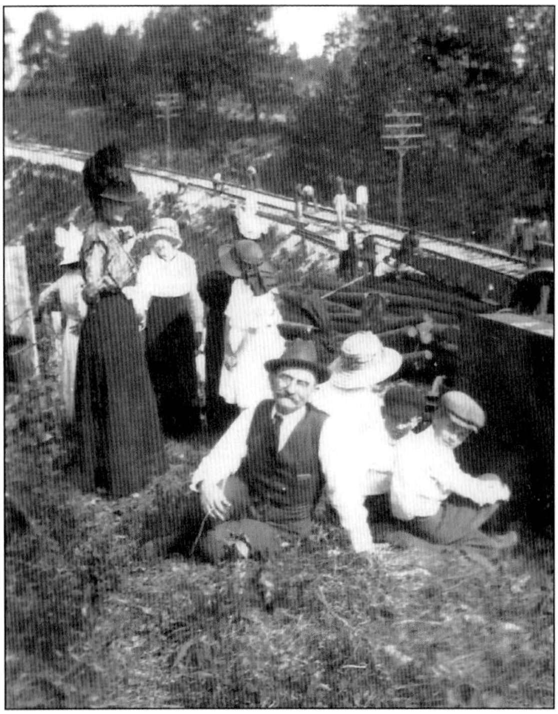

As the track was being laid southward, spectators came out to watch the progress of the Kansas City, Ozarks & Southern Railroad line. It was a festive mood, with people arriving in their Sunday best to picnic along the ridges. Railroad officials decided there would be seven stops between Mansfield and Ava. These stops were Flat Rock, Slate Hill, County Line, Alwanda, Mulligan's Gap, Mt. Zion, and Spurlock.

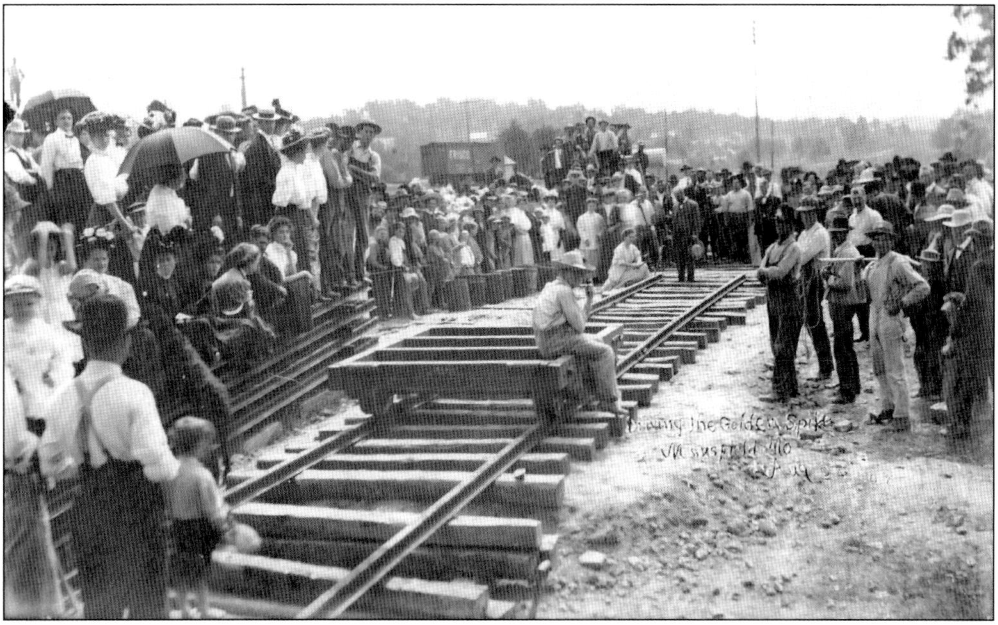

August 24, 1908, was a day of celebration in Mansfield. Huge crowds, which included the Wilder family, were in attendance for the driving of the golden spike. This gala occasion topped off the completion of the Kansas City, Ozarks & Southern Railroad, better known to locals as the Ava Southern. The highlight of this celebration was the driving of the last spike by Ava Quigley, daughter of railroad promoter J.B. Quigley.

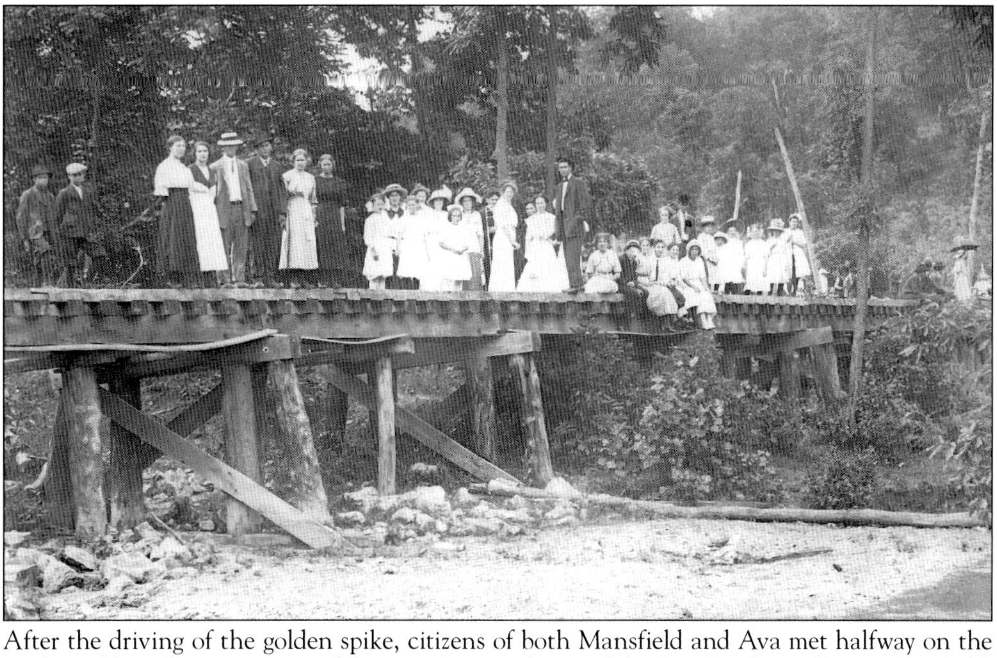

After the driving of the golden spike, citizens of both Mansfield and Ava met halfway on the tracks at Alwanda to continue celebrating the completion of the Ava Southern. A picnic was held, with both towns bringing their bands to provide merry music for the occasion. Mansfieldians, dressed in their finest, walked to the location by following the rails. This included crossing the newly-constructed wooden bridge over Bryant Creek.

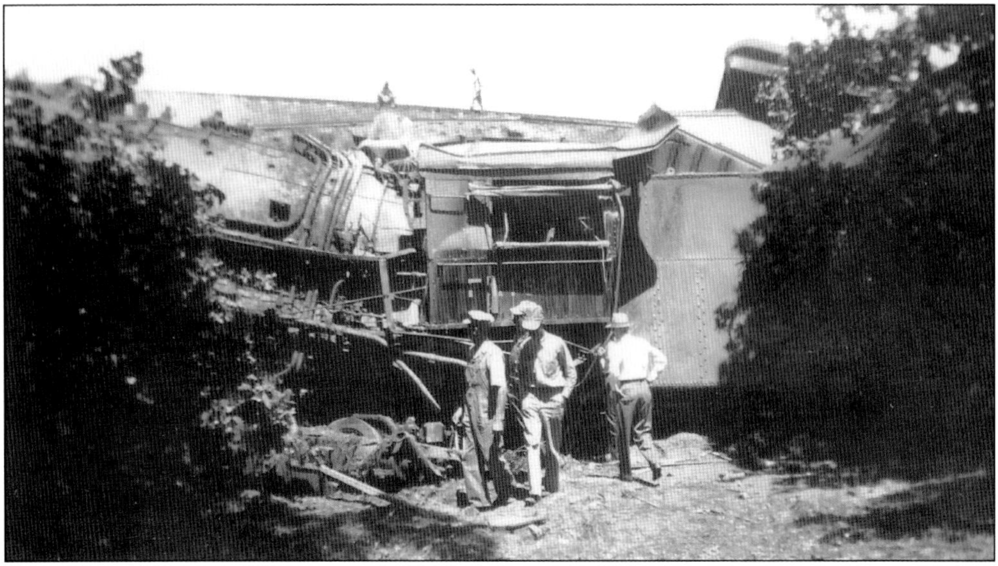

The second highest point on the Frisco Railroad is located just west of Macomb. Several train wrecks have occurred on this stretch of track. The worst one, shown in these four pictures, occurred on Memorial Day 1947. At 1:47 a.m., the Florida Special passenger train, containing the engine, two express cars, a baggage-mail car, four baggage cars, three coaches, a dining car, and three sleeping cars, derailed due to a broken rail. The locomotive and several cars plummeted down a 35-foot embankment, destroying 150 yards of ties and rails. Engineer Byrd Duncan and fireman Lewis Sanders were killed, scalded by steam. First on the scene were Bill Greenwood, the adjoining farm owner, and highway patrolman Earl Barkley. Cozella Greenwood, holding a lantern, directed traffic through their farm all night. There were no serious injuries to passengers.

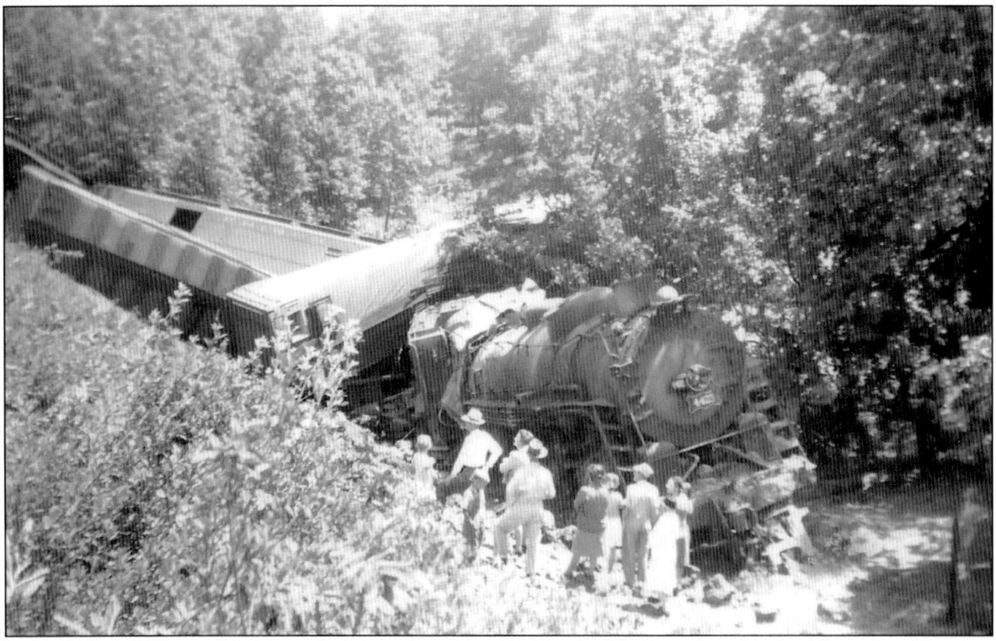

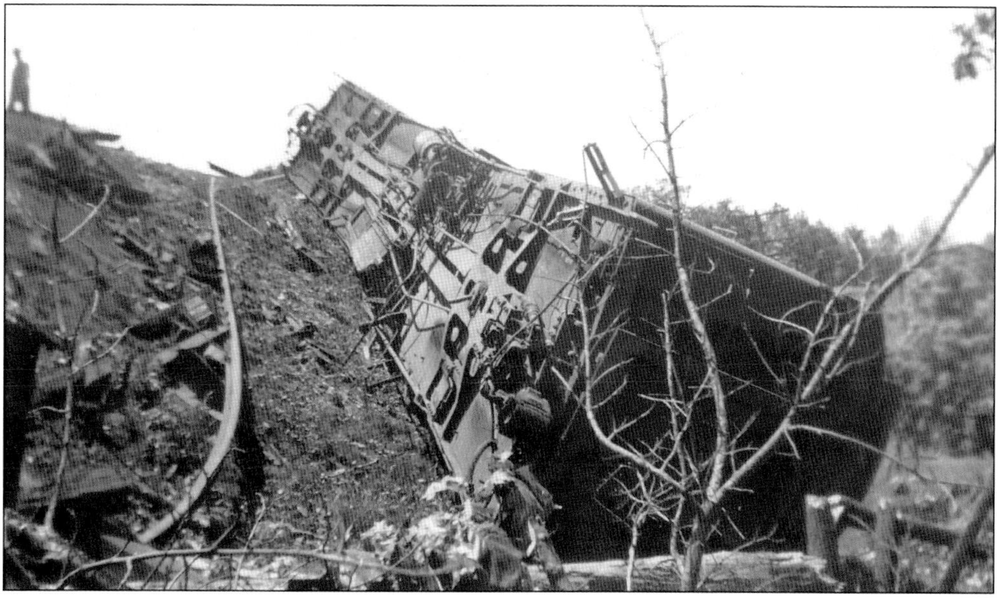

Macomb has a colorful past in railroad history. On January 3, 1899, three men boarded Train No. 4 at Norwood. One mile west of Macomb at the Blue Cut, they forced the engineer to stop the train. Four other bandits joined them, and they used 26 sticks of dynamite to blow up the baggage car. The seven split the loot of $364. By January 7, all had been captured. Sam Erwin, one of those guarding the prisoners, said George Shepherd, a former member of the James Gang, "could slip out of a pair of handcuffs faster than we could put 'em on him." The preliminary hearing was held at the Blue Goose Saloon in Mansfield, with the prisoners being held at the Mansfield Hotel. Kansas City bandit Jack Kennedy, the ringleader and gunman, received the stiffest sentence at their trial in Hartville.

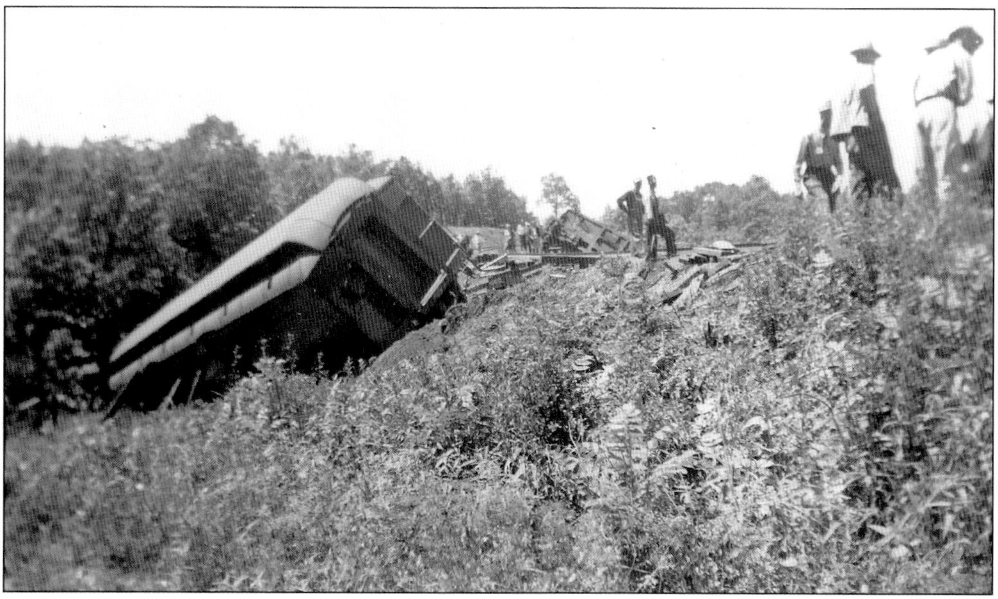

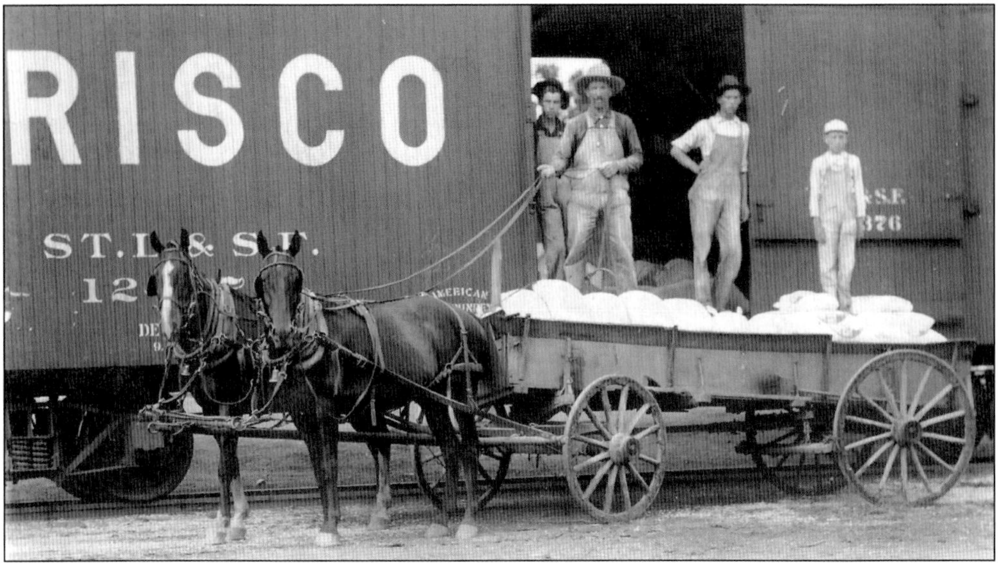

Due to the volume of freight passing through the Mansfield Depot, contracted services were needed to handle it. In the late 1800s, this was provided by the Cooley Dray Service. After Mr. Cooley's death, Almanzo Wilder purchased his dray wagon and team. He continued the service until he sold out and began to work for a kerosene company. By 1900, Joe Turner was the primary freight hauler in Mansfield. He employed several men to help with the loading and unloading of freight. Pictured above are, from left to right, Lester Stone, Joe Turner, unidentified, and Alvia Turner. Below are, from left to right, John Garner, Fred Grover, and Joe Turner. Turner's freight wagon was powered by the horse team of Bill and Barney. Numerous freight trains still continue to roll through Mansfield daily.

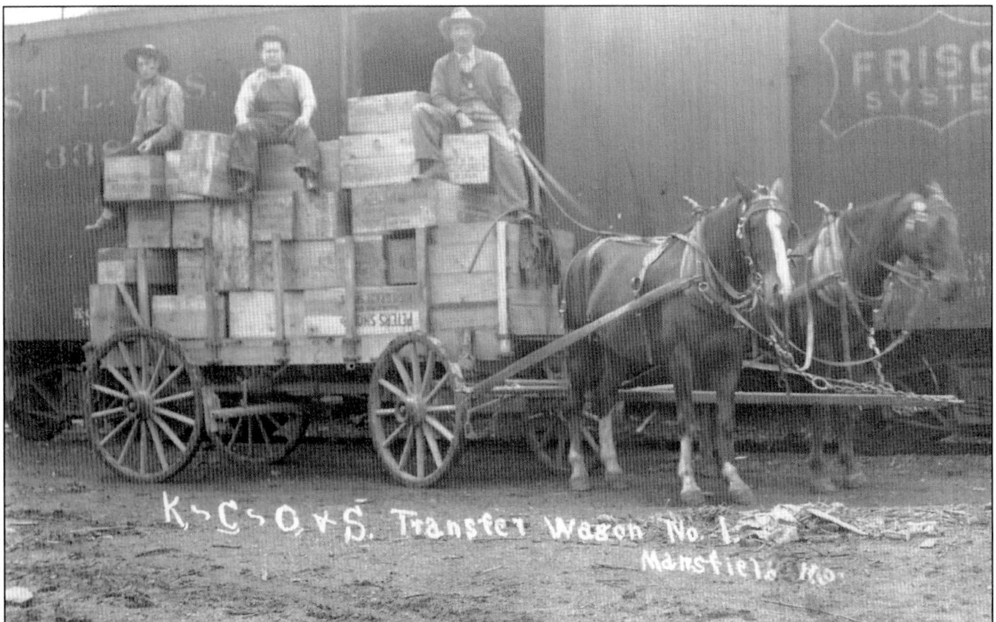

Two

Gem of the Ozarks

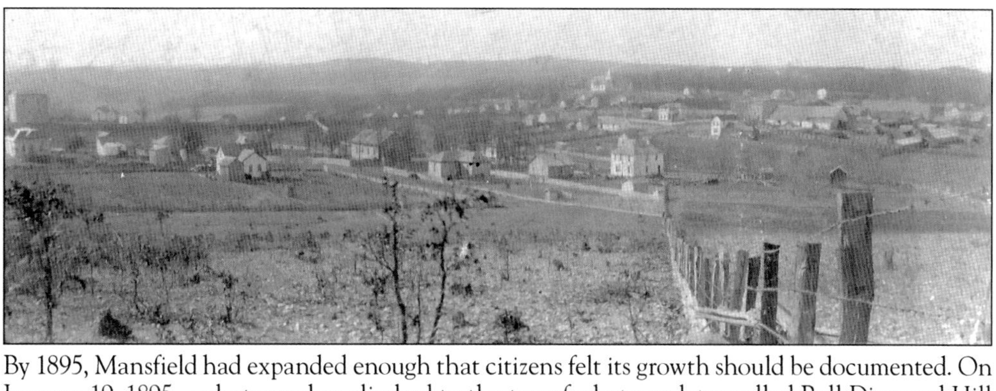

By 1895, Mansfield had expanded enough that citizens felt its growth should be documented. On January 19, 1895, a photographer climbed to the top of what was later called Ball Diamond Hill to take a panoramic picture of the prosperous town. Early landmarks in the photograph include, from left to right, Freeman Eagle Roller Mill, the railroad tracks, the school, the Presbyterian church, and Hoover's Livery Stable.

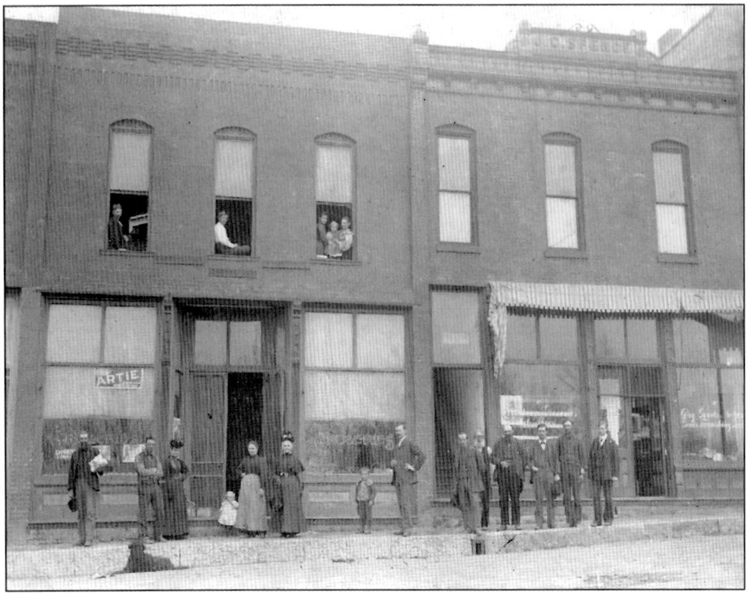

Mansfield's early business district was located on the east side of the current park square. The first buildings were the post office, with Edward B. Young as postmaster, and three businesses run by I.I. Hart, M.D. Gorman, and S.W. McCall. These buildings were first built of lumber, but as time progressed, they were covered over with bricks produced at the brickyard in town.

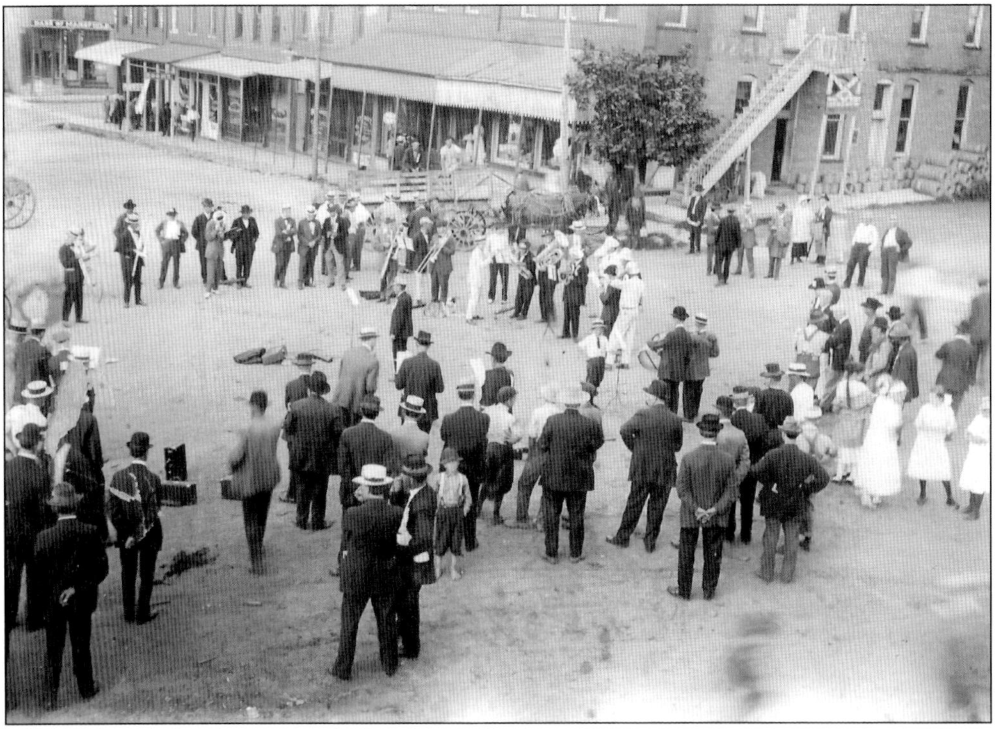

Often, dignitaries arriving on the train were welcomed by the music of the town band. While waiting for the visitors to arrive, residents leisurely strolled on the sidewalks along the east side of the square, gazing at the latest shipments prominently displayed in store windows. Some travelers stayed at the Ozark Hotel, seen in the upper right corner, while they conducted their business.

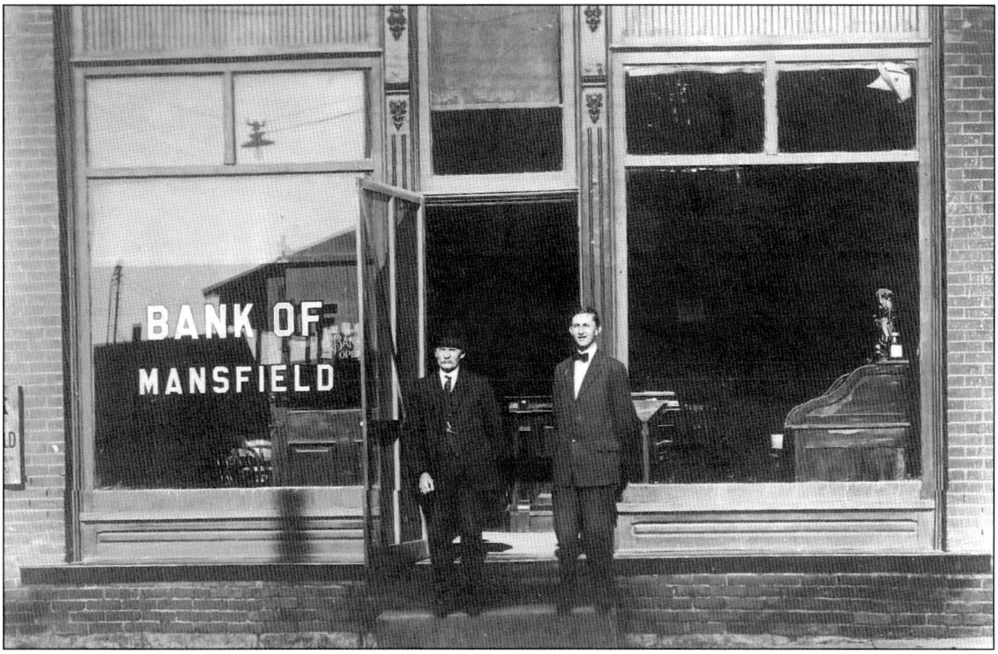

G.W. Freeman and his son M.A. Freeman stand before the first Bank of Mansfield, a family-owned business, which was founded in 1892. This is the only original business that is still in operation today. The Bank of Mansfield loaned the Wilders the $200 needed to buy property owned by the bank. On September 24, 1894, they used Laura's $100 bill that she had hidden in her lap writing desk for the down payment on Rocky Ridge.

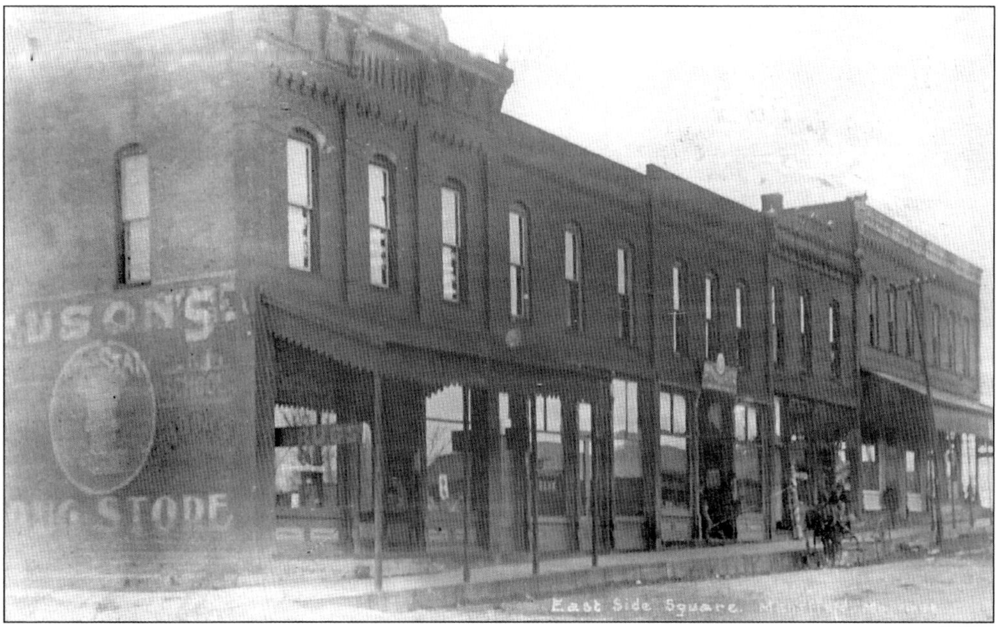

Industry continued to grow in Mansfield. In 1918, businesses lining the east side of the town square included Fuson's Drug Store, the dentist office of Dr. F.H. Riley, P.W. Newton Grocery, Dave Ellis Produce, Manie Freeman Dry Goods, Jodie Freeman Hardware, and Milton and Henry Dennis General Store.

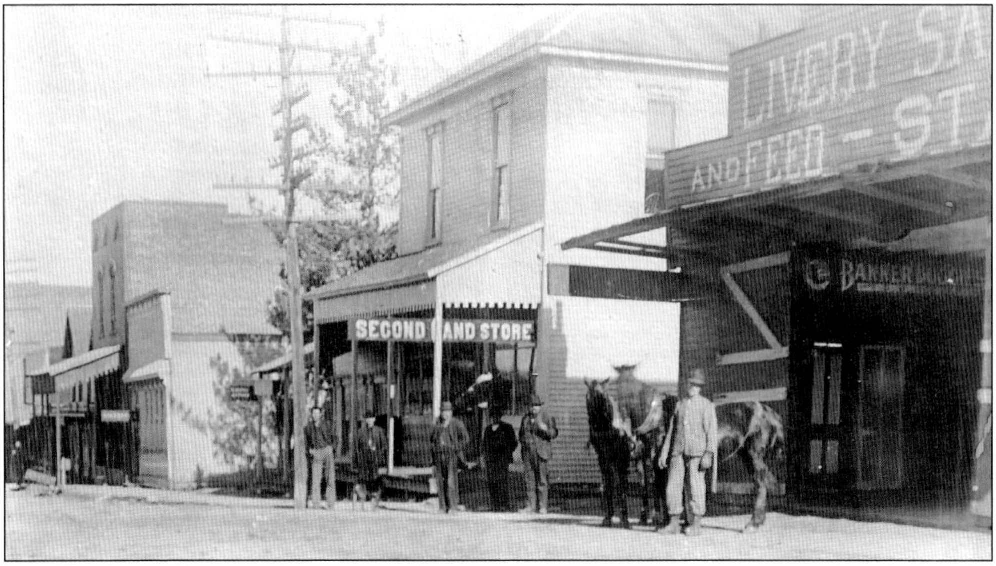

As time progressed and the area population grew, the business district expanded to the north side of the square, as pictured above. The Bank of Mansfield, needing more space, constructed a new building on this side. A second-hand store opened, specializing in household goods. Another business on the north side was Young's Feed and Livery, seen below, which served many purposes. The owners stabled and groomed horses and sold buggies. Young's also bought hay and grain from local farmers to feed the horses and rented the horses out to people needing transportation. When travelers did not have enough money to stay at the hotel, they often slept inside the livery, either on their wagon beds or on piles of hay.

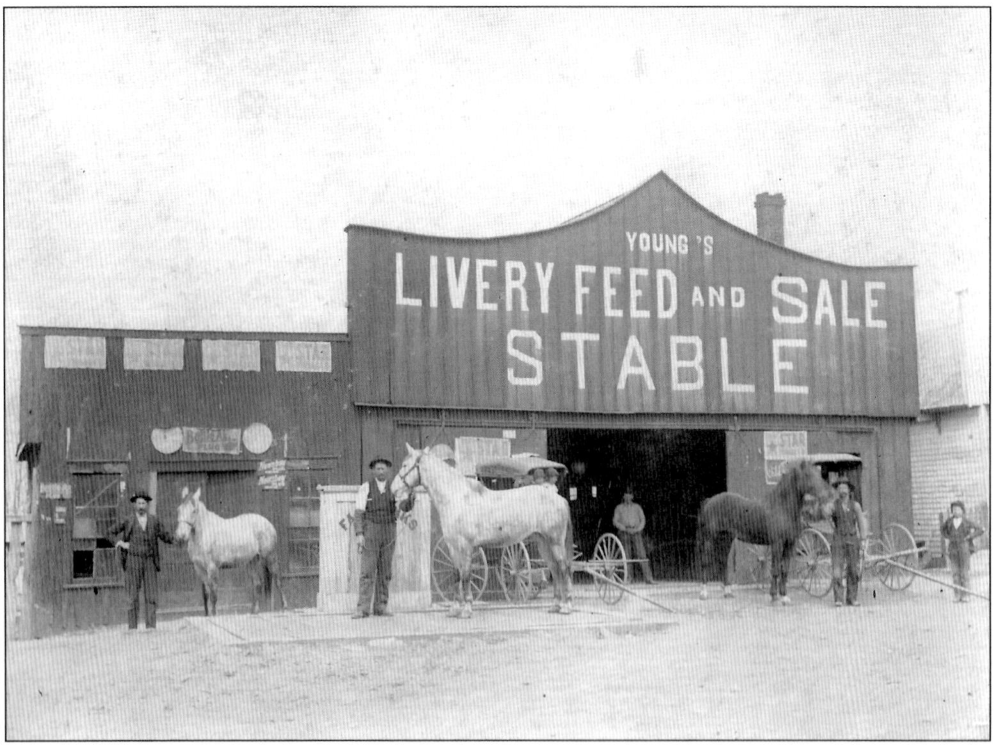

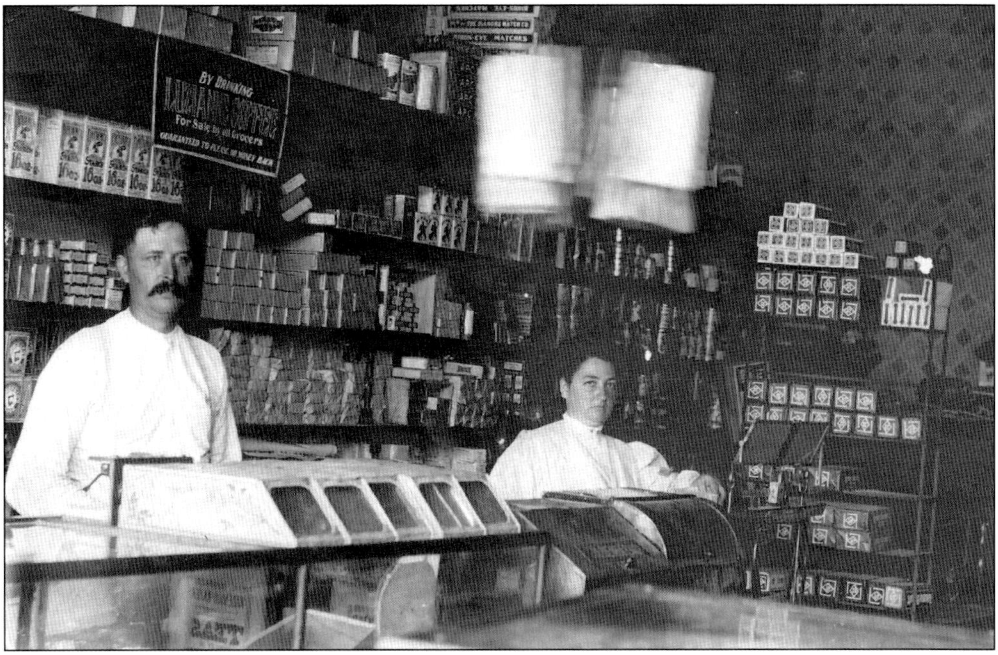

The P.W. Newton Grocery Store was located on the east side of the Mansfield Square. Its slogan advertised, "Everything Good To Eat." Customers' orders were filled promptly by the proprietor, his wife, or an employee. Many store owners provided credit to their patrons and also took eggs or chickens for trade. P.W. Newton, owner, is shown here with employee Cora Herod.

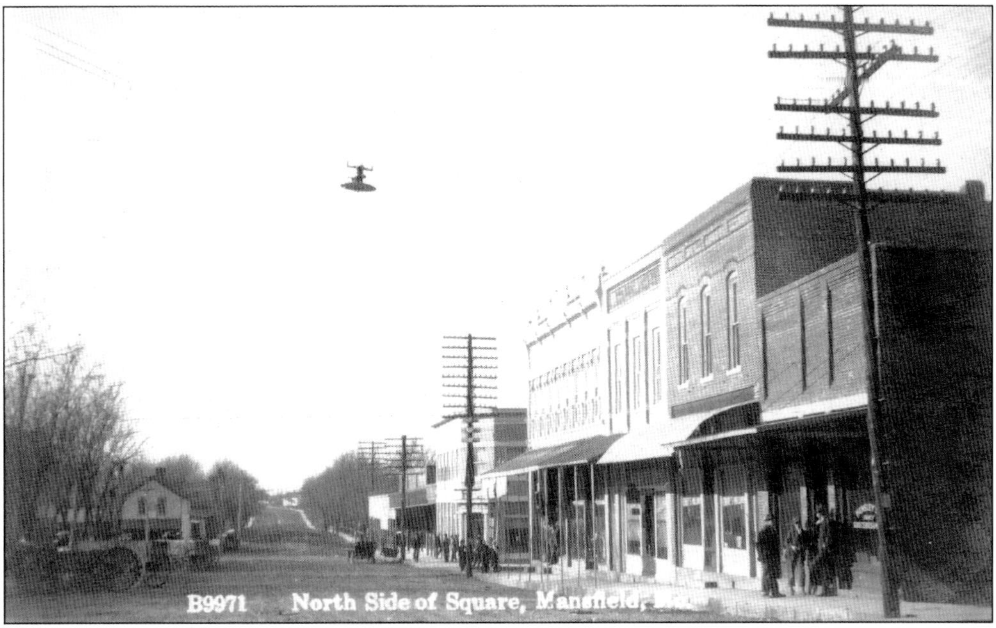

In the early 1900s, the Reynolds Building dominated the northeast corner of town. The business was a two-story brick mercantile, which J.D. Reynolds and family ran for over 40 years. Merchandise included dry goods, groceries, and hardware; Reynolds also purchased lumber, produce, and railroad ties for resale. An elevator went up to the second floor where buggies, wagons, and farm machinery were displayed. Later, Reynolds sold Maxwell cars.

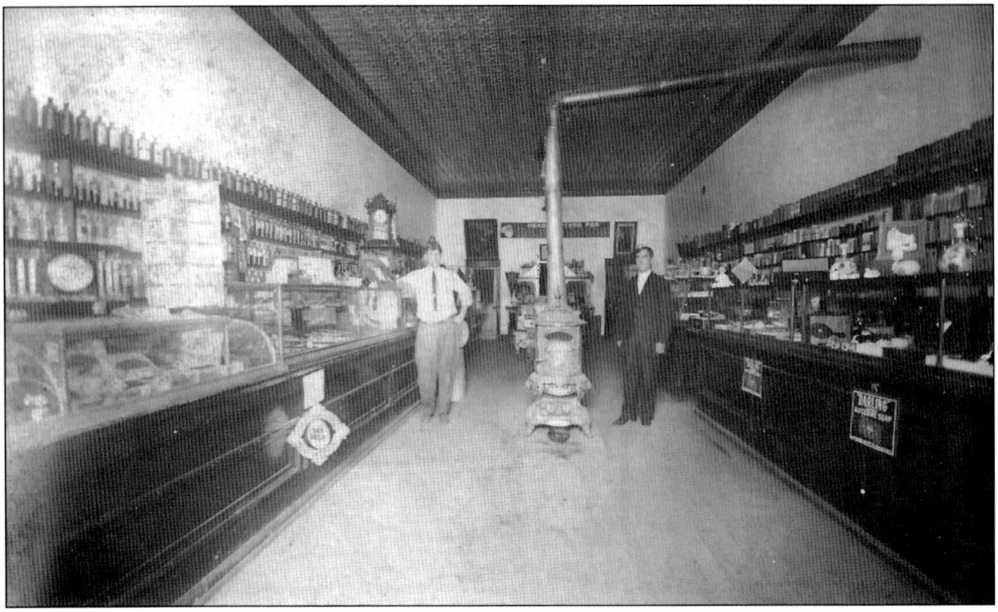

Brasher Drug Store, pictured in 1915, was located west of the Bank of Mansfield. It had a single, wide aisle, which was flanked by wooden, glass-topped cases. A potbelly stove, centrally located, provided the heat. Lining the shelves on the left side of the store were rows of elixirs, tonics, and patent medicines that all promised to "cure what ails you," everything from summer complaints to fainting spells.

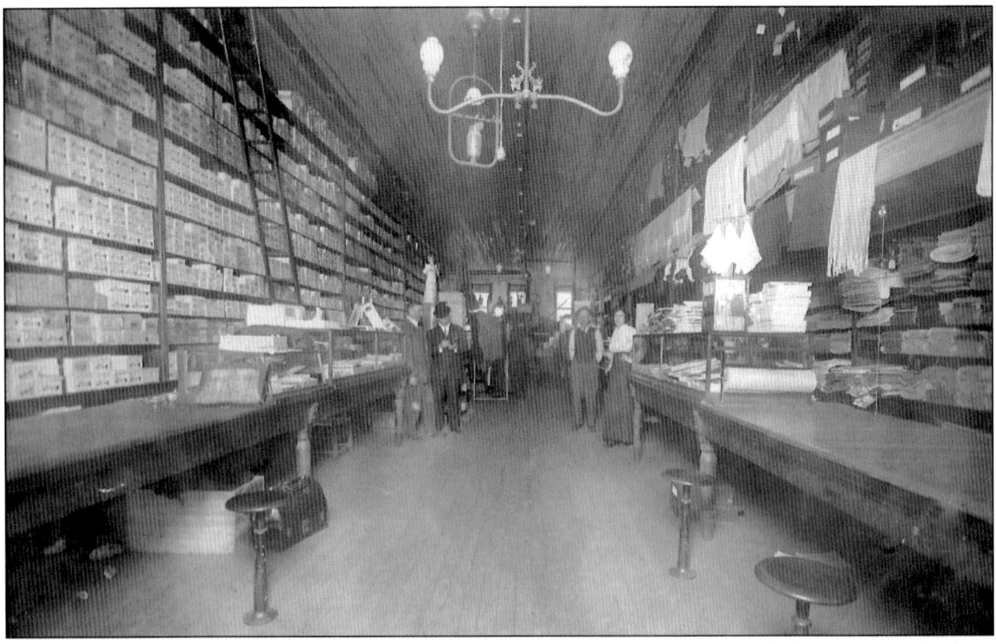

In the G.W. Freeman and Son Mercantile, gaslights illuminate the goods that are stacked on shelves up to the ceiling. A ladder stands ready to access those items out of reach. Oscar "Buster" Brown was employed there. Because the store sold Buster Brown shoes, his daughter thought they were named after her dad. Supposedly, the 1899 Macomb train robbers purchased material here for their hold-up masks.

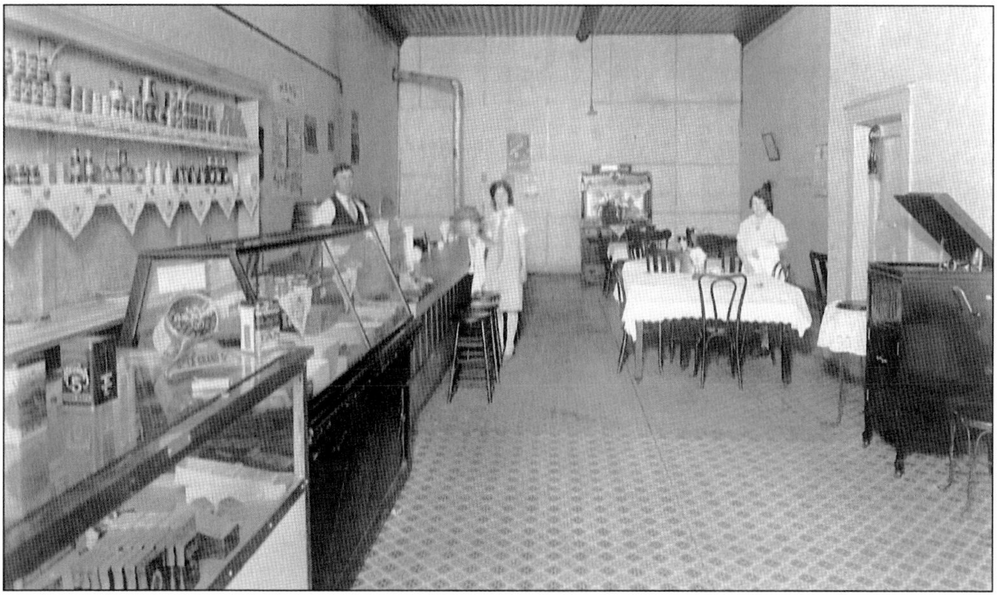

For many years, if people wanted to purchase a meal, they could eat in a hotel dining room or buy a meal from local housewives who advertised on signs outside their homes. While the Wilders lived in town, Laura Wilder made extra money cooking for guests. Soon, small cafes, like the one above, began to open. Seating consisted of tables for diners who wanted to chat and stools around the lunch counter.

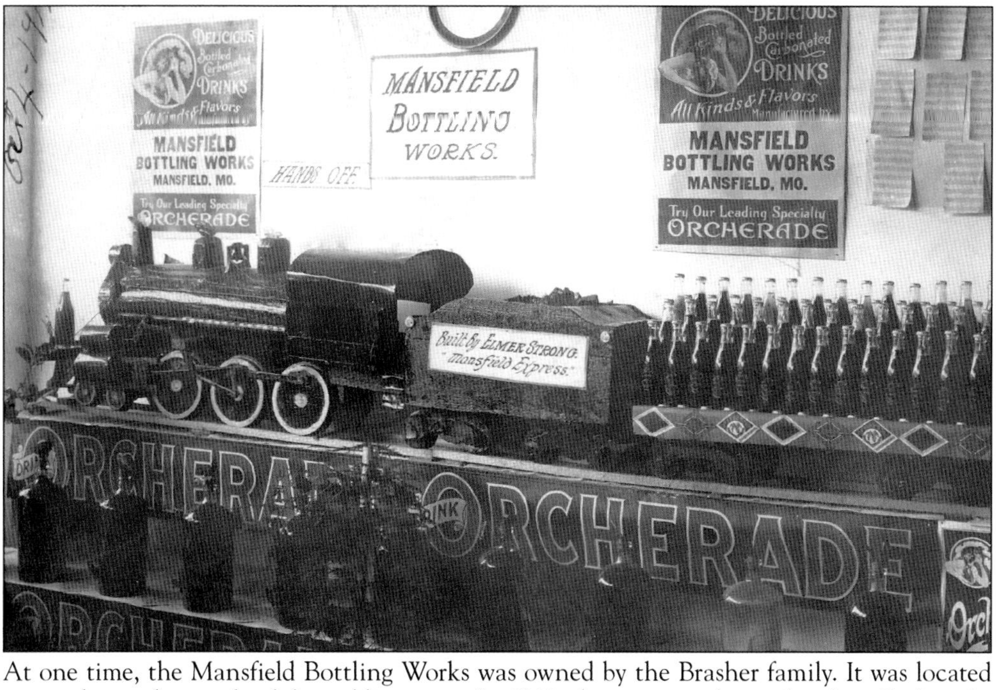

At one time, the Mansfield Bottling Works was owned by the Brasher family. It was located across the tracks, south of the public square. In 1912, the company began bottling Orcherade, soon followed by Orange Crush and Grapette sodas. Shipments were made nationwide. Once in a great while, a clear glass bottle embossed with Mansfield Missouri can still be found in flea markets and antique stores.

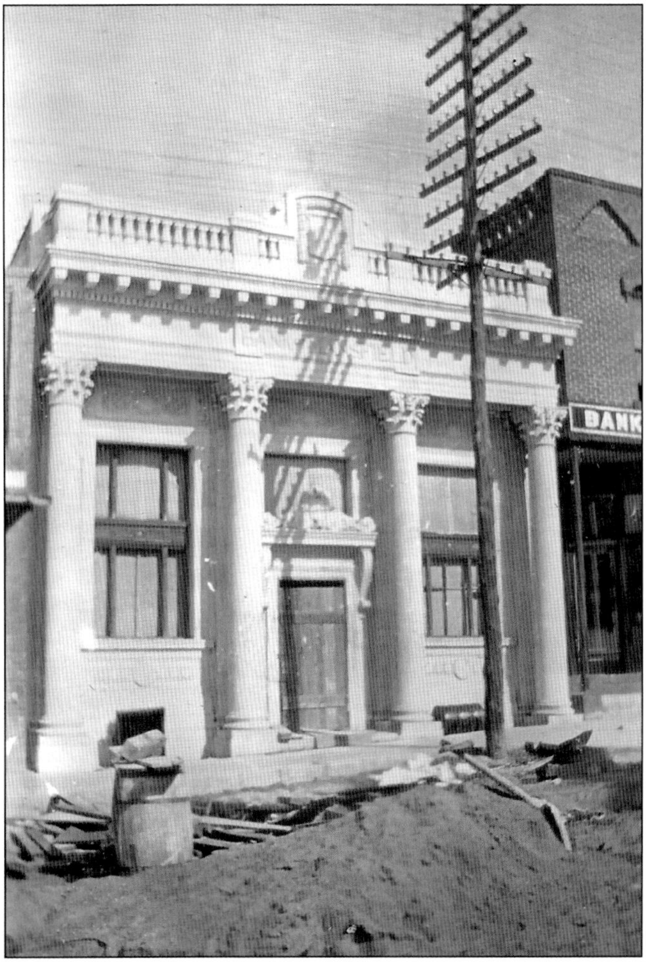

Established in 1892, the family-owned Bank of Mansfield is the oldest business in town. The Freeman line of ownership continues today through the Coday family. A new building, seen at left, was under construction in 1910. Although this building has been enlarged, the original portion still welcomes all who enter the door. In 1908, a second bank was established in Mansfield with the founding of the Farmers and Merchants Bank, below. J.D. Reynolds was the first president. As a testament to the banking industry in Mansfield, it too still exists today as a branch of Great Southern Bank. In 1952, the Missouri State Banking Department decided to make banking hours uniform by ruling that all institutions must close by 3:00 p.m. Only three banks in the state were still open until 4:00 p.m., and two of those were in Mansfield.

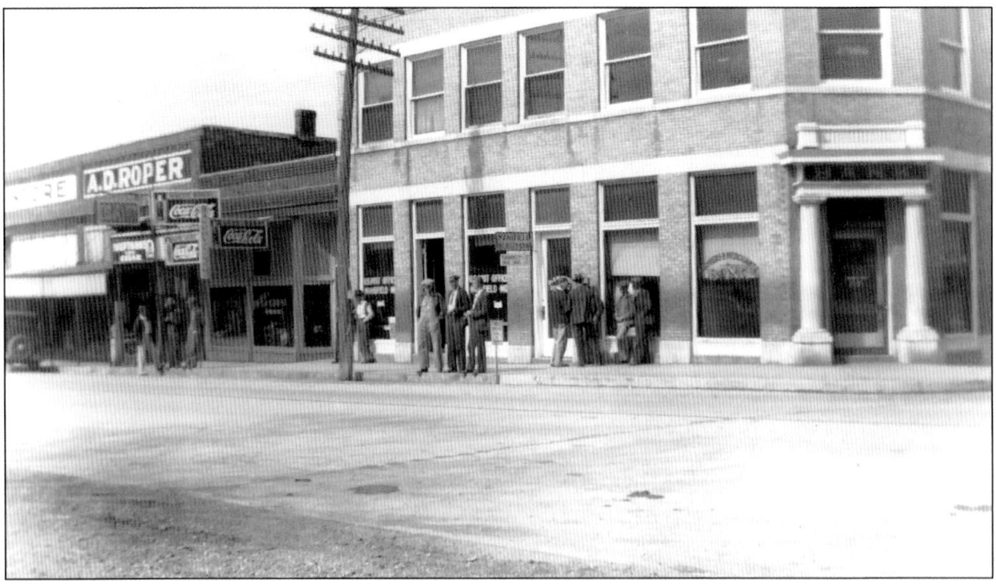

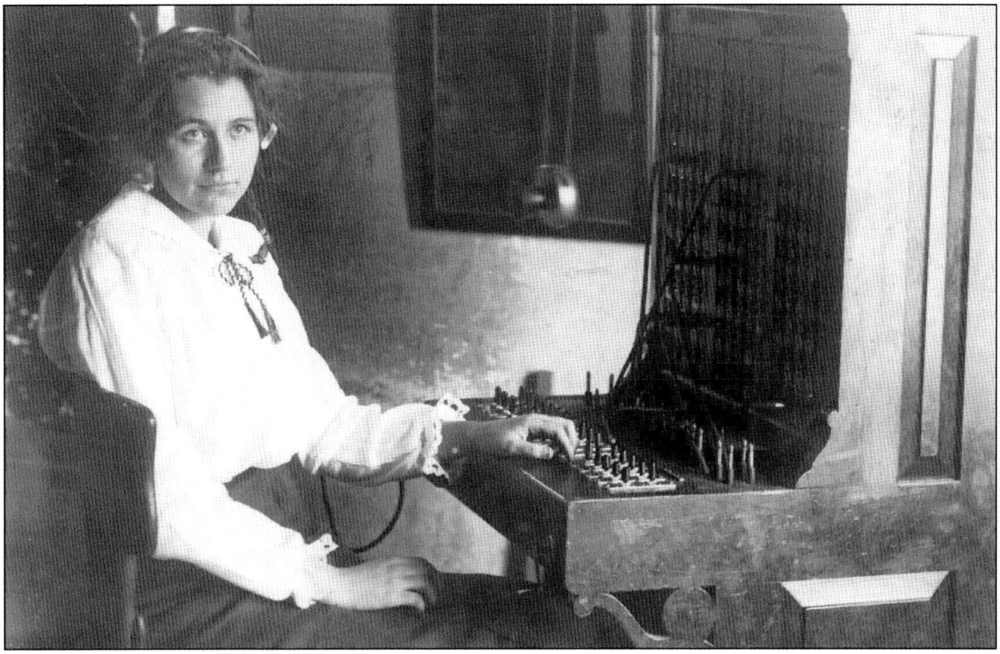

Early communication in Mansfield was primarily by mail or telegraph, and the depot agent was usually the telegraph operator. Agent George Burney taught both his daughter and Rose Wilder the operation of the telegraph and Morse code. By 1895, telephones dotted local homes; in 1900, telephone service became citywide. Mae Benjamin, first telephone operator in Mansfield, worked in an office on the second floor of the Farmers and Merchants Bank.

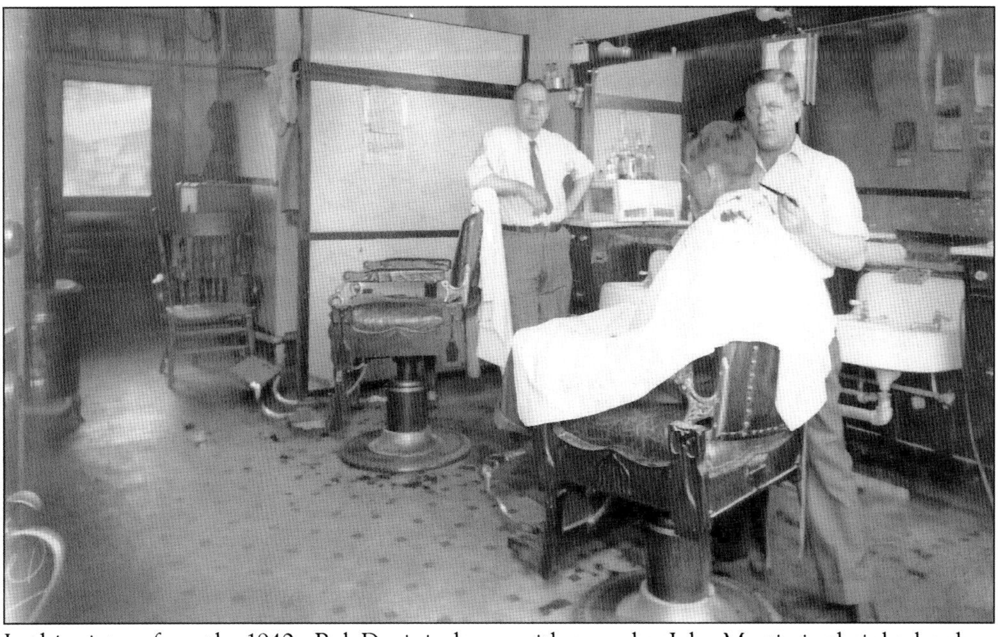

In this picture from the 1940s, Bob Davis is shown with coworker John Martin in their barbershop on Commercial Street. Martin (right) is trimming customer Raydene Ray's hair. A patriotic picture of General McArthur hangs between the mirrors. At this time, two of Davis's sons were fighting in the war overseas. Later, Davis sold the shop to longtime Mansfield barber Clifford Cooper.

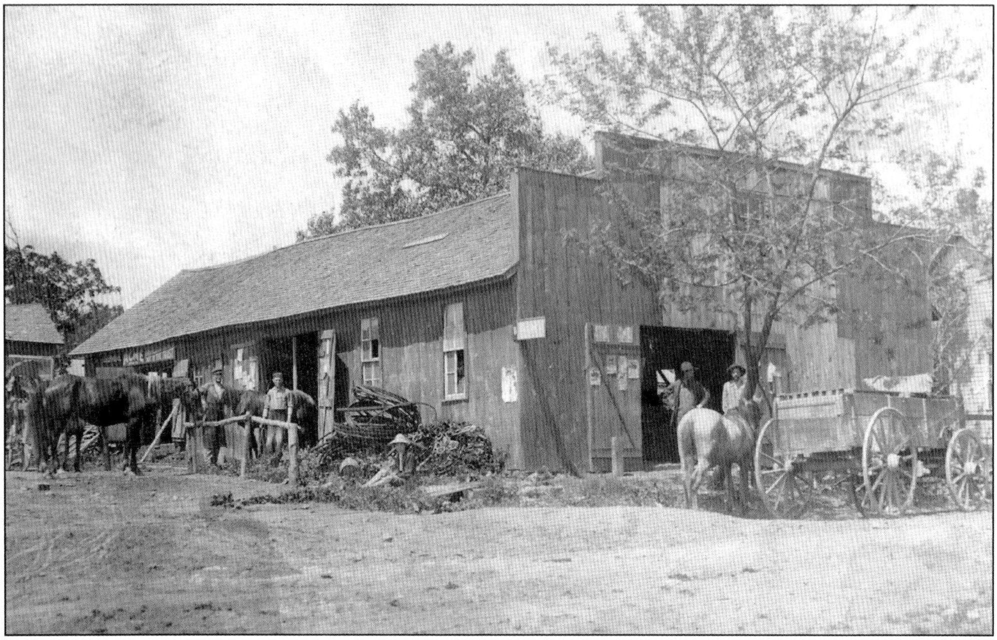

By the 1850s, blacksmith shops dotted the rural landscape of southern Wright County. The need for their work was not isolated to the farm; blacksmith shops were some of the earliest businesses in Mansfield. On a quiet side street behind the public square stood the Joe Carter Blacksmith Shop. This 1910 photograph shows the horses unharnessed from the wagon and waiting to be shod.

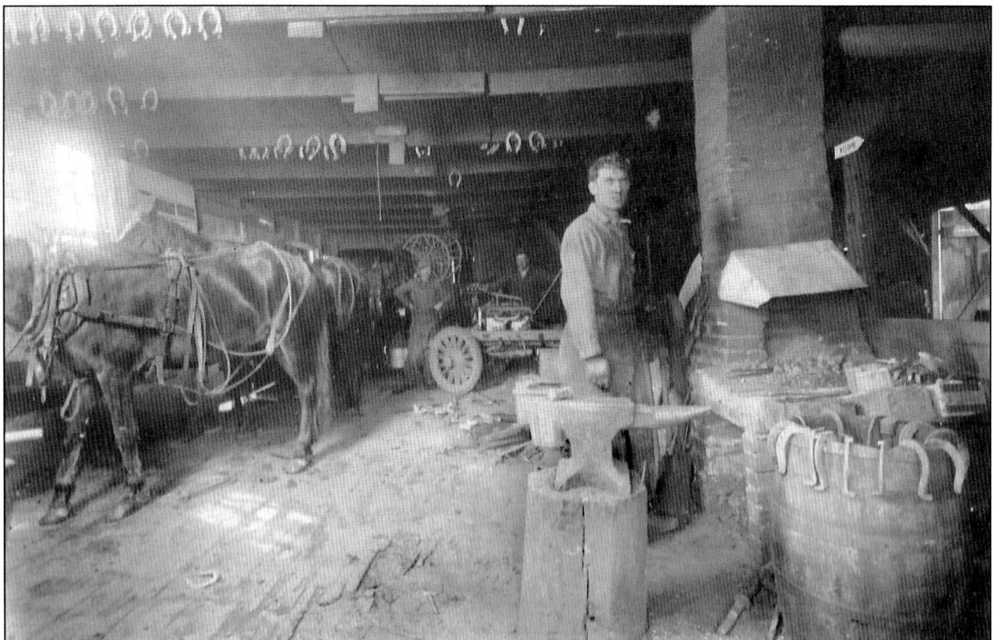

Joe Carter is shown forging horseshoes for a team of waiting horses. Shoes were custom fit by hammering the hot metal on the anvil. After the correct shape was achieved, dipping it in a barrel of water set the shoe. The mark of a good blacksmith was making the anvil sing. When Bill Caskey worked at the anvil, he hammered and whistled in time to "Turkey in the Straw."

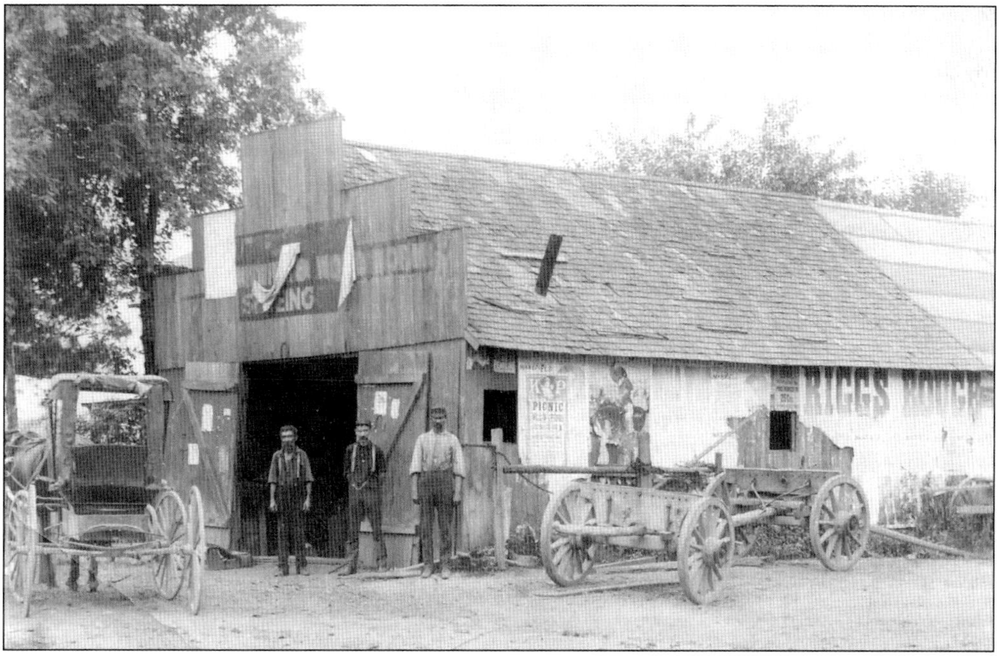

Three generations of the Short family operated blacksmith shops in the Mansfield area, beginning in 1870. The first was Jay Short, followed by Els Short, and last were Herb and Loney Short. The Short family bought the Carter shop around 1916 and continued business there for 60 years. Not only was it a business, it was also the social hub for area hunters and storytellers.

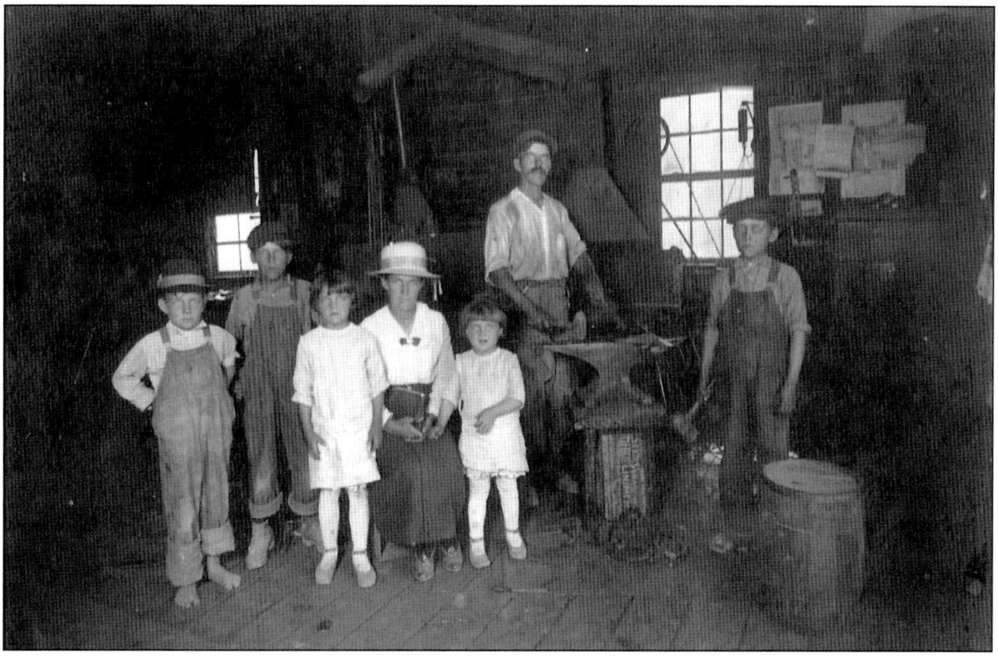

Whether a blacksmith shop was on a farm or in town it was considered a family business. The father worked the metal while his sons turned the forge to keep the coals hot. The children kept the coal bin full, swept the floors, and hauled manure outside. The mother often kept the books, paid the bills, and washed the extremely dirty clothes.

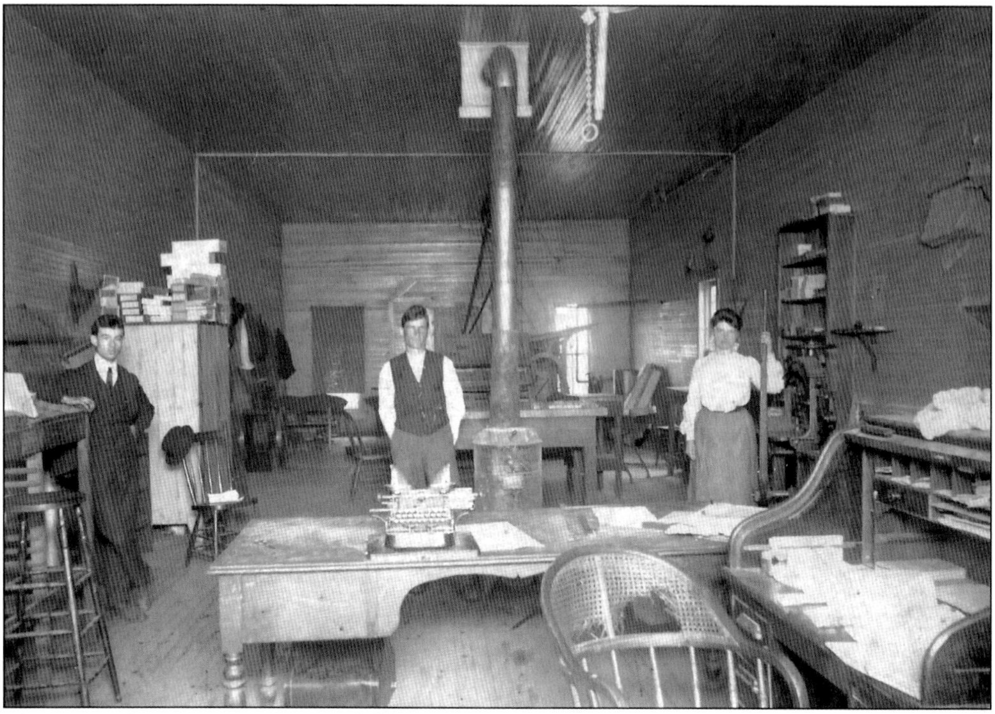

The town's first newspaper, *Mansfield Press*, was established in 1908 with W.H. Pyles as editor. In 1912, it was purchased by W.A. Black and renamed the *Mansfield Mirror*, so chosen because he said, "Everyone takes a look in the mirror." In 1919, Black became Mansfield's postmaster and subsequently sold the newspaper to O.B. Davis.

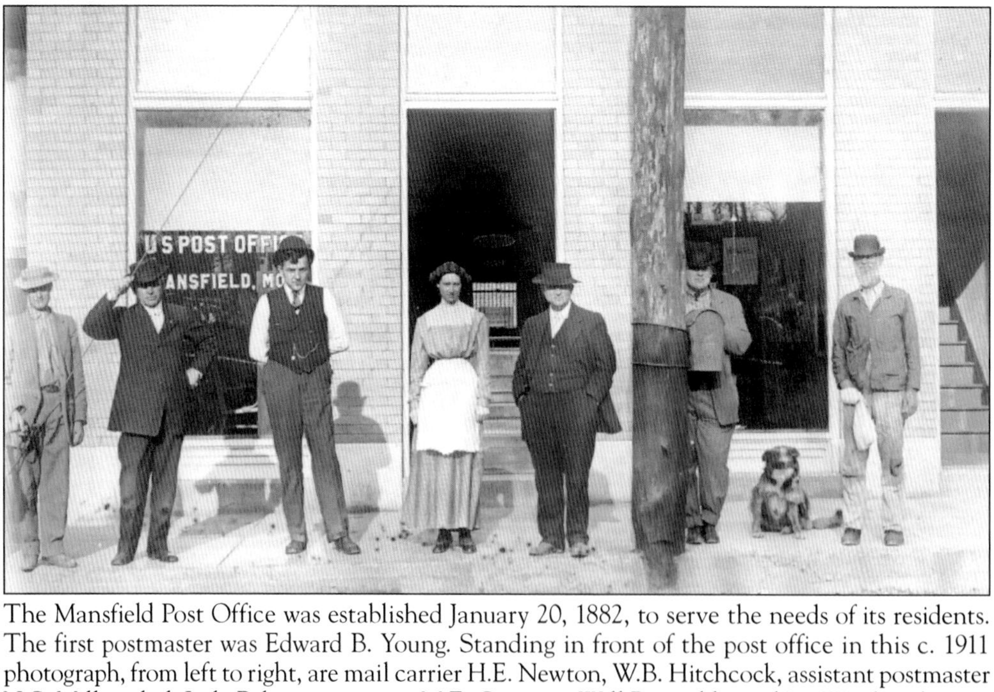

The Mansfield Post Office was established January 20, 1882, to serve the needs of its residents. The first postmaster was Edward B. Young. Standing in front of the post office in this c. 1911 photograph, from left to right, are mail carrier H.E. Newton, W.B. Hitchcock, assistant postmaster N.S. Miller, clerk Lula Riley, postmaster M.E. Gorman, Will Reynolds, and Ira Westbrook.

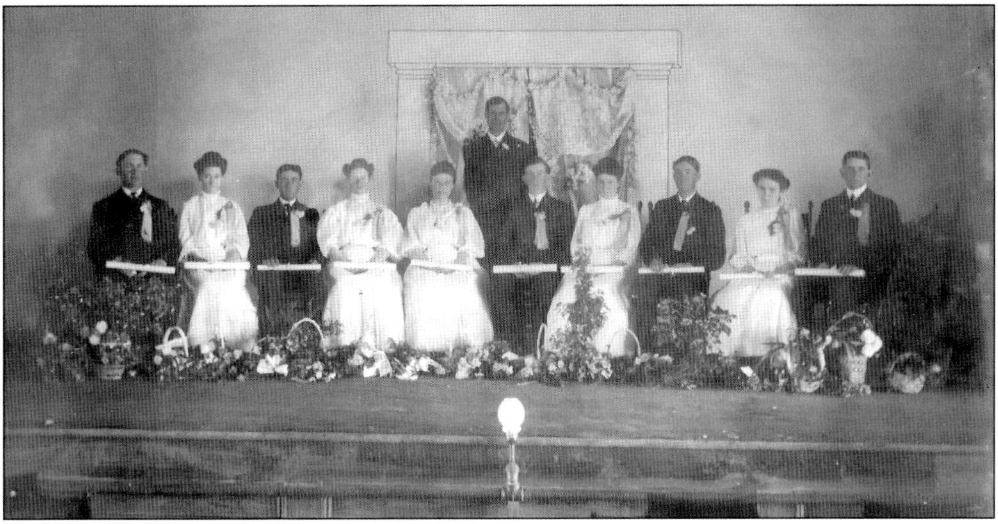

The Opera House, located on the west side of the public square, was the setting for graduation exercises for the Mansfield High School class of 1907. Gas lights in front of the stage showcased the honorees. Graduates are, from left to right, Russel Rogers, Frona Rippee, Ernst Brentlinger, Lula Riley, Lula Hitchcock, Elmer Gaskill, Ora Rippee, Brad Taylor, Tiny Russell, and Frank Brentlinger. Prof. J.A. Hylton is standing in the back.

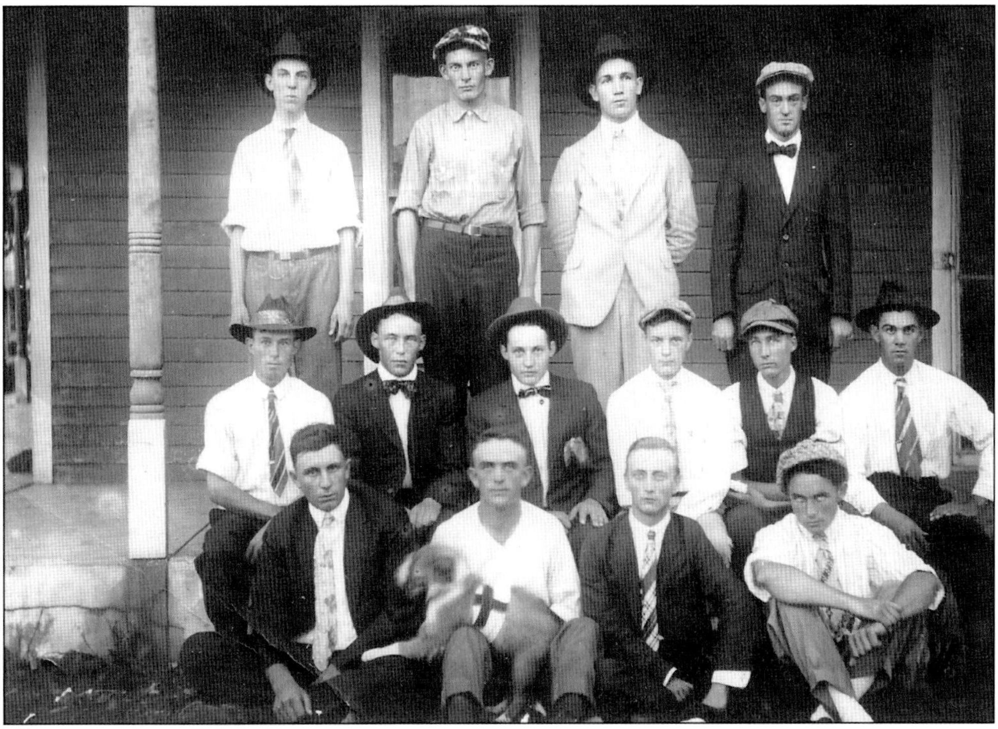

These Mansfield-area World War I soldiers made up the Supply Company of the 140th Infantry, 35th Division. From left to right are (first row) Roy Handy, Howard Claxton, Roy Norcross, and Garrett William Carter; (second row) Claude Tripp, Alva Carter, Glenn Craig, Robert Viles, Clarence King, and Clyde Tarbutton; (third row) John Potts, R.R. Whittaker, Frank Hoover, and Walter Coday. The American Legion is named after Clarence King, Mansfield's first war casualty.

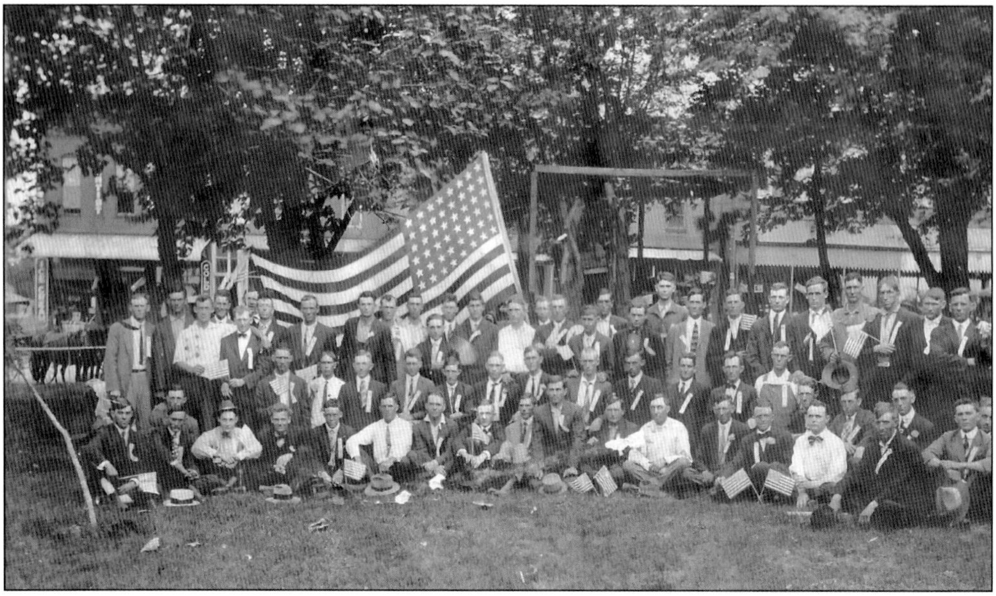

During World War I, Mansfield became an embarkation point for servicemen. Registration Day was held on June 15, 1917, at the Mansfield Park where J.W. Gilley's American flag was prominently displayed. Men between the ages of 21 and 31 were required to register for the draft. The area men pictured above who were prepared to serve their country included Alva Carter, Gus Brazeal, Glen Craig, Bob Davis, Marve Dennis, Roy Dennis, Dee Gaskill, Ernie Gaskill, Roy Huggins, Ira Keeling, Jim Morris, Al Newton, Mose Newton, Roy Norcross, Frank Peacock, Ray Riley, Clyde Tarbutton, O.K. Tripp, and Carl Turner. The Park Square gazebo, seen below, proudly served as the focal point for the festivities honoring these men. Residents partook of a basket dinner while enjoying a patriotic program of songs, music by the town band, and special speeches.

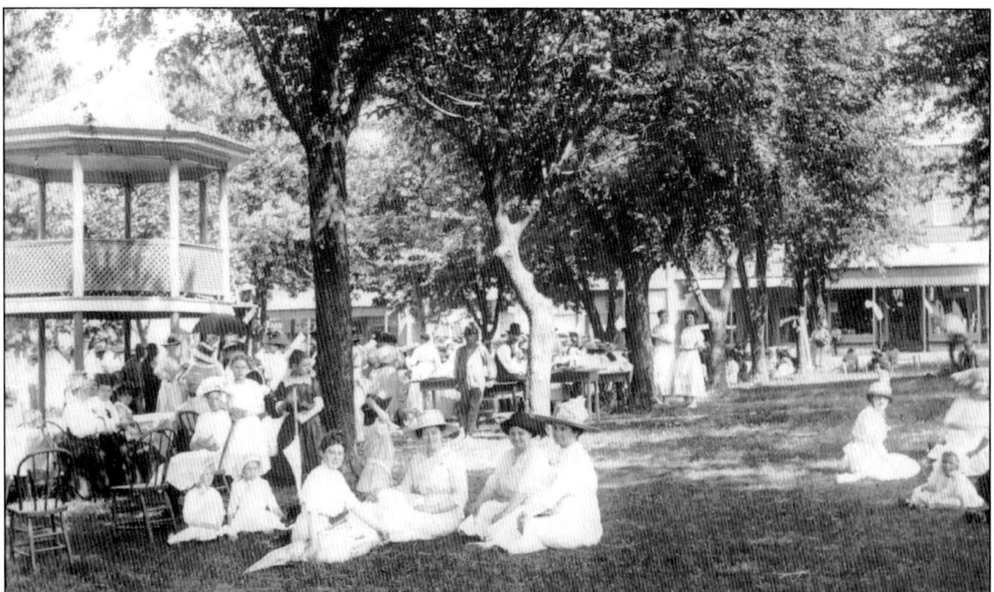

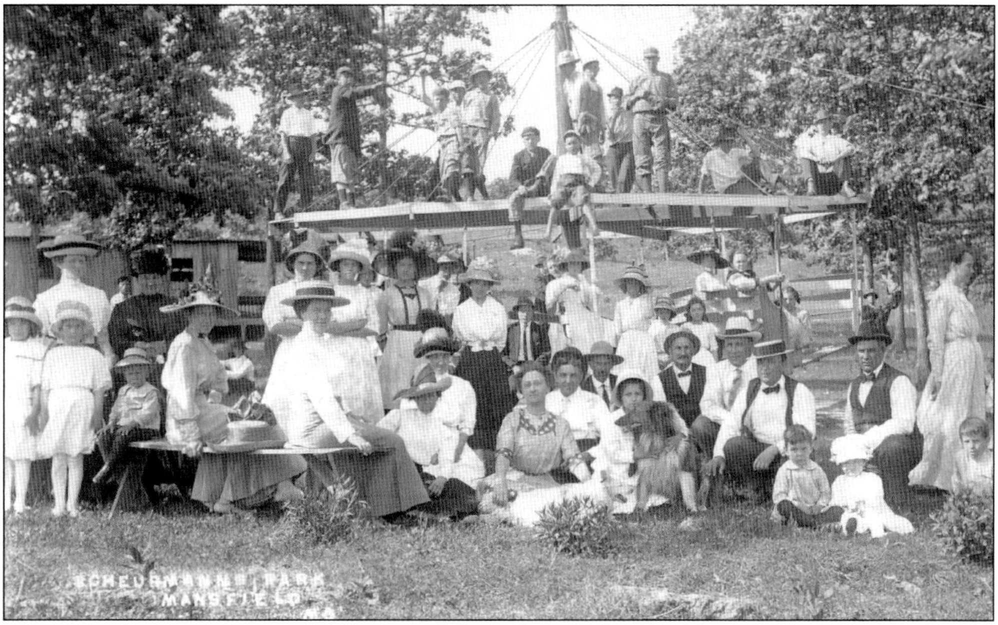

Scheurmann's Park provided an area of relaxation to visitors and residents alike. The wooden merry-go-round was a place for the energetic youngsters to play while still in sight of their watchful parents. Ladies came to town dressed in their finest, including stylish hats to keep the sun off their faces. This park was located across the railroad tracks from the southeast corner of the Mansfield Square.

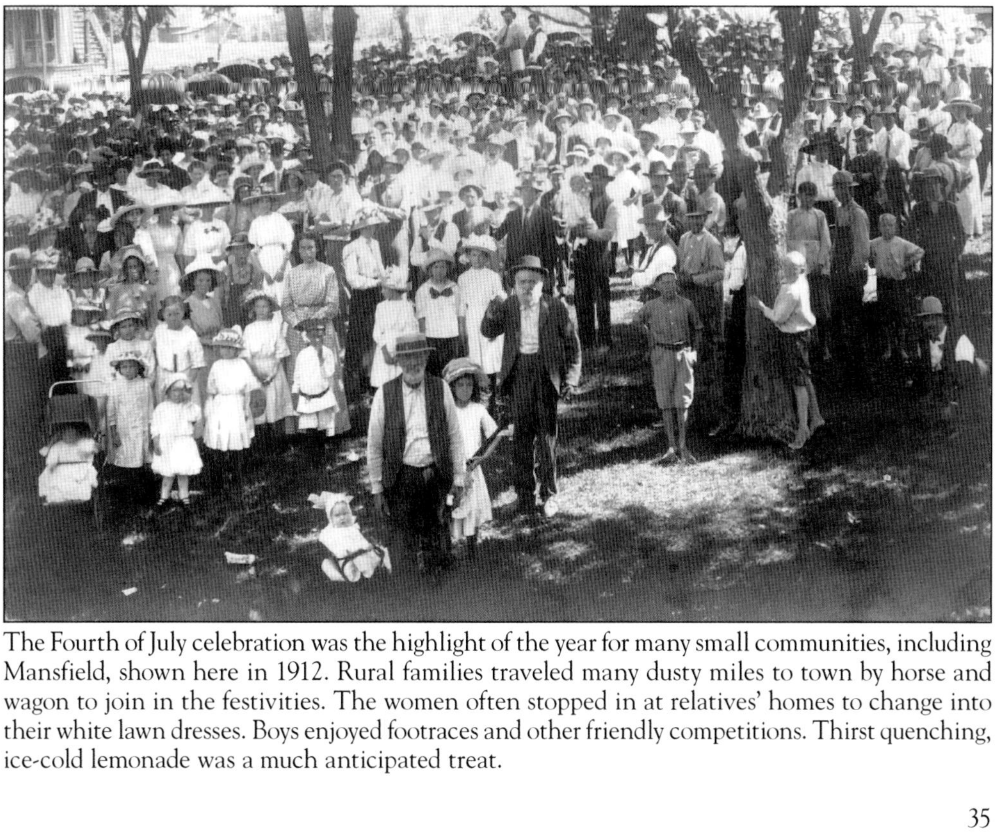

The Fourth of July celebration was the highlight of the year for many small communities, including Mansfield, shown here in 1912. Rural families traveled many dusty miles to town by horse and wagon to join in the festivities. The women often stopped in at relatives' homes to change into their white lawn dresses. Boys enjoyed footraces and other friendly competitions. Thirst quenching, ice-cold lemonade was a much anticipated treat.

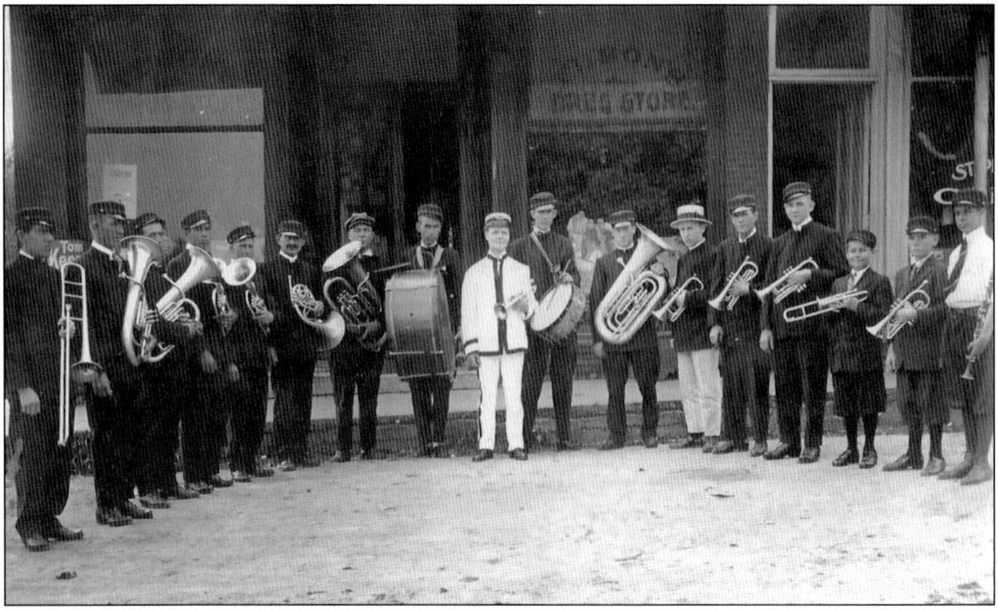

An excerpt from the *Mansfield Mirror* reads, "Mansfield boasted a lively band, a credit to the community, playing at various city functions and adding gaiety to all occasions." Members pictured are, from left to right, Edgar Sisk, Elmer Strong, Charley Newton, Cecil Brazeal, Ray Riley, J.D. Reynolds, R.N. Farren, Burl Stone, director Cal Hunsaker, Oscar Coday, Walter Coday, Pete Freeman, Ezra Dennis, Herve Coday, Ben Grover, Snyder Craig, and Ralph Hylton.

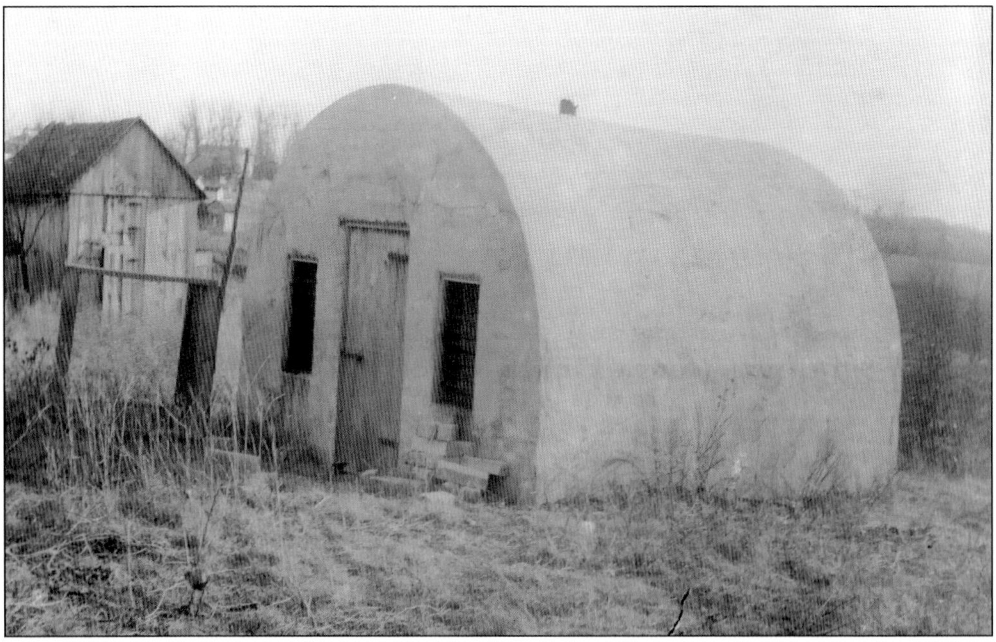

Mansfield's first jail was this dome-top building located south of the railroad. Basically standing in a field, the unusual structure was made of stone blocks. The small size, along with the two barred windows and wooden door, undoubtedly served as a deterrent to crime. Those committing minor infractions were housed here in the "hoosegow," whereas those arrested for more serious crimes were incarcerated at the county jail in Hartville

Three

A Trail Through Time

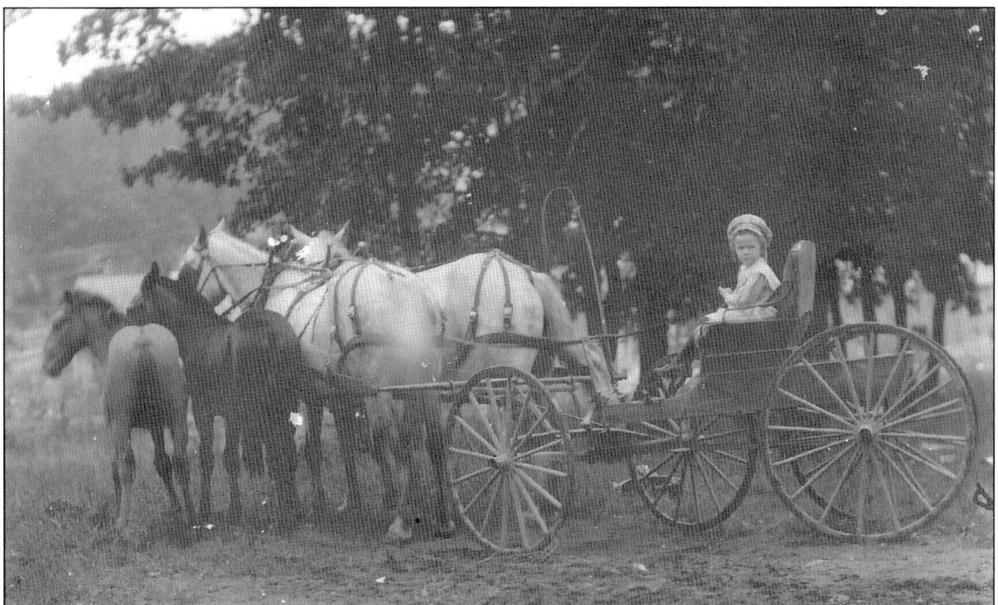

Most people hoped to own at least one team of horses to be used for both work and pleasure. Teams matching in color were all the more valuable. Young men spent all day working their teams in the fields; then, they cleaned up, hitched the team to their buggy, and went "a-courtin'." The owner of these horses was fortunate to have both a matched team and two colts.

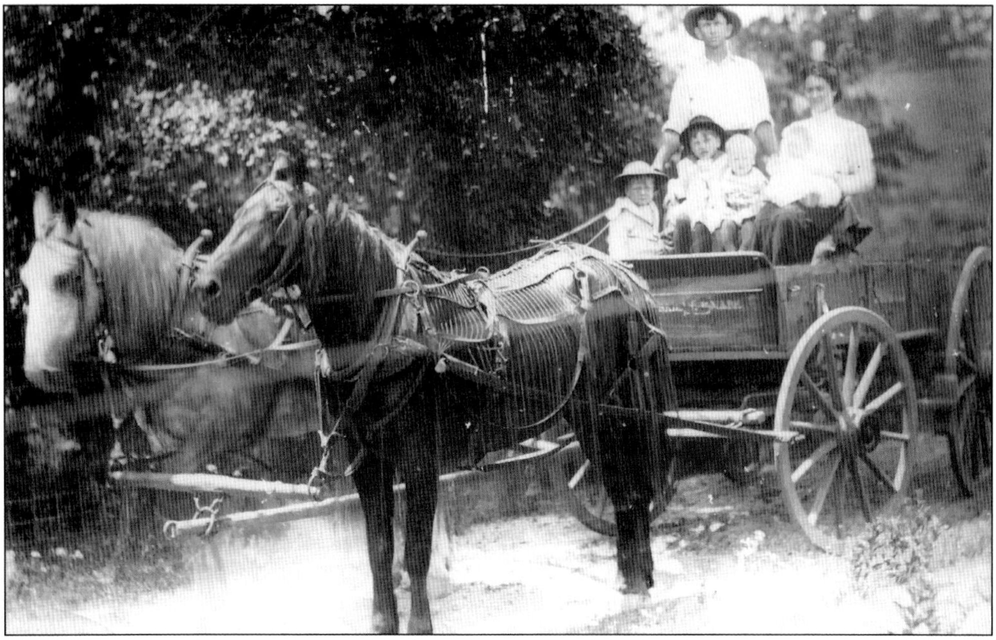

Farmers used wagons to haul crops and transport the family. In the early 1900s, Leonard and Laura Miller, with four of their nine boys, travel in a Springfield wagon pulled by a team with leather fly strips attached to the harnesses and bridles to keep flies from biting them. The Springfield Wagon Company was located in Springfield, Missouri. In 1872, it began producing "farm and road" wagons, constructed from Ozark hardwood.

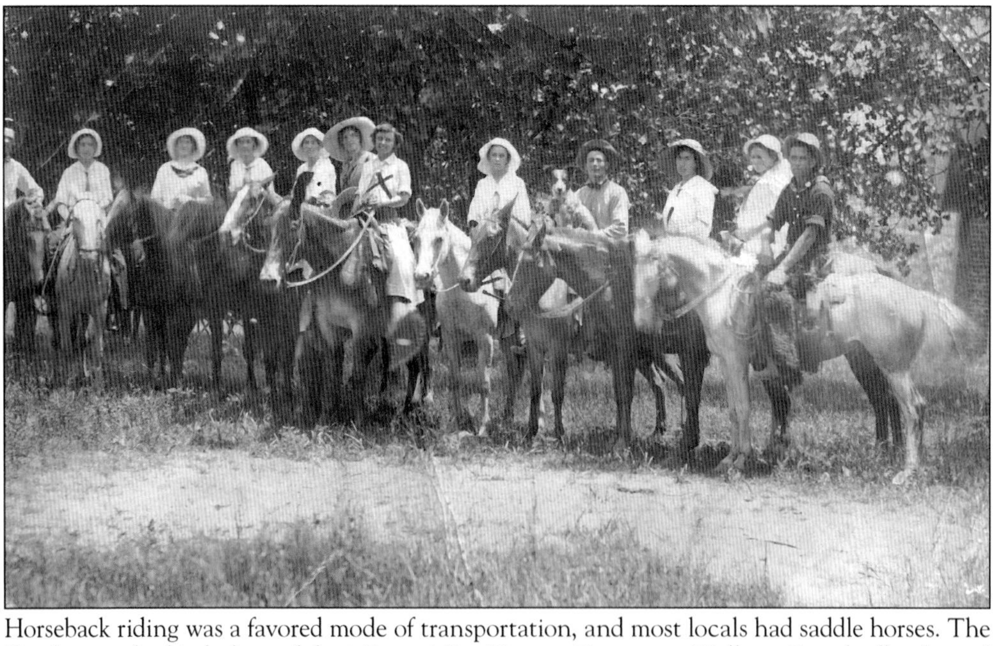

Horseback riding was a favored mode of transportation, and most locals had saddle horses. The Ozarks was the birthplace of the Missouri Fox Trotter. Tennessee Walkers, Standardbreds, and Morgans were used to breed this sure-footed, easy-riding horse. Young men and women, like those seen here, used afternoon rides as a means of socializing. Although most women rode side-saddle, many in the Ozarks rode astride, which was shocking to people outside the area.

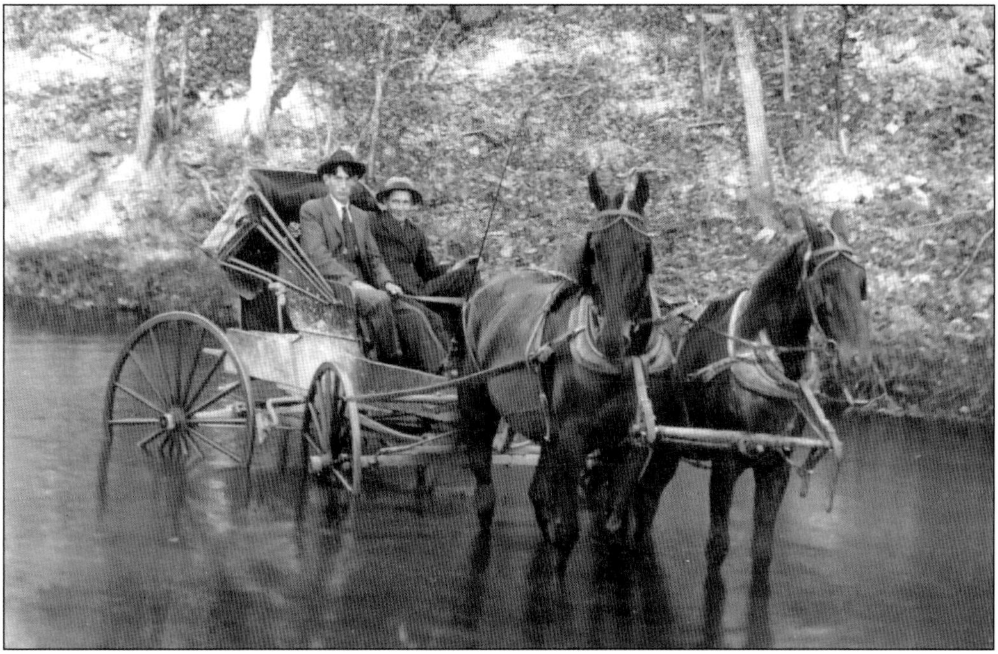

For much of the year, travel in the Ozarks was quite difficult. Roads, which were primitive and unkempt, were merely streams of mud during the rainy seasons. Early roads traversed the wilderness, often following the Native American paths. As time passed and more and more wagons and buggies traveled over them, the roads became even more rutted. Horse-powered vehicles were often forced to detour around the rolling hills and rocky outcroppings. When roadbeds became impassable, many travelers, like those above, turned to the streambeds. With numerous creeks, streams, and rivers, travelers found it easier to drive through them than to drive on the roadbeds. The Dye and Molly Bell family, pictured below, demonstrate how treacherous early roads could be.

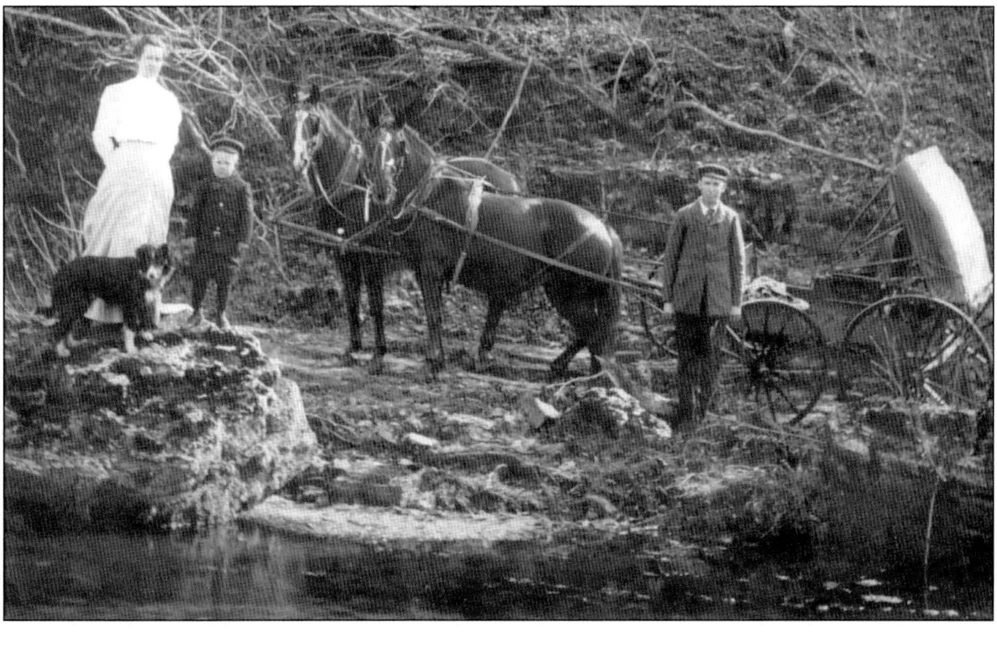

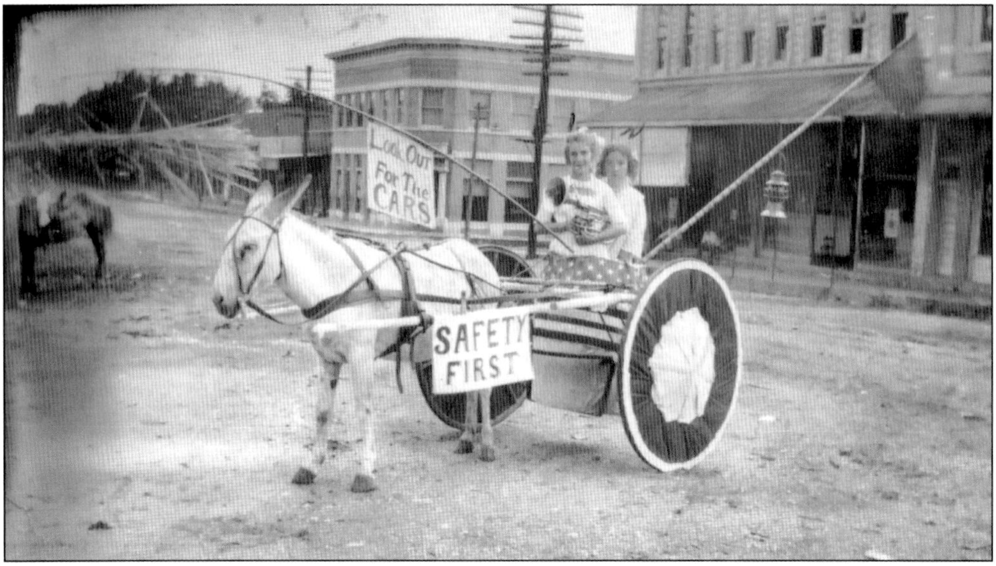

With the introduction of Henry Ford's Model T, the age of the automobile arrived in Mansfield. Improvement of area roads was necessary for these early vehicles to travel through the area. The Good Roads movement was the driving force behind the needed improvements. Driving their decorated donkey-drawn float, Leona Hoover and an unidentified friend draw attention to the importance of safety and good roads.

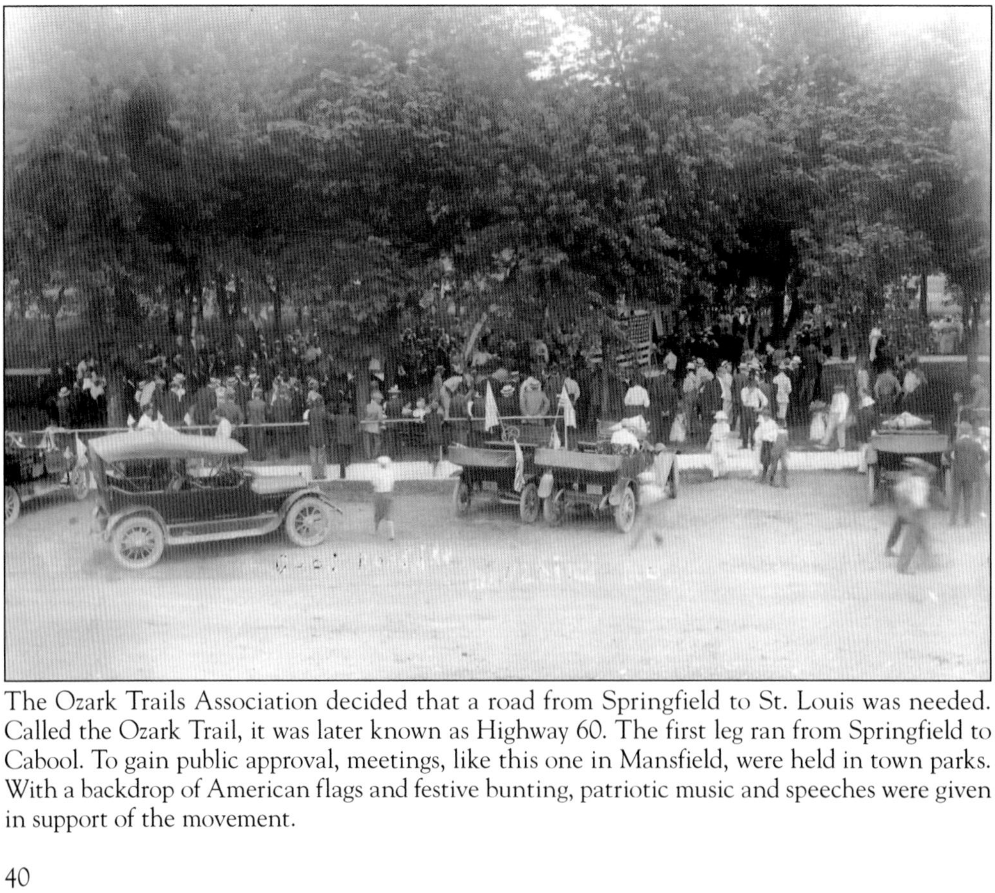

The Ozark Trails Association decided that a road from Springfield to St. Louis was needed. Called the Ozark Trail, it was later known as Highway 60. The first leg ran from Springfield to Cabool. To gain public approval, meetings, like this one in Mansfield, were held in town parks. With a backdrop of American flags and festive bunting, patriotic music and speeches were given in support of the movement.

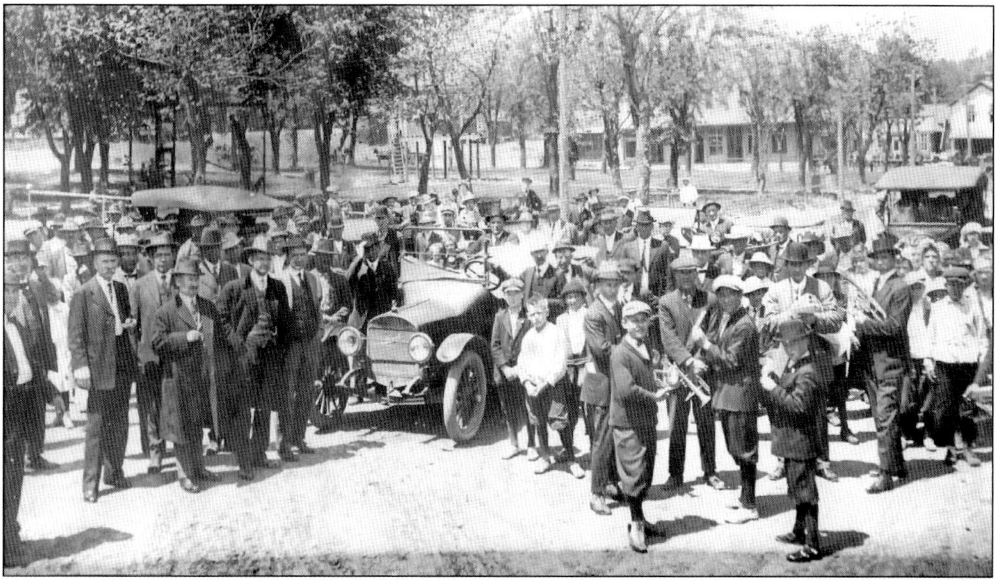

An article in the December 18, 1915, issue of *Scientific American* showcased the Mansfield Good Roads movement. As reported, the "Gem City of the Ozarks" was gaining national attention for its Good Roads work. In August 1915, the town fathers declared a Good Road Day, and all local businesses closed. Above, supporters gather on the square to celebrate. Below, Dr. F.H. Riley, mayor and one of the three road commissioners, stands in front of the sign with a shovel in his left hand. His goal was to see permanent roads extending towards the county seat. The town voted to issue $20,000 in bonds to continue the building of permanent roads, and it was expected that within a year, 35 miles of roads in the Mansfield district would be as improved as those in any other county.

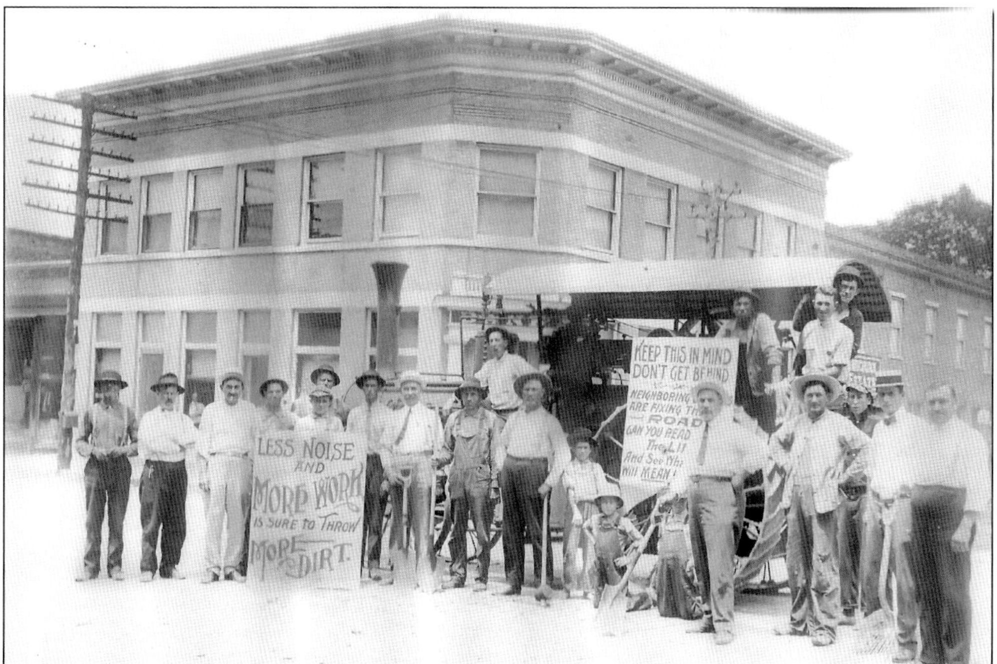

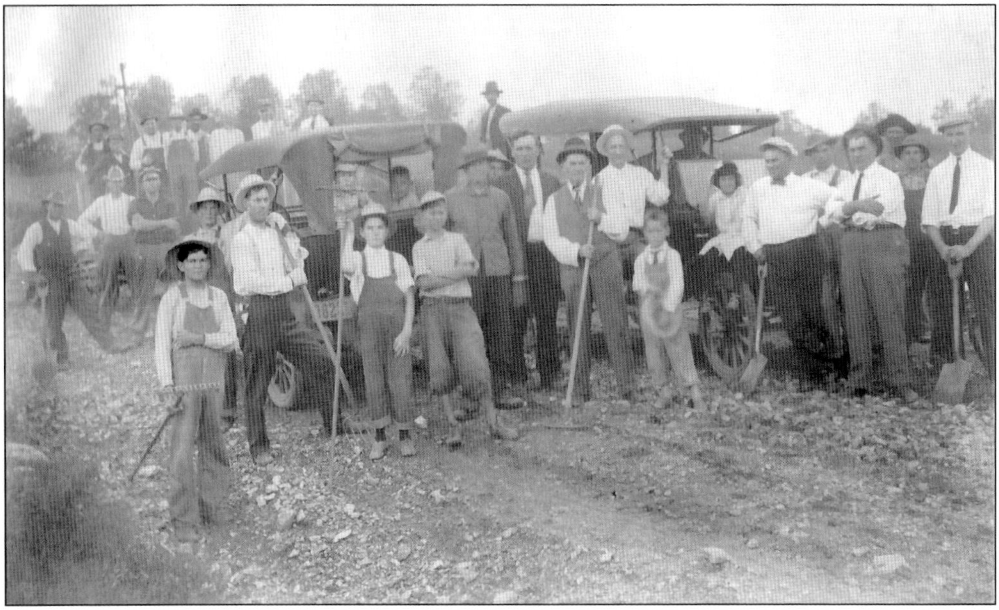

Dr. F.H. Riley established a boys' Good Roads Club with more than 50 members. In September 1915, they made this second trip to work on county roads, inspiring local men to become involved. The boys picked and hauled more than 200 loads of rock, which were used to resurface rough spots and to build a concrete culvert. Ten teams of horses and mules hauled gravel from creek beds.

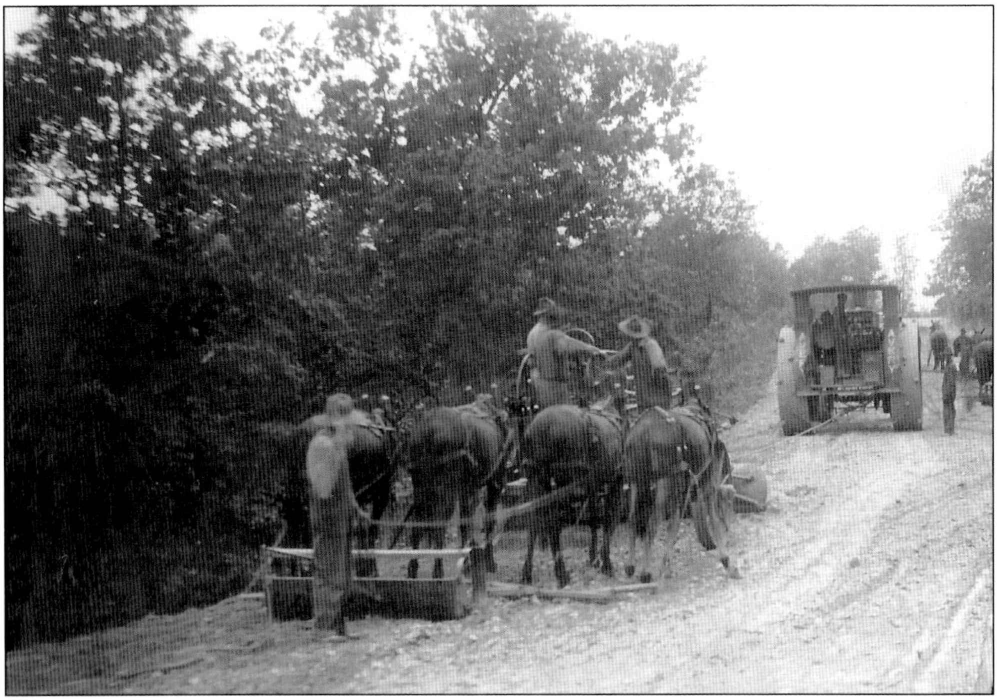

Money collected from the road tax was used for the upkeep of local roads. Taxpayers could choose to either pay the tax or work on the roads. Working on the road, as seen here, was an arduous task. An Avery steam tractor pulls a road grader to flatten the road. Behind this, a man drives a four-hitch of horses pulling a scraper to level the surface.

Gas tanks of early vehicles were usually in the front, making it hard for cars to go down hills because the gas would slosh, causing the engine to flood. Many old-timers said that their dads had to drive backwards up hills because they could not handle the steep embankments. At some creeks, steel bridges, like this one at London, were constructed. The bridge frame was made of steel; the floor was made of wood planks.

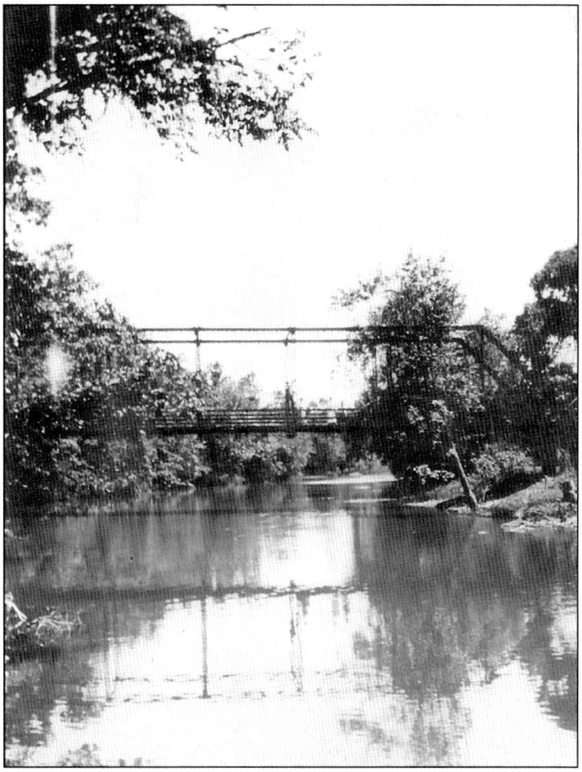

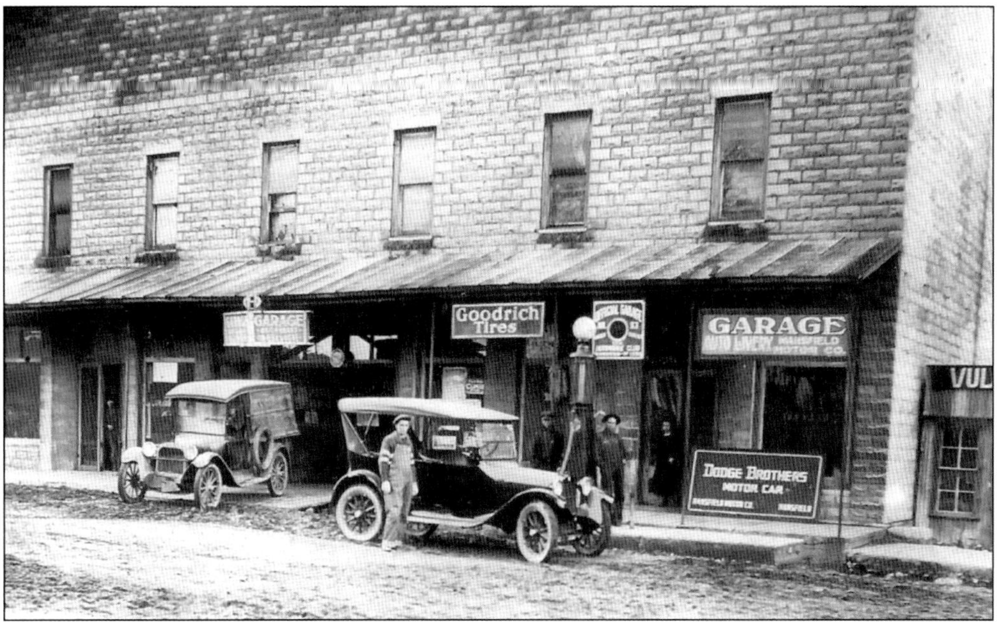

Located in the Miller building, the Van Ness garage was the Ford dealership in the early 1900s. Model Ts were shipped by rail in crates, which were placed on a hand-cranked conveyor belt and moved to the upstairs showroom to be displayed. When a vehicle was purchased, it was sent back down the conveyor belt and reassembled behind the building. The wooden crate became the floorboard.

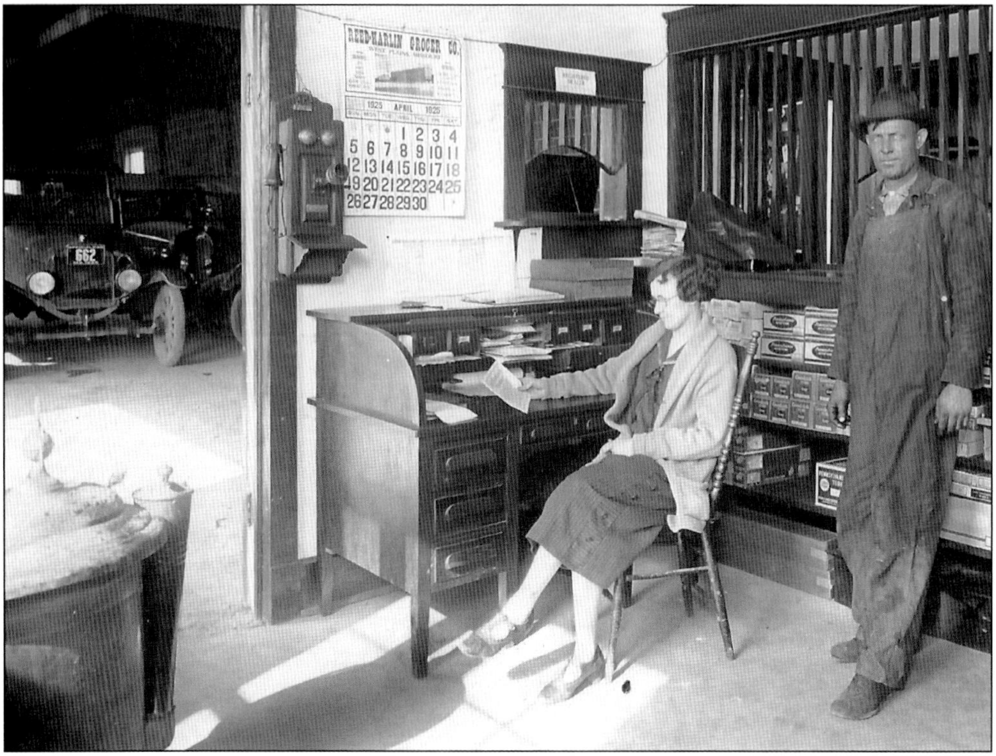

Elmer and Jessie Strong are seen above inside their Maxwell dealership. Between 1917 and 1918, Mansfield Motor Company, with R.N. Farren as manager, began selling Maxwell cars to the residents of Mansfield and Wright County. In 1924, when Elmer Strong and Mr. Tarbutton purchased the dealership and changed the name to Strong and Tarbutton Motors, they built this structure. The building served as a showroom, a garage for repairs, and a service station. Next to it stands the *Mansfield Mirror* and part of the west wall of the rock Missouri Farmers Association building. Huge wooden signs outside Mansfield welcomed travelers to town and also advertised the dealership, the service station, and a ladies' waiting room.

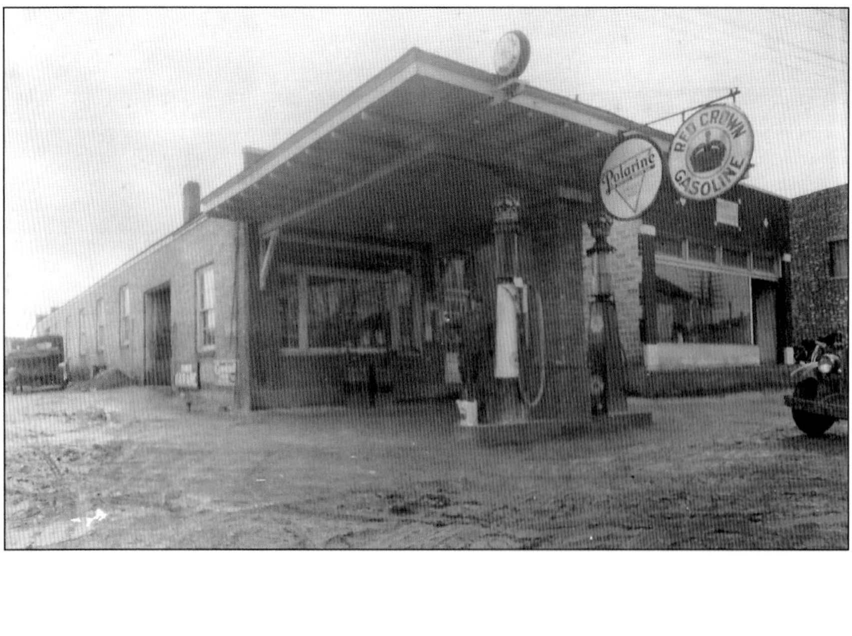

George Samuel of Cedar Gap, a motorcycle enthusiast, poses with one of his cycles. Samuel began cycling in 1912; his first cycle was a 1911 Metz that cost $25. While employed by Erb Fruit Company at Cedar Gap, he rode a Flying Merkel Twin. When Samuel worked as a motorcycle dispatch rider during World War I, he rode an Indian. After his discharge from the Army, he bought a 1916 Indian.

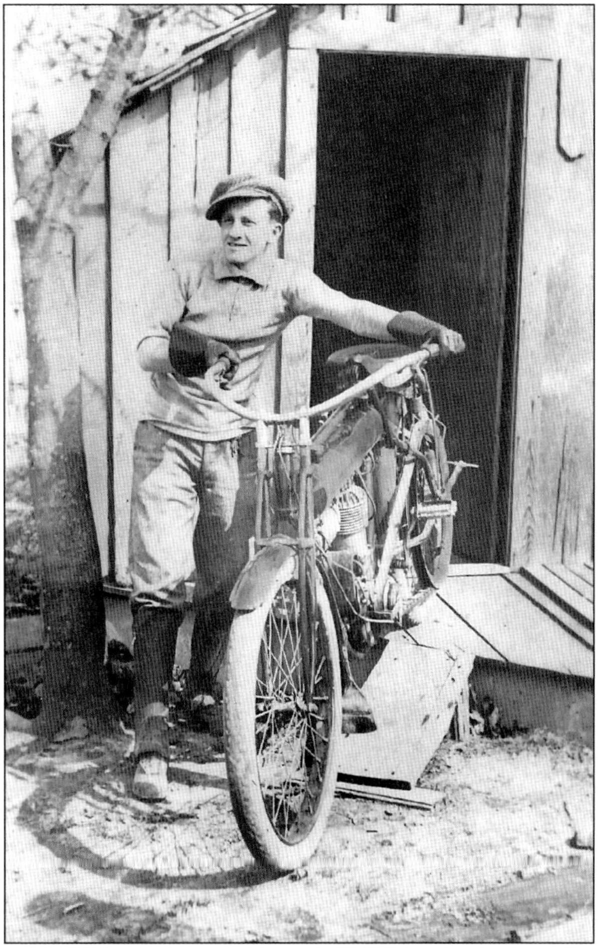

In the early 1900s, many motorcycles were imported into the United States. They were mainly used by travelers and commuters because they were less expensive than automobiles and cheaper to operate. The first motorcycles were actually bicycles with small engines installed on them. These cycles sparked some creative individuals to motorize their own bicycles. Below, dapper Hosea Newton was definitely an eye catcher riding around town on this motorcycle.

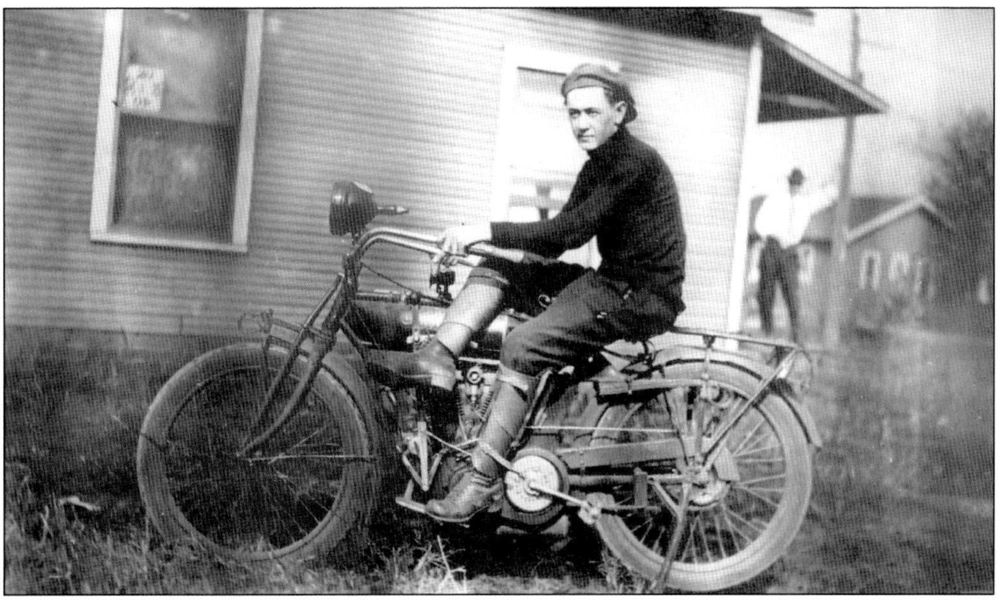

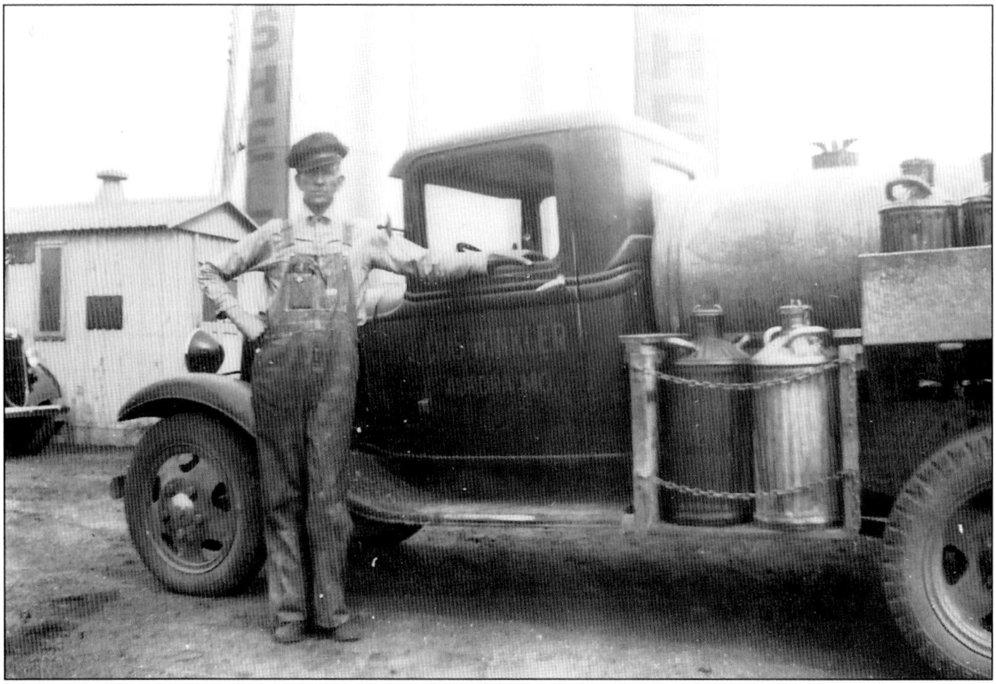

With more automobiles on the road, the need for more readily available gas brought about a new business opportunity. The distribution of gas, referred to as oil, required large, filled tanks to be hauled in on the rails. Lige Craig owned the oil tanks, which were on the south side of the tracks. Gasoline was loaded onto oil trucks, like the one pictured here, and distributed to outlying areas.

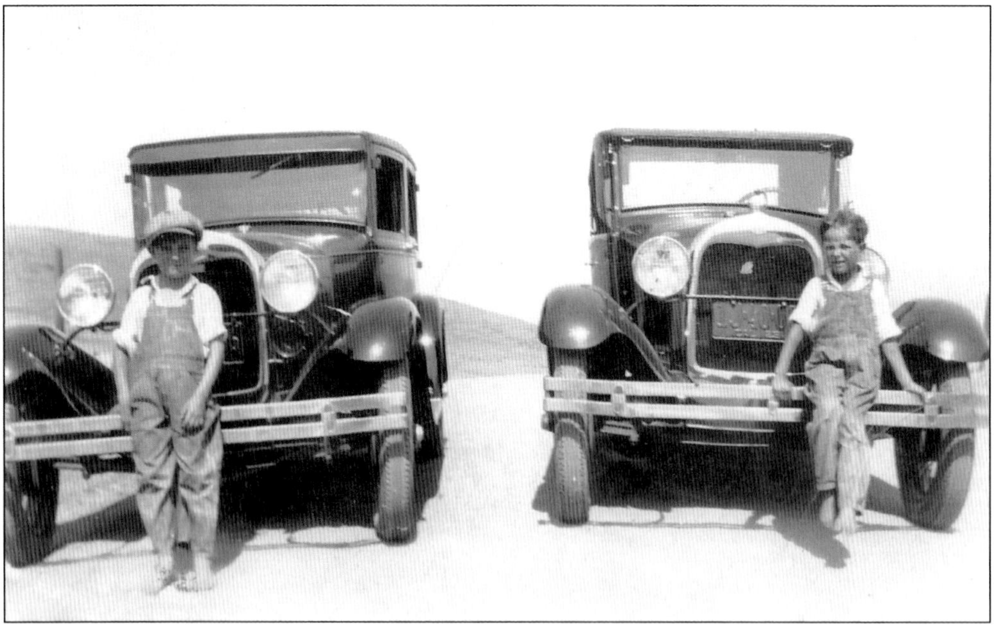

This was the end of a 14-day cross-country journey made by the Moody, Stout, and Fagan families from Mansfield, Missouri, to California in the spring of 1928. For Hosea Stout (left) and Cecil Duquesne (right) it was a grand adventure as they camped along the road at night under a blanket of stars. Other families, seeking a milder climate and jobs, made the same trip on Route 66.

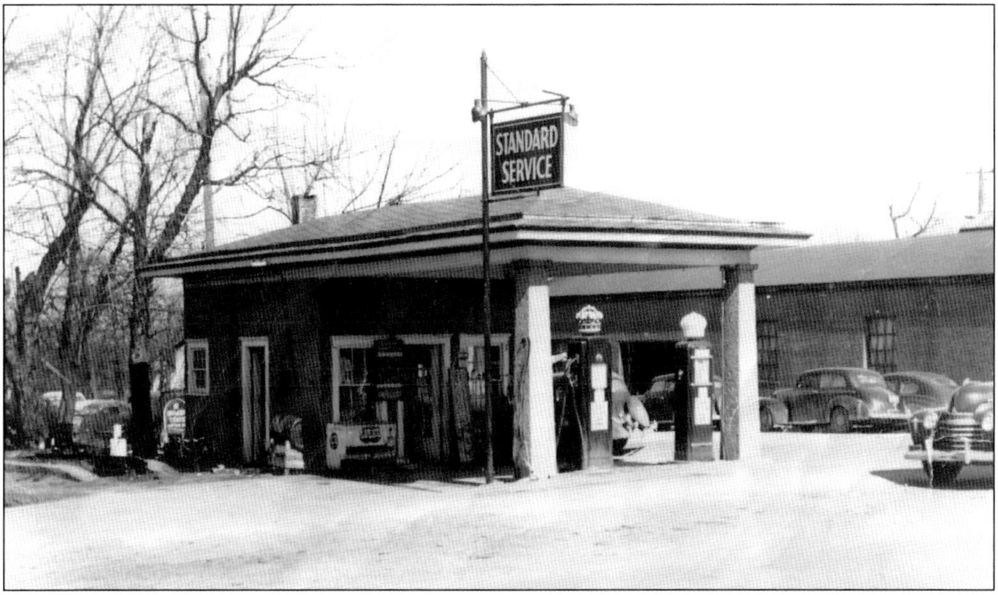

One day, Almanzo Wilder pulled into Silas Seals's service station. Seals checked the tire pressure, the water in the radiator, and washed the windows before ever asking if Wilder wanted to buy any gas. Reportedly, Almanzo said, "Seals, you don't know if I'm even going to buy gas." Seals replied, "Mr. Wilder, you have to have air in your tires, water in your radiator, and a clean windshield." When this photograph was taken, the station was owned by Chet Taylor.

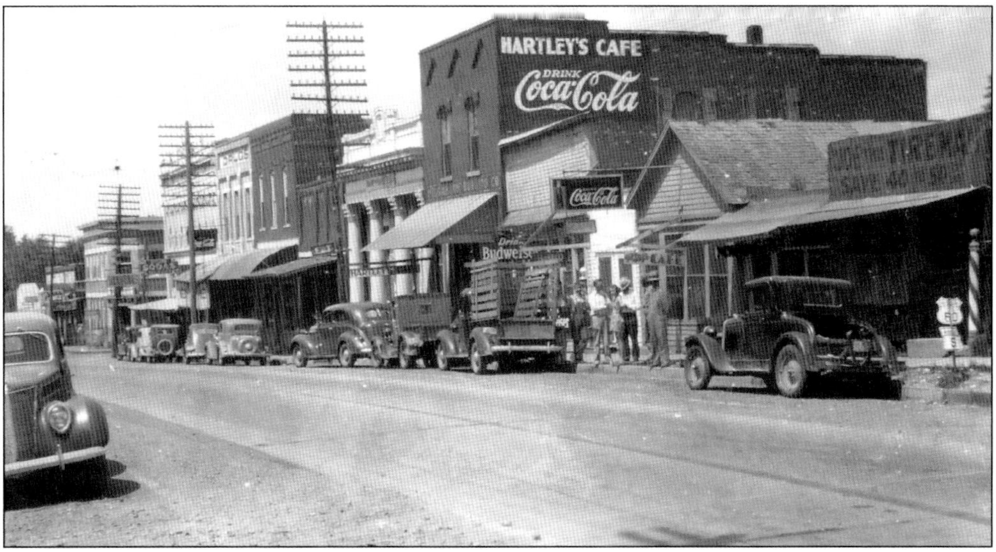

The 1930s brought change to the face of Mansfield. Automobiles replaced horse-drawn vehicles. Cement sidewalks replaced the wide wooden boardwalks. The paving of Highway 60 brought a totally new and updated look to the downtown area. This 1940 photograph shows that most of the original wooden structures were replaced with brick buildings. Although the business section has been paved, the shoulders are still either gravel or dirt.

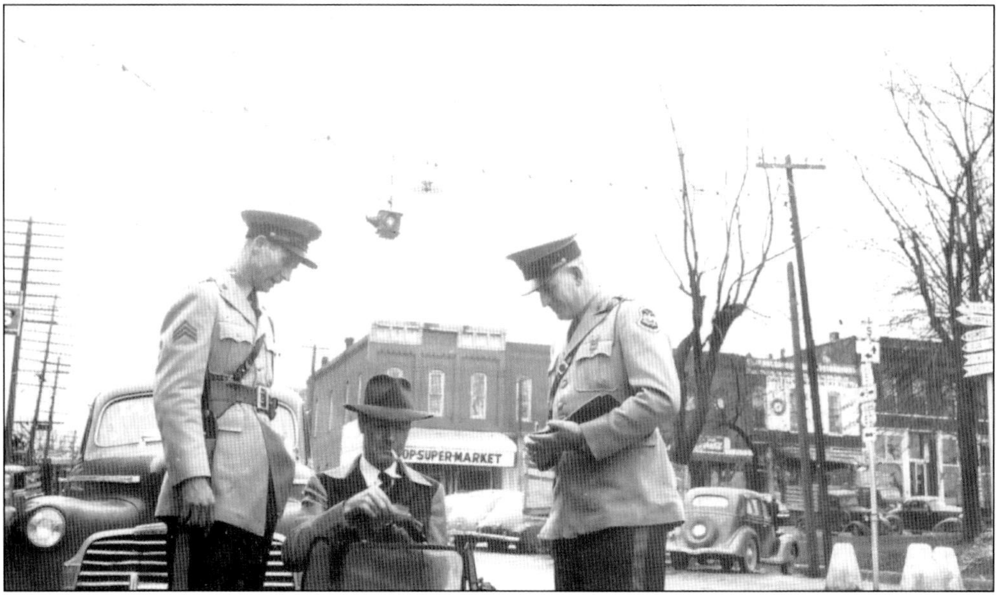

In 1946, P.E. McCracken dared Snyder Craig, an employee with Farmers and Merchants Bank, to drive a battery-operated toy car, belonging to McCracken's three-year-old son, through Mansfield's intersection of Highway 60 and Highway 5. In this staged photograph, Craig is being lightheartedly "arrested" by highway patrolmen Ted Taylor and Earl Barkley.

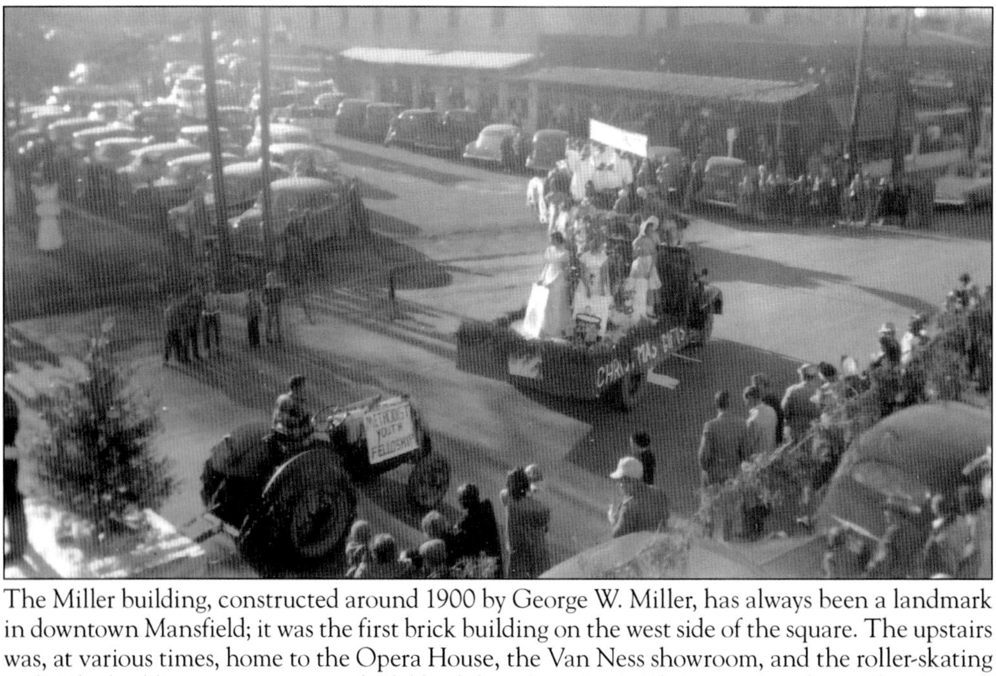

The Miller building, constructed around 1900 by George W. Miller, has always been a landmark in downtown Mansfield; it was the first brick building on the west side of the square. The upstairs was, at various times, home to the Opera House, the Van Ness showroom, and the roller-skating rink. The building serves as a wonderful backdrop for a 1940s Christmas parade winding its way around the square.

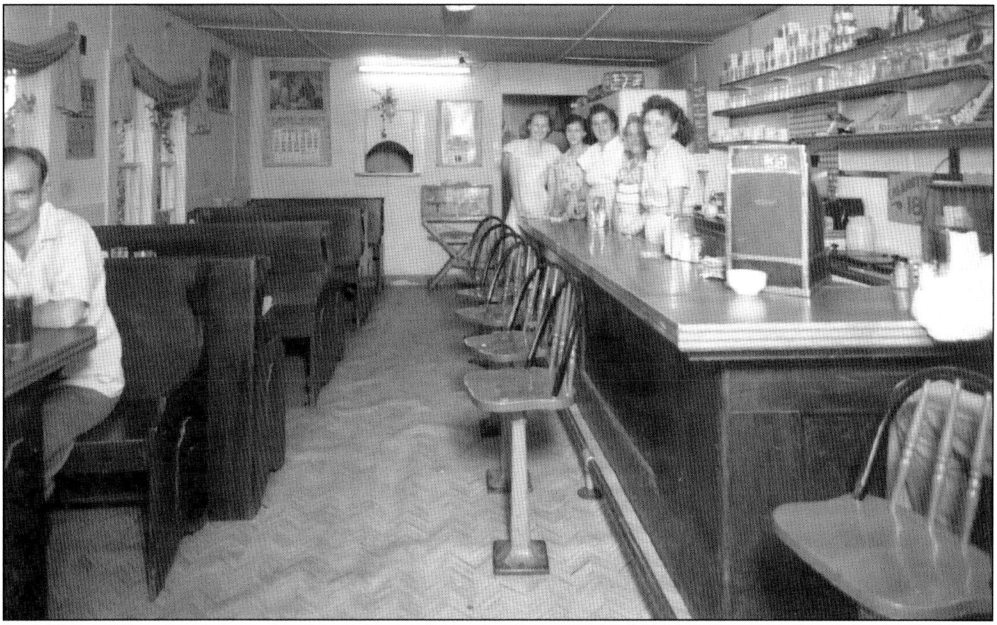

With the introduction of cars, the face of America changed. During this golden age of the automobile, new highways were built and paved, providing easier access to travel, but there was one problem: where would travelers eat and sleep while on the road? Camp Summit, seen in both photographs, was a prime example of a solution to this problem. Camp Summit was composed of three different businesses, all catering to the automobile and its owner. A station provided gas to refuel the vehicles, a cafe afforded food and drink to the travelers, and cabins allowed them to rest up for the next day's travel or enjoy an extended stay. The waitresses working in the cafe at the time of this photograph are, from left to right, Ruby June Drake, Gloria Bogart, Fern Veit, Edna Rippee, and Mabel Thompson.

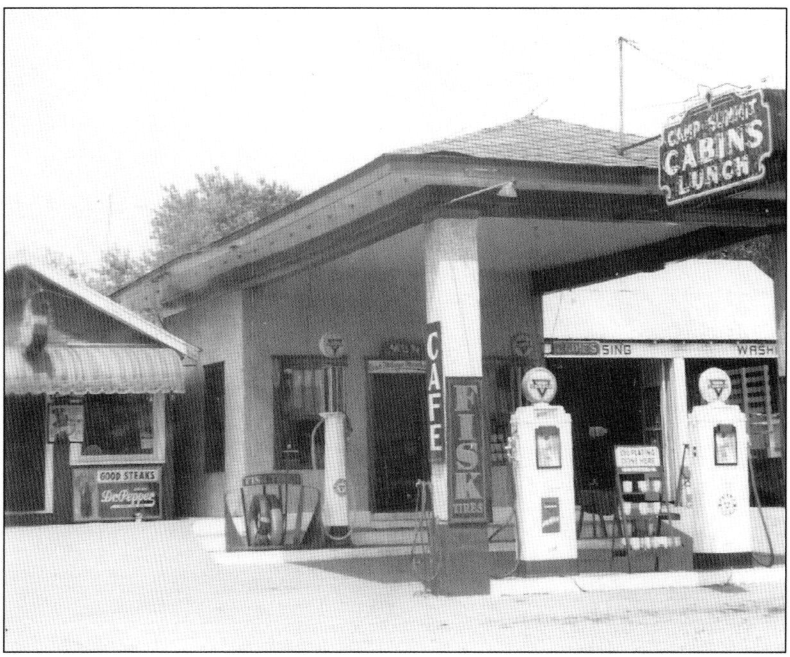

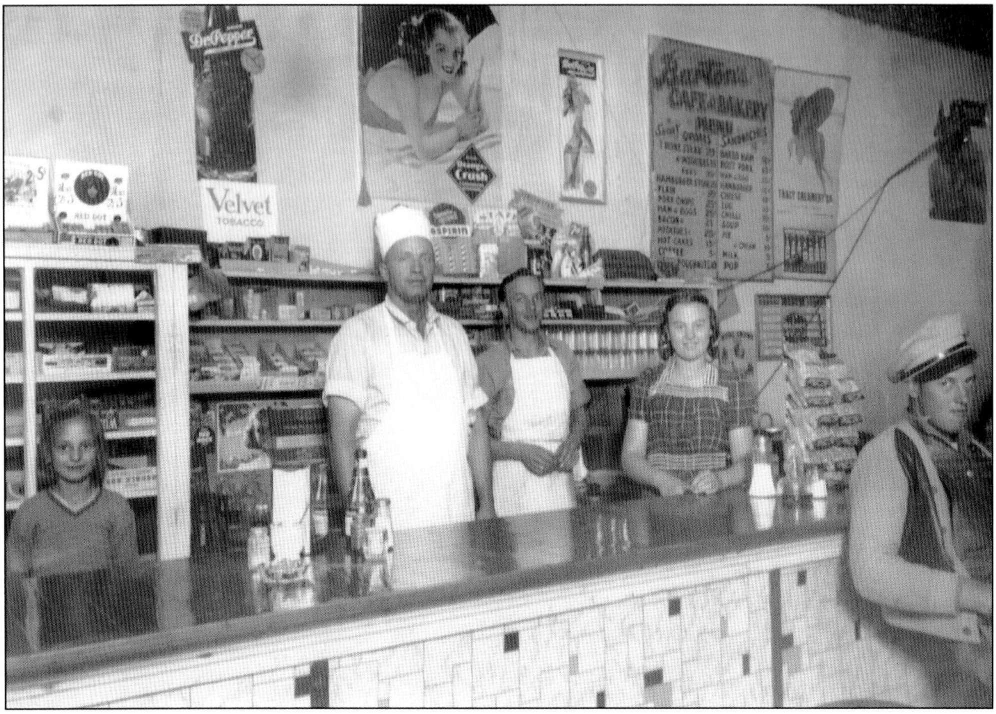

Another well-known Mansfield eatery was Barton's Cafe & Bakery. The owner and main baker was W.C. "Bake" Barton, who was noted for his pies. This 1940 picture shows, from left to right, Daisy Barton, W.C. Barton, Shelby Barton, Mary Barton, and unidentified. Some items listed on the menu included ham and eggs (25¢), hamburger steak (25¢), chili (10¢), pie (5¢), and coffee (5¢).

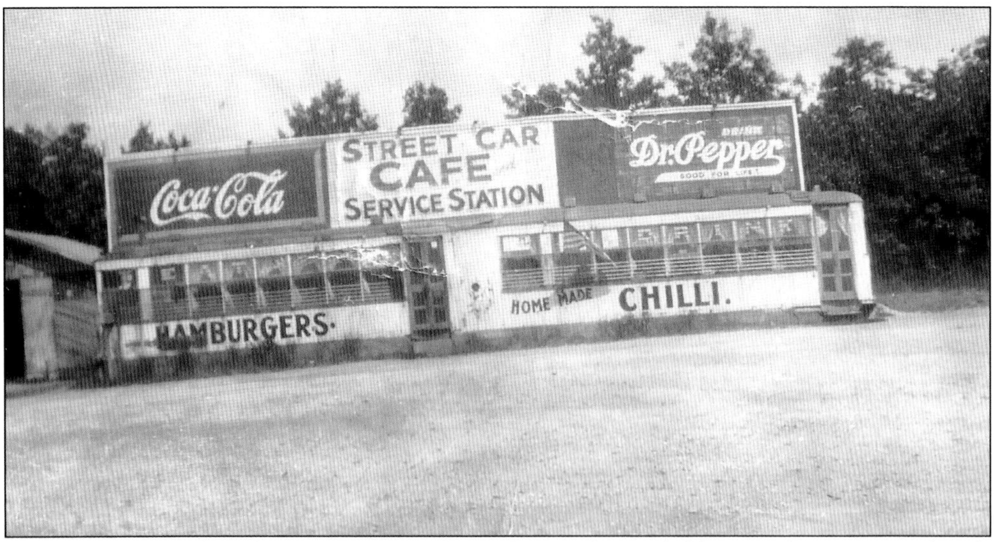

The Street Car Cafe and Service Station, located west of Mansfield on Highway 60, was handy for travelers just wanting a quick bite. It was also Mansfield's only honky-tonk, with a bar and dance hall. Many locals recall weekend dates consisting of parking in the woods on the right just to see who went inside. The numerous fights outside the cafe provided entertainment, some so rowdy that they sometimes stopped traffic on Highway 60.

Four

Benches and Blackboards

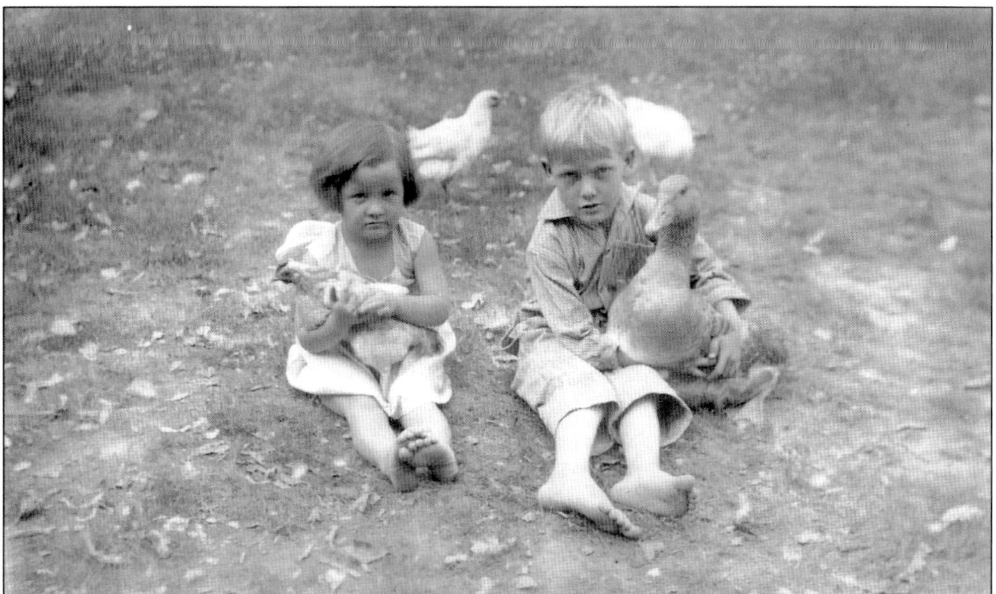

Shoes were cast aside by the eighth day of May, when fear of frost had passed. Barefoot summers filled with playtime and chores all too soon gave way to hand-me-down clothes and resoled shoes when "books took up" in the fall. Students were schooled in the three Rs: reading, writing, and arithmetic.

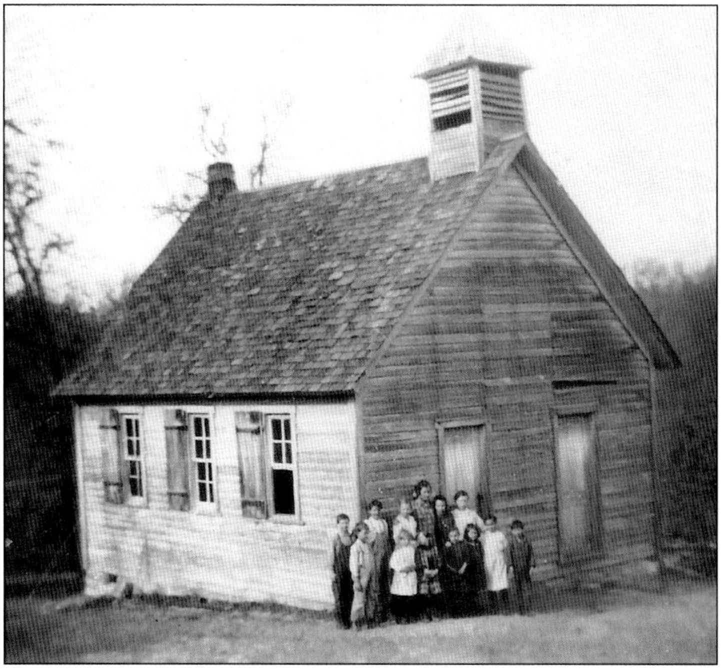

Early schools were one-room log structures. Later, sawmills produced lumber for frame buildings, utilizing the abundant native timber. Flat boards painted black hung on the wall for ciphering. Family-owned textbooks were passed down to younger siblings, and the schools were always strapped for money. Besides teaching all eight grades, teachers were also responsible for building a fire, and sometimes, a pot of beans simmered on the stove. Pea Vine School, pictured above, was located south of Mansfield. It boasted a belfry, shuttered windows, and a hand-hewn, shake-shingled roof. Schools often shared the name of the family that donated the land. Johnson School, seen below, was named for grantor Calvin Johnson. Although area springs provided clear, cool water for many rural schools, Johnson was fortunate to have a well with a hand pump.

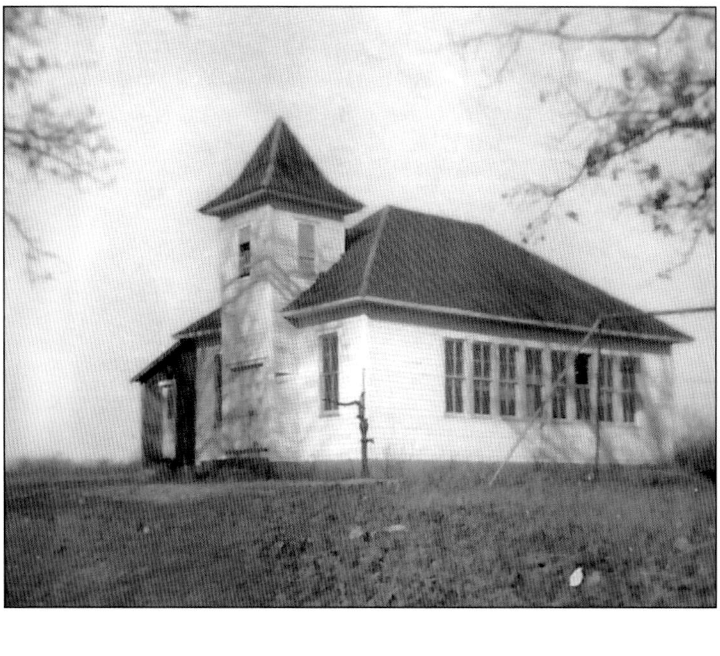

No. 5 School, so named because it was the fifth school in Gasconade Township, was located on the Lick Fork of the Gasconade River between London and Pleasant Valley. Teachers boarded with families who lived near the school. Teacher Amel Long and student Scotty Brazeal stand in front of the Brazeal home with lunch pails in hand, ready for another day.

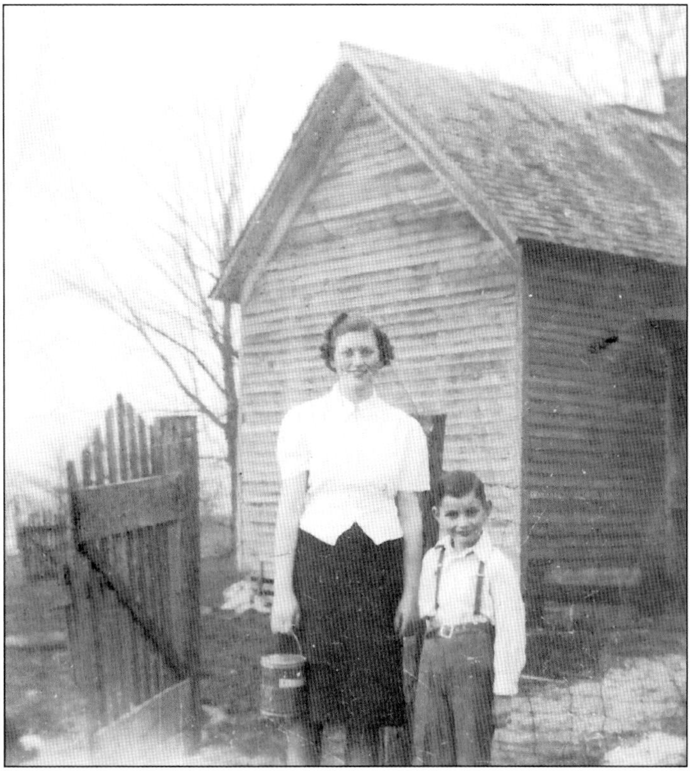

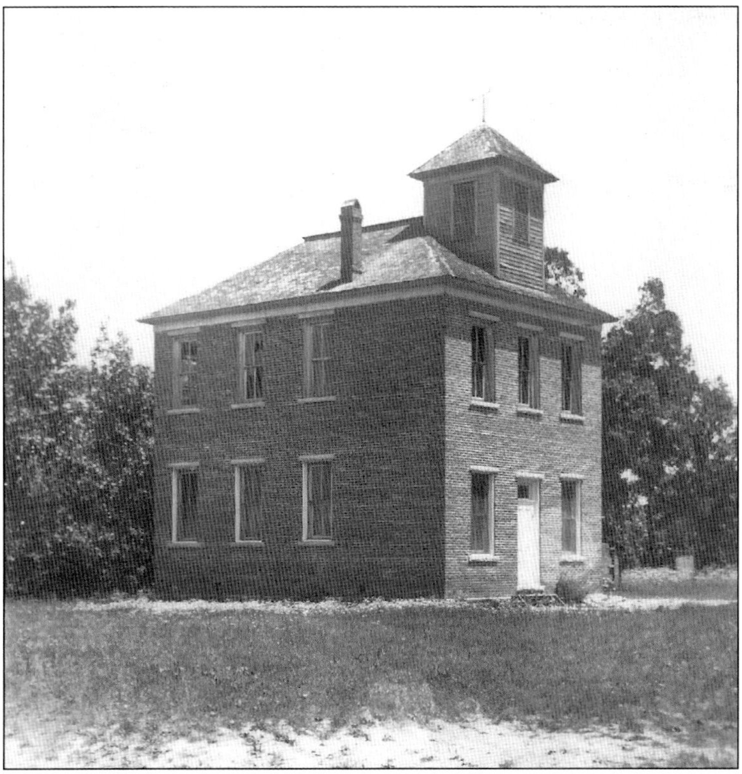

In the early 1900s, the original frame school building at Cedar Gap was destroyed by fire, and a new two-story brick building with its own belfry was erected. Early teachers of this school included Frank Foster, Fred Gates, and W.R. Reed. Cedar Gap School district consolidated with Mansfield Schools in 1949.

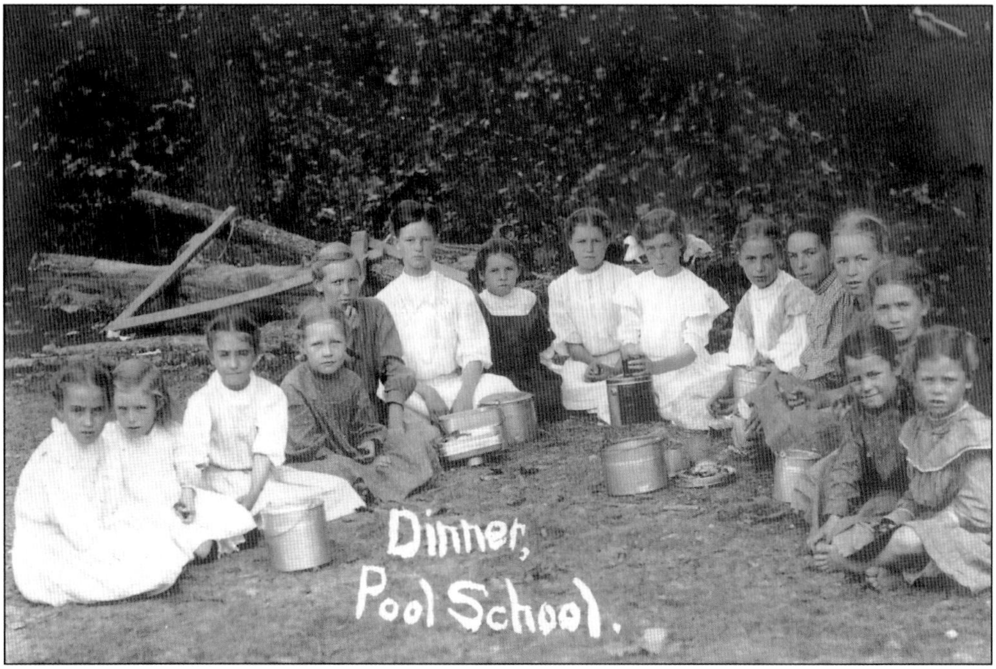

Prior to the advent of cafeterias, most students carried their lunches to school in lard buckets. Staple items included leftover biscuits or cornbread sandwiched with ham or bacon. These were readily swapped for "store bought bread." It wasn't until cafeterias were added in the 1930s that hot lunches were provided. Above, students of Pool School, located two miles northwest of Mansfield, enjoy their dinner outside. This district consolidated with the Mansfield School system around 1927. Oak Ridge School, below, was also located northwest of Mansfield on F Highway, formerly known as Rockbridge Road. This brick school was built in 1905. The cafeteria, located on the right side of the school, was added later. Although Oak Ridge consolidated with Mansfield in 1948, classes continued there for an additional two years while Mansfield built more classrooms to accommodate the increased enrollment.

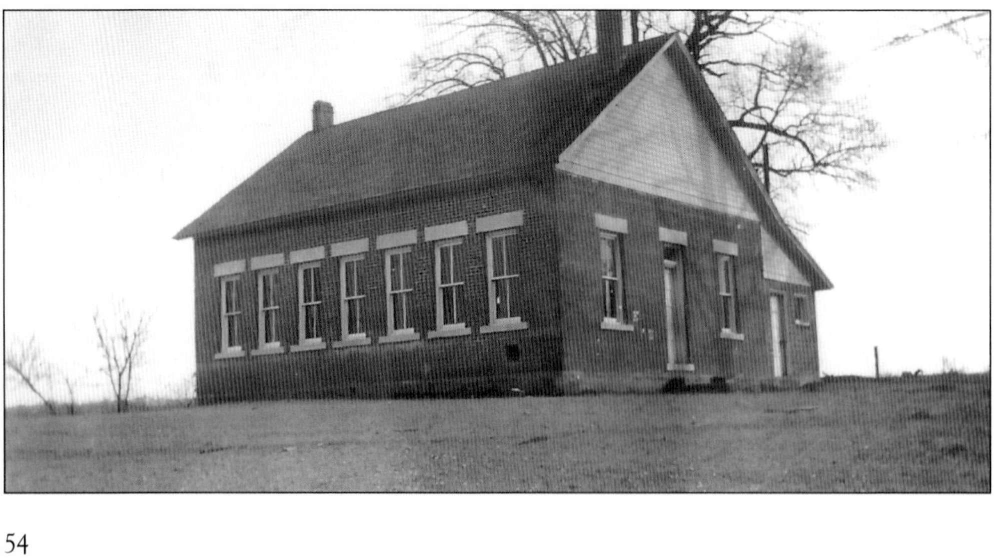

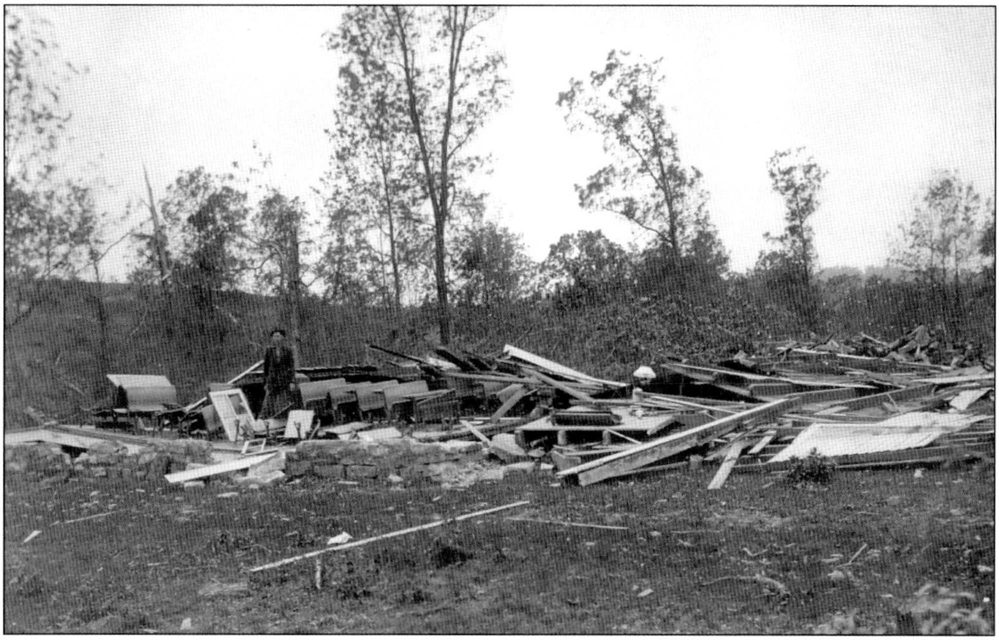

Flat Rock School, also known as Slate School, was situated south of Mansfield near Bryant Creek. In 1917, a cyclone started at Flat Rock and continued northeast until it reached the home of the Whites, just south of the railroad tracks in Mansfield. Although all records from Flat Rock were lost, some of the desks and the teacher's coal oil lamp survived.

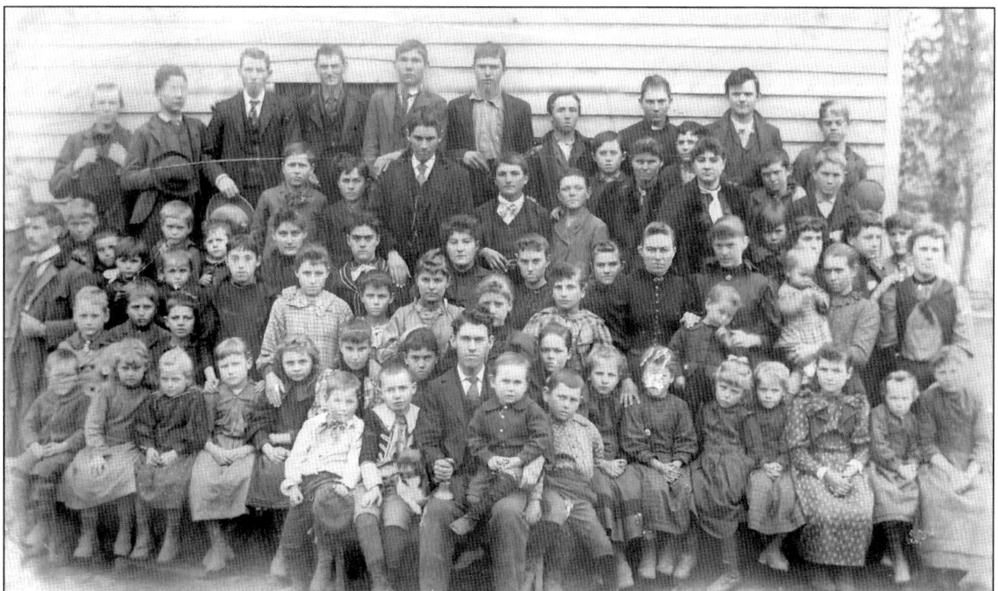

Pea Ridge School, located north of Mansfield, was named for the ridge road running through the Umpire community. A log school was constructed in 1860, followed by a frame building. Directors, students and families, and teacher C.M. Kincheloe, holding the bell in the front row, gather for a special occasion on January 21, 1896. Textbooks used at this time included *Walter's Spelling*, *McGuffey Readers*, *Spencerian Writing*, and *Ray's Arithmetic*.

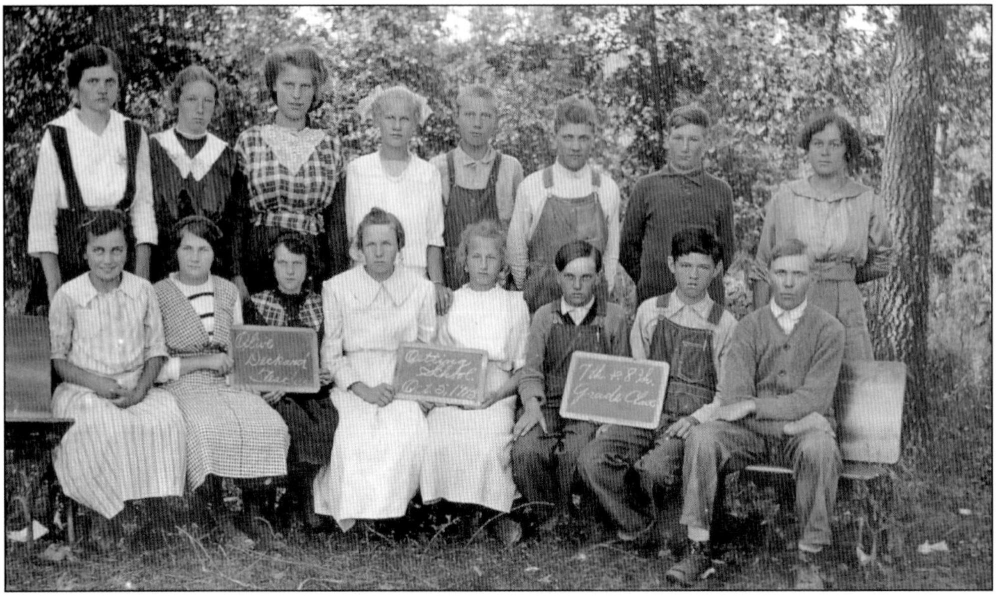

In 1895, Dietrich Oetting and Joe H. Dennis led the movement to establish Oetting School. The first teacher there was Jane Poort. In this 1915 picture, teacher Olive Deckard poses with her seventh- and eighth-grade classes. Surnames of some families residing in this community included Oetting, Lakey, Ingerson, Matlock, Adamson, Sikes, Ivy, Dennis, and Gutchke. A new sandstone school building was constructed in 1940 by the Works Progress Administration (WPA) and still stands north of Mansfield.

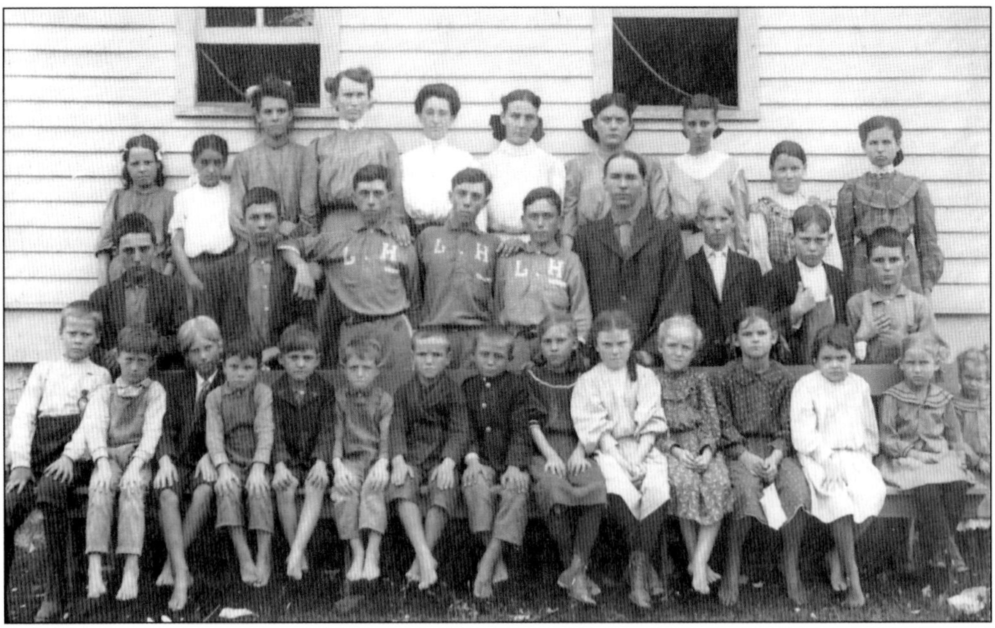

Lead Hill School, which was also used for church services, was built in 1870 on land donated by the Reverend O.B. Whittaker. Frona Rippee, a 1907 Mansfield High School graduate, was teaching these students in 1908. Family names of those attending Lead Hill included Crider, Morris, Cameron, Douglas, Goss, and Davis. Baseball games highlighted Friday afternoons at rural schools. Harry, Fred, and Claude Crider proudly sport their Lead Hill baseball uniforms.

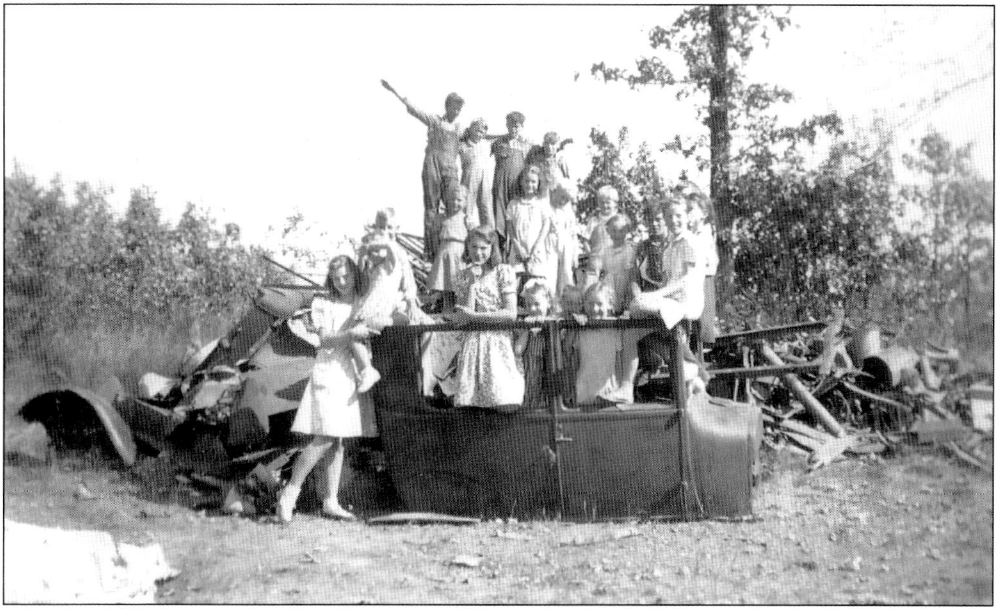

Fagan, another one-room school, rallied to answer Franklin Roosevelt's challenge to collect scrap metal for the World War II effort. Evelyn Moody Duquesne (standing front left) and her classmates present the pile they accumulated, everything from buckets, old car bodies, tractor parts, and wheel rims. The scrap was loaded onto railroad cars or government trucks and sent to factories to be melted into items for the troops.

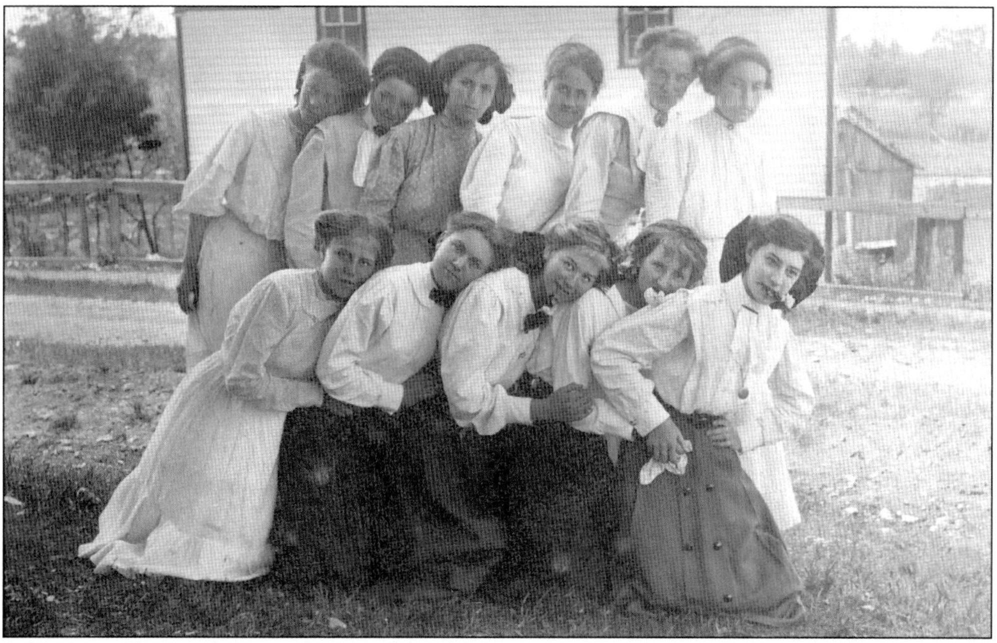

Schools taught social graces along with book learning. Young women were taught the art of being ladylike, while their male counterparts learned how to behave like gentlemen. Life-long friendships often developed. Shown cutting up after class, from left to right are (first row) Maude Coday, Bess Turner, Veda Coday, Clara Hensley, and Corene Hitchcock; (second row) Audrey Deaver, Veda Teftteller, Magg Turner, Myrtle Campbell, Zenna Reynolds, and Lula Carter.

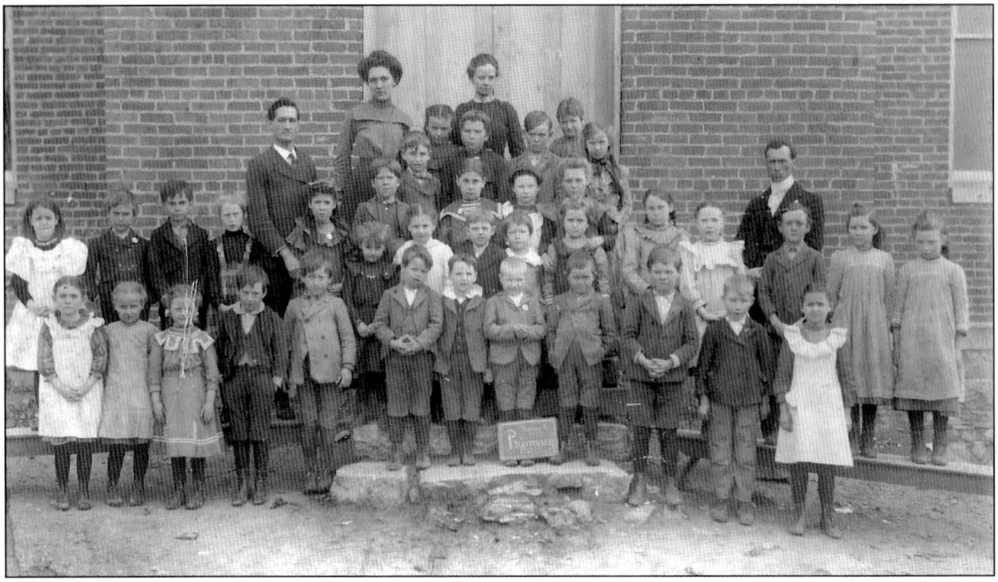

In 1883, Mansfield erected its first school east of the square. Drinking water had to be carried from a spring south of the railroad tracks, as there were few wells in town. Early instructors included professors ? Hickman (1884), ? Moore (1885), ? Caldwell (1886), Annie Miller (1887), Houston Freeman (1888), and J.G. Siler (1889). A new four-room, two-story school, shown above, was built in 1891 on the hill at the east edge of town, which remained the school site for the following 80 years. The first 10th grade graduation was in 1904. The 1905 primary class, composed of first through third grades, pictured above, boasted 38 students. The school was destroyed by fire, as shown below, in 1908. A new building was finished in 1909; however, it was 1920 before the first class graduated from Mansfield's four-year high school.

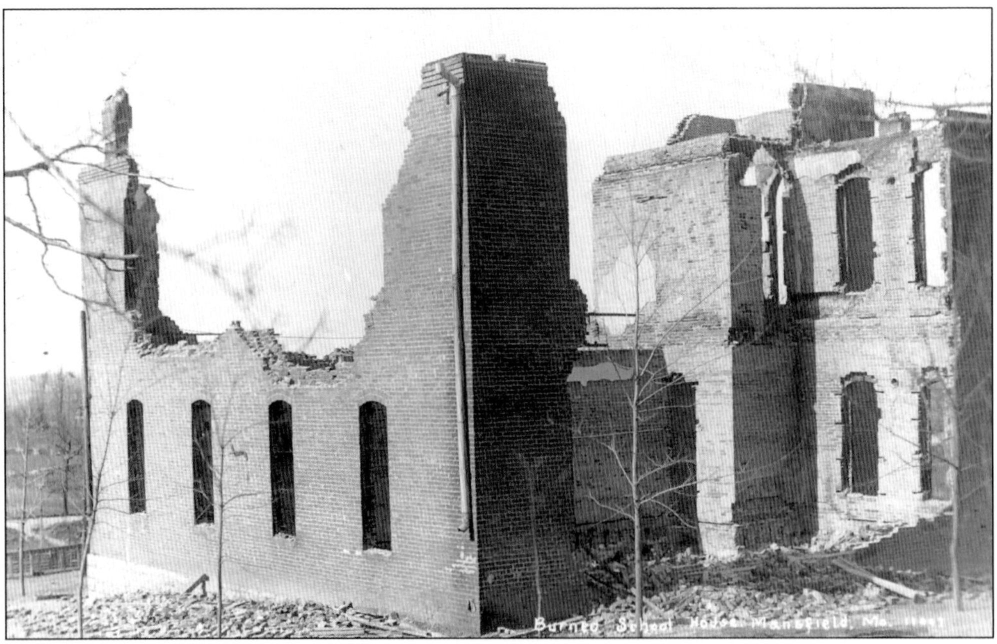

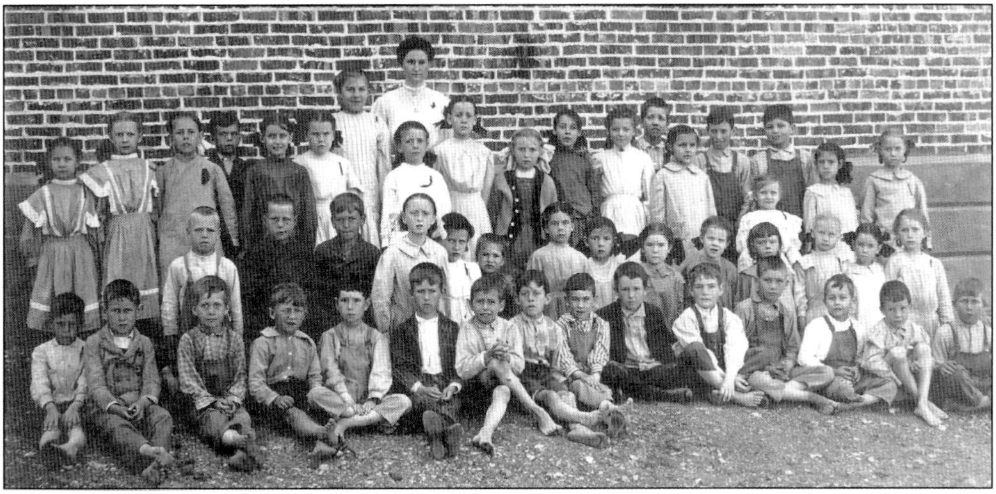

In 1910, Mansfield students returned to a new brick school building recently constructed on the original site. The primary class of 1910 is pictured in front of the school as they begin a new school year. Evidently, the weather is still warm, as evidenced by all the bare feet displayed in the front row. Ora Rippee is the teacher.

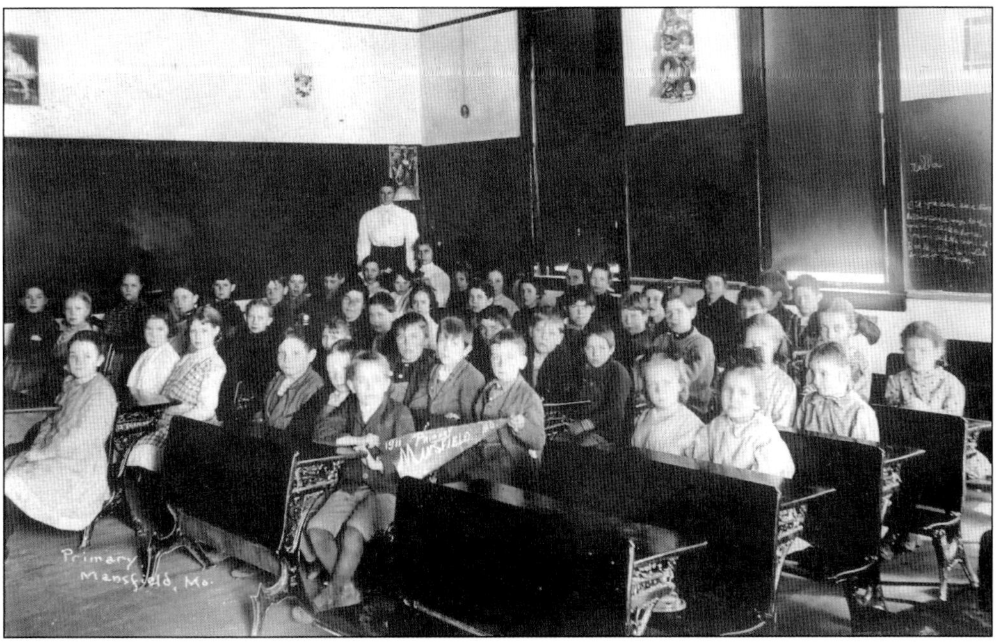

In 1911, the school reported an enrollment of 220 students. The first PTA was organized the same year. The primary class is shown in room no. 1 of the four-room school. This class, usually consisting of the first three grades, was taught by two teachers. The walls were lined with blackboards so that lessons could be taught to different grade levels simultaneously.

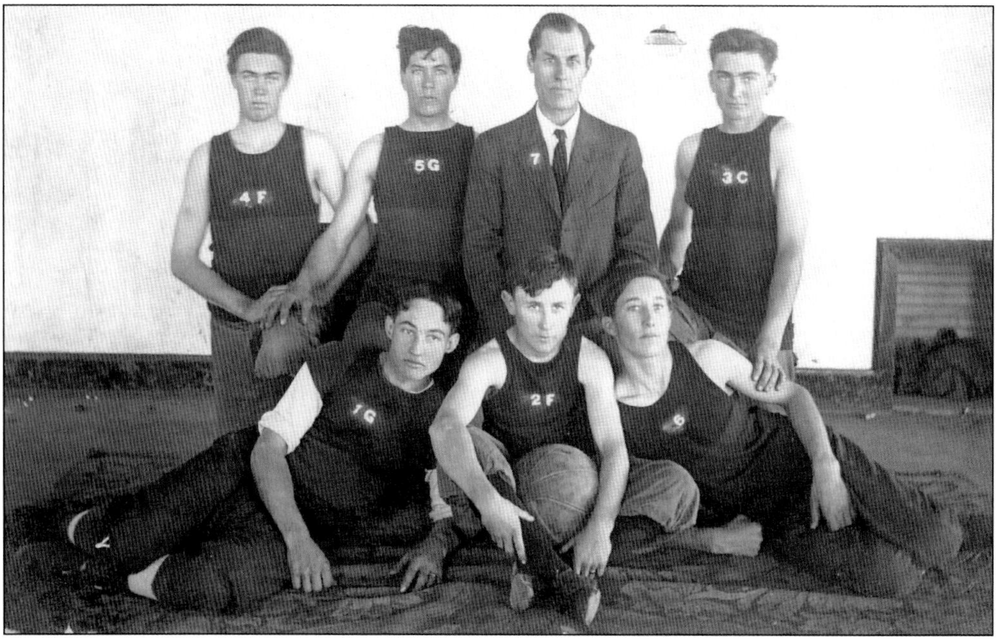

In 1913, six boys formed the original basketball team. For six years, their games were played on the second floor of the Reynolds building on the north side of the square. In 1919, the first frame gym was built. Team members are, from left to right, (first row) Glen Craig, Pete Freeman, and Morris Berry; (second row) Clifford Seals, unidentified, coach J.A. Hylton, and Herb Short.

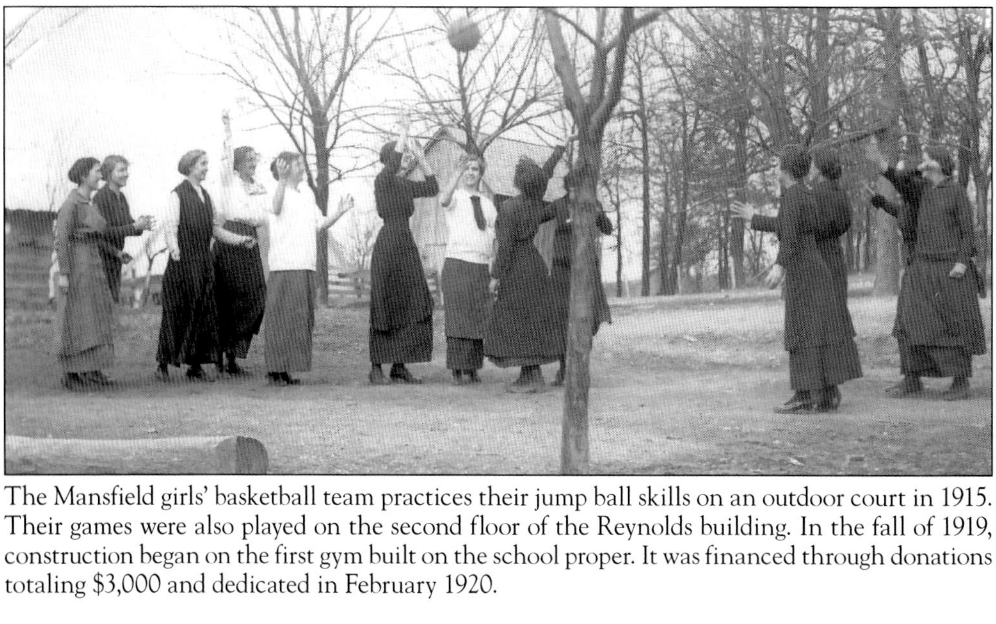

The Mansfield girls' basketball team practices their jump ball skills on an outdoor court in 1915. Their games were also played on the second floor of the Reynolds building. In the fall of 1919, construction began on the first gym built on the school proper. It was financed through donations totaling $3,000 and dedicated in February 1920.

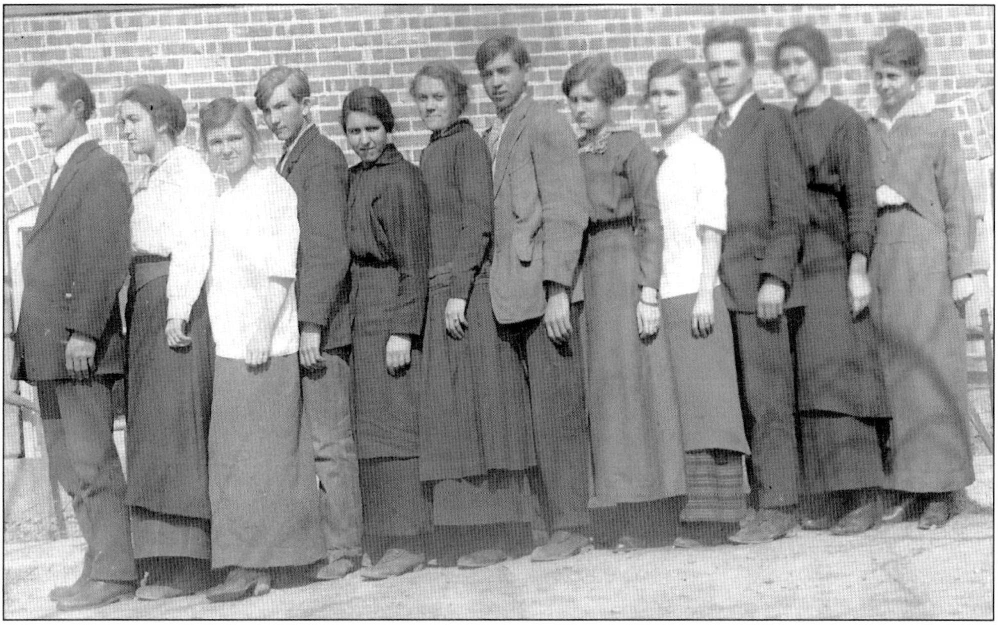

Farm children wanting to further their education often boarded with relatives in town so they could attend high school. Since boys were needed to work on the farm, girls were more likely to take advanced classes. Members of the 1914–1915 junior class were, from left to right, Supt. Joe Hylton, Mable Coday, Mable Hoover, Jordan Bogart, Minta Avery, unidentified, Cecil Brazeal, Minnie Dennis, Opal Hoover, Cecil Gladden, Alice Tomblison, and unidentified.

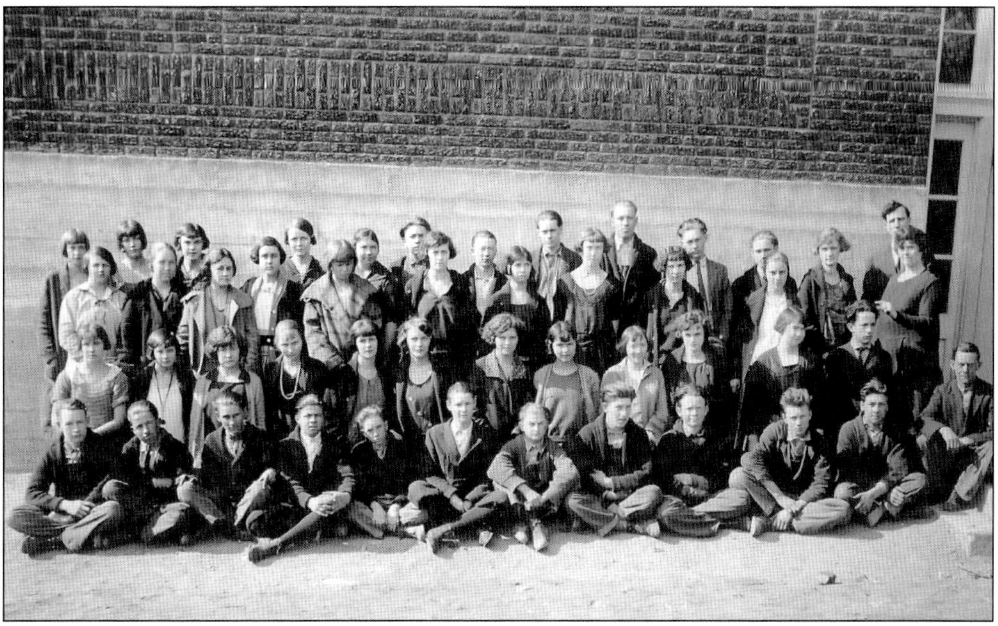

In 1922, Mansfield's school suffered yet another fire. The gym, built in 1920, was divided into four classrooms to temporarily accommodate the lower grades. The high school students met in a private home nearby. Bonds approved in the amount of $11,000, combined with the insurance settlement, covered the $25,000 cost of a new building. The class of 1924, shown here, was the first to graduate from the new brick school.

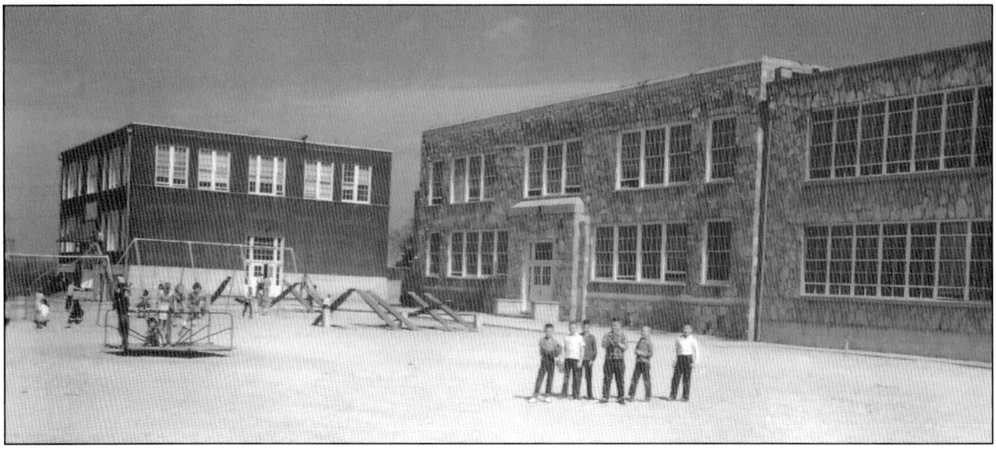

In 1937, a sandstone building containing an elementary school and a gym was erected, completely funded with WPA funds and labor. The old frame gym building was razed at this time. In 1940, a new two-story building for agriculture, shop, and music was completed. Later, this building was joined to the elementary by a cafeteria with classrooms above. An addition was added to the east of the elementary providing dressing rooms for the gym.

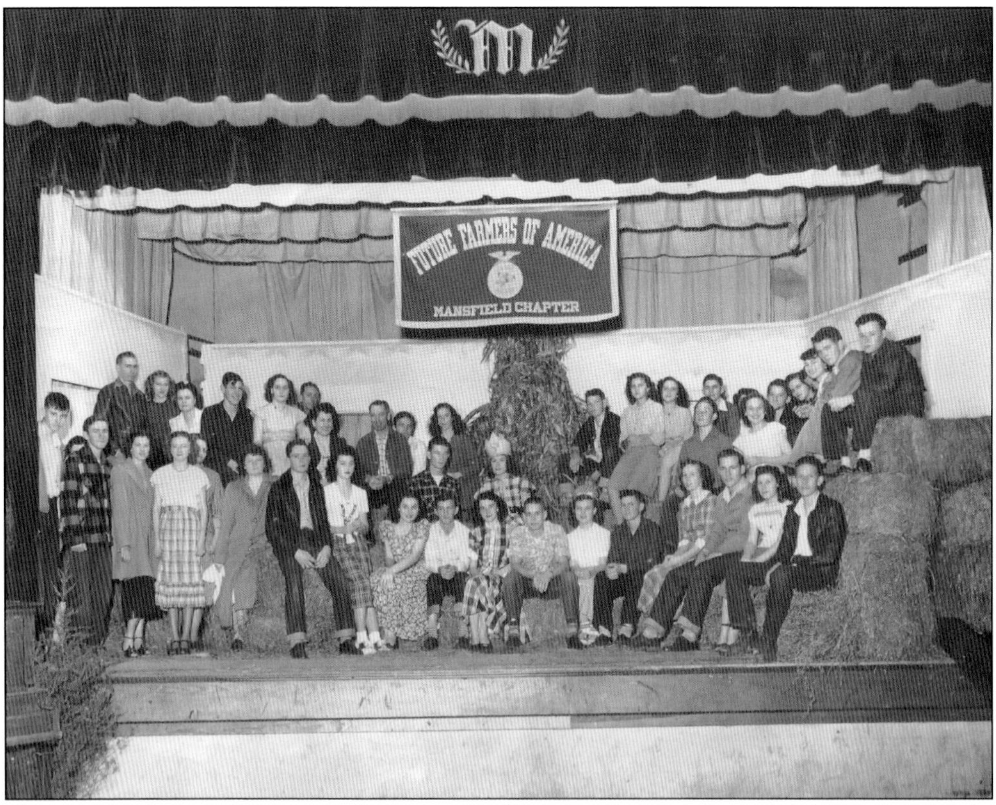

The Future Farmers of America held their annual barn warming activity each fall. Around 1950, members and their dates fill the stage, decorated with hay bales and corn shocks. The gym was the setting for many school and community events, including Christmas programs, school plays, physical education classes, basketball, volleyball, the winding of the May pole, and fundraisers, such as donkey basketball games.

Five

Fruits of Their Labor

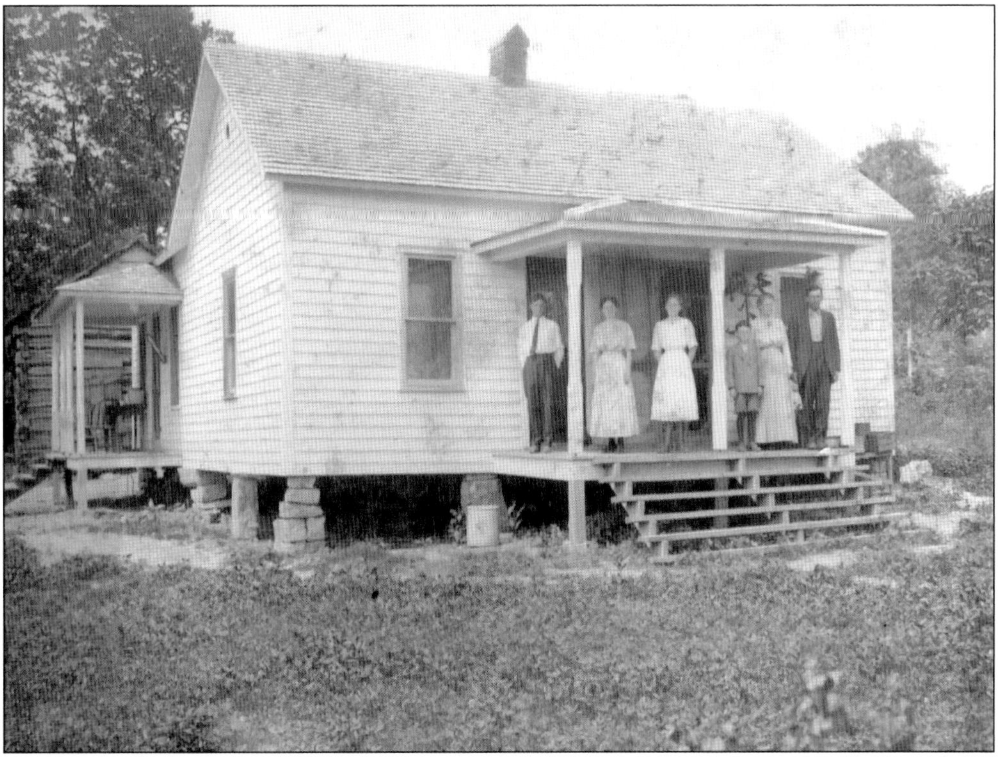

The Martin Gaskill home was typical of the type of house that often replaced the cabins of early settlers. The fireplace and foundation were made of native stone. Preserved meat was kept in the smokehouse, and a back porch served as a clean-up area. Members of the Gaskill family are, from left to right, Ernest, Opal, Stella, Roy, Alice, and Martin. Stone crocks, like the one on the ground beside the porch, collected rainwater for bathing and laundry.

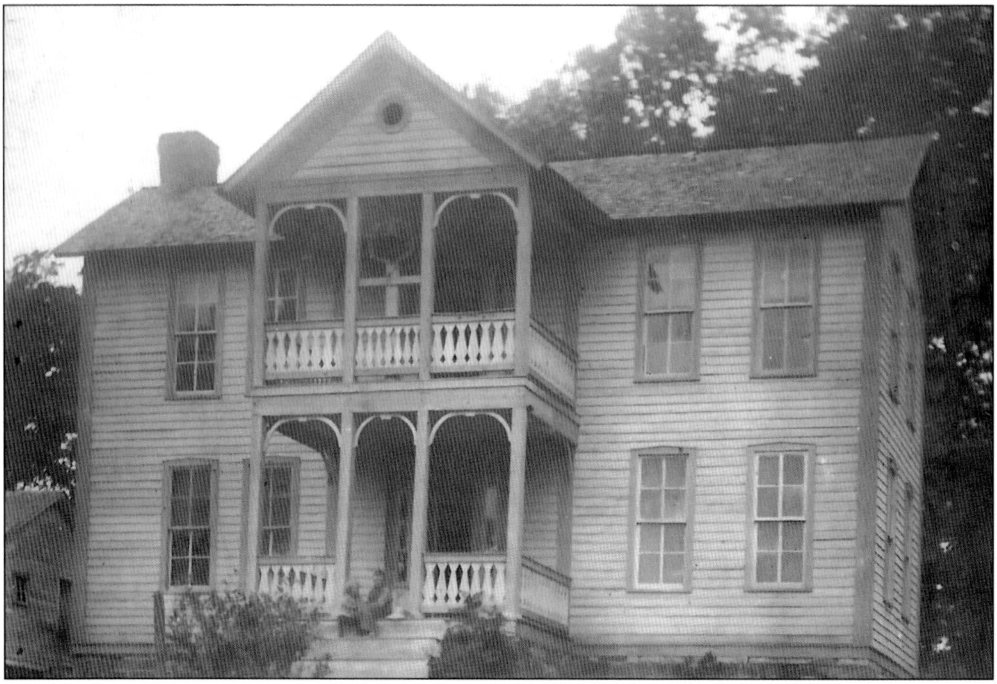

Most farmhouses were one-story bungalows or two-story rectangular homes, like this Van Ness house. Generally, the downstairs contained a parlor, bedroom, kitchen, and dining room. The second floor might have four to six bedrooms. Most had a front porch; upstairs porches were used for sleeping areas during summer. A hitching post and a yoke bell, used to call in workers, were common.

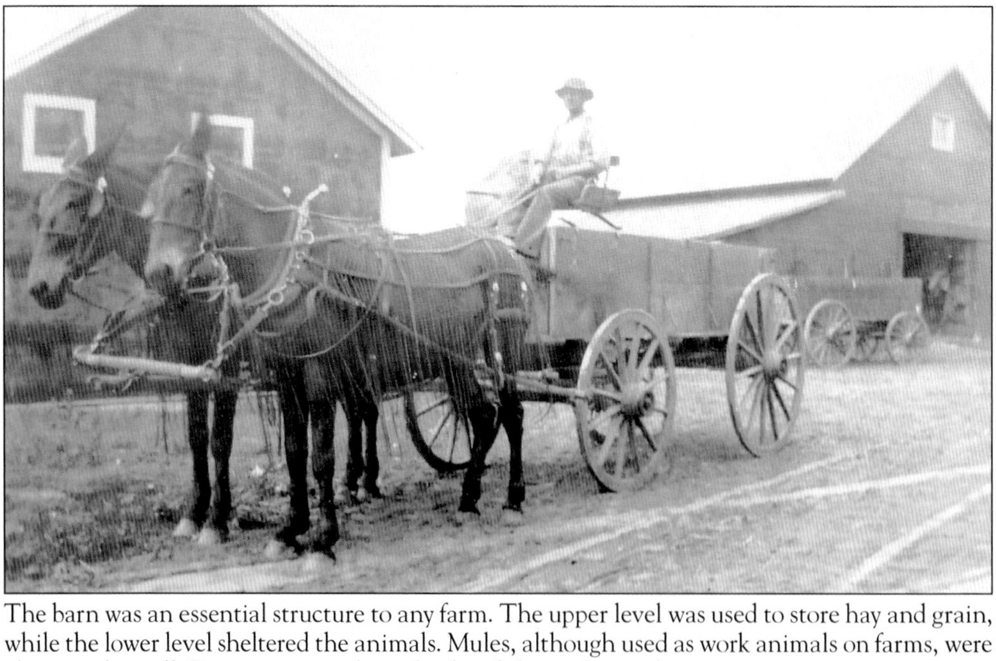

The barn was an essential structure to any farm. The upper level was used to store hay and grain, while the lower level sheltered the animals. Mules, although used as work animals on farms, were also raised to sell. Buyers put together a load and shipped it to the cotton states or mining states of the west. The state became well known for its Missouri mules.

Wooden silos, such as this one on the Reese farm, were held together by steel cables and used to store silage, a chopped animal feed. Neighbors worked together to cut and bundle the grain in the field. Children often tamped down the silage so that more could be added. Some homesteaders lined the bottom of the silo with empty crocks to catch the juice for fermentation.

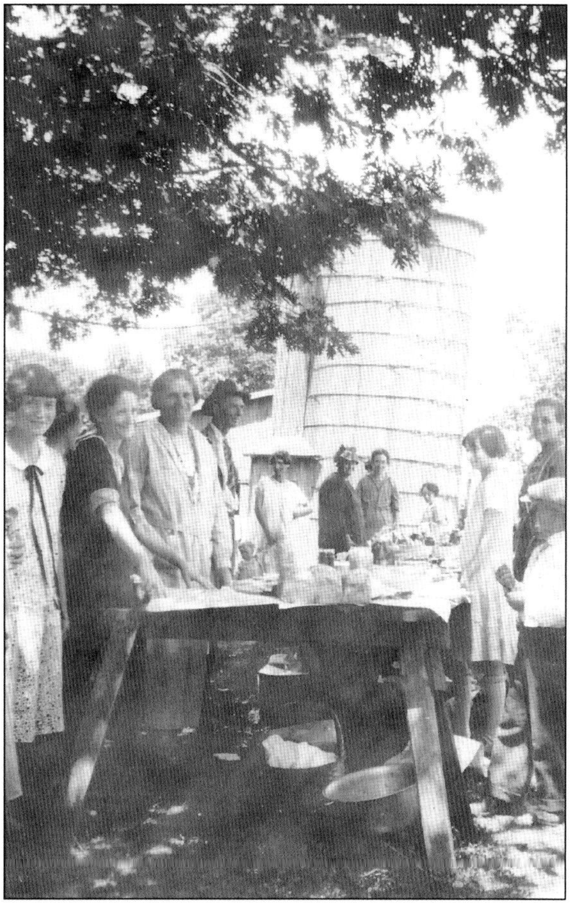

Oliver Riley proudly stands beside his prize bull. The split rail fence behind him was designed to contain the animals and yet was easy to repair or move, if need be. This style of fence required no nails or hardware; just a strong back and a sharp axe. During the Civil War, the fences were used by both sides as a major source of firewood.

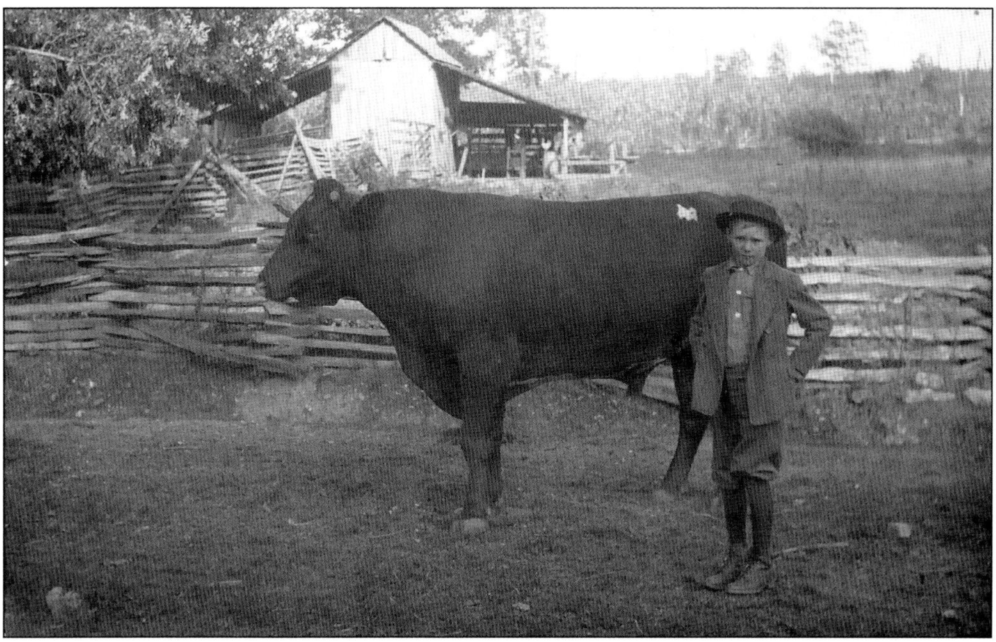

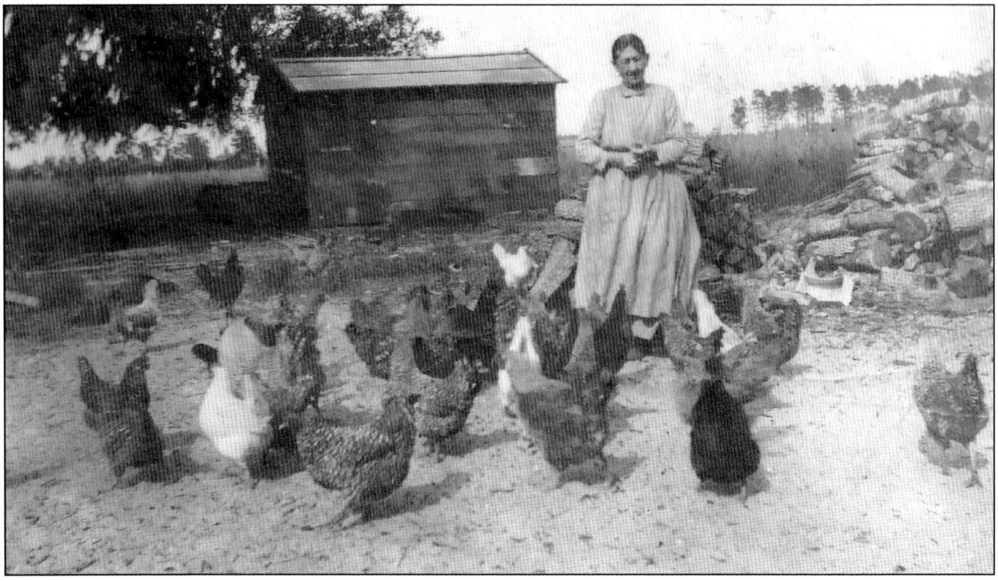

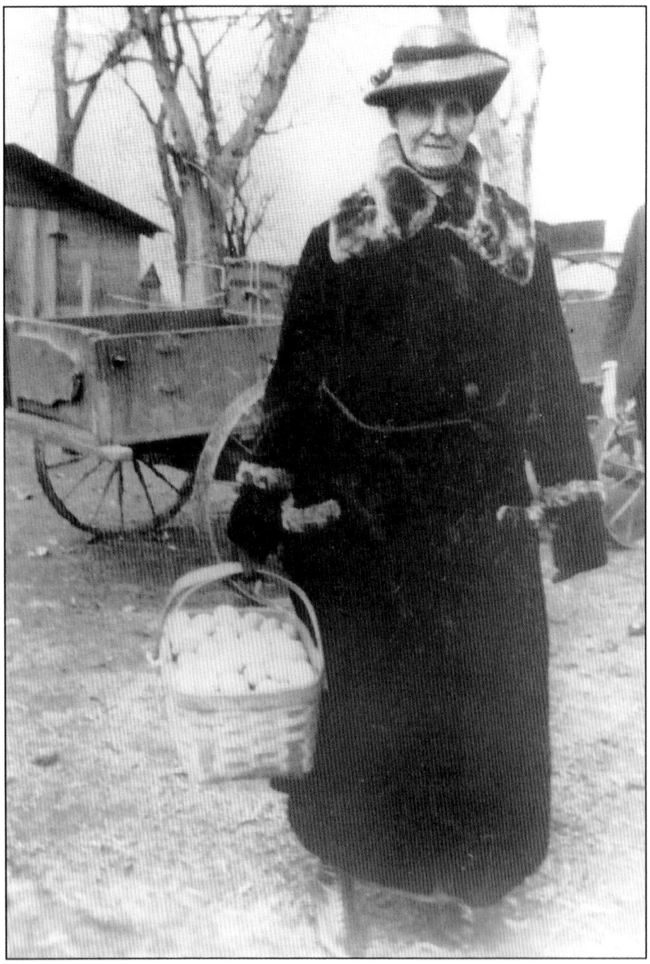

Flocks of chickens were found at almost every home. The birds were granted free range during the day and protection from predators at night when they were rounded up and herded into coops. In return, families enjoyed fresh eggs and meat, as well as stuffing for featherbeds and pillows. Most farmwives took pride in tending the flocks. Eggs were generally gathered once a day and then washed and dried. Often they were sold or bartered for goods at the general store as a welcome contribution to the family's economy. In later years, eggs were sold to the MFA store, where they were candled and then shipped to Springfield. Above, Zella Todd Newton feeds her chickens while Mary Newton, pictured at left, takes her eggs to market. Laura Ingalls Wilder was well known around Mansfield for her eggs and chickens.

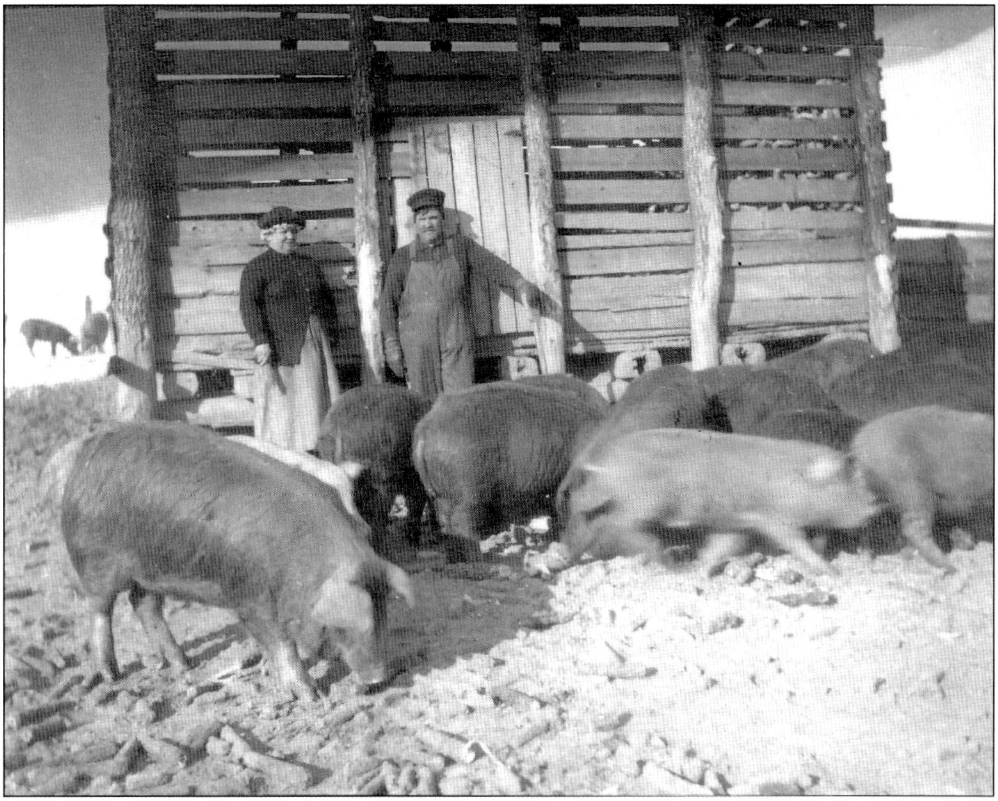

Hogs were fattened out on field corn that had been dried and stored in a corn crib, which was built up off the ground and latticed in order to prevent molding. Slopping the hogs was a most dreadful chore. The smelly concoction of slop contained everything from vegetable peelings to table scraps. Come fall, neighbors and families worked together to accomplish the day-long process of butchering.

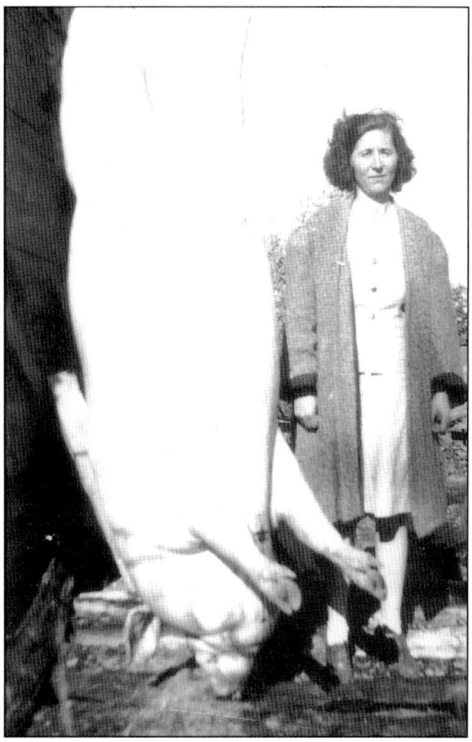

Pork was a main source of protein for families. Some hogs fattened out nicely, such as this one hanging next to Gladys Blankenship. Sausage was ground and seasoned, hams were smoked, and side meat was salted for preservation. While adults enjoyed scrambled eggs and brains, the children enjoyed a tasty treat of cracklins, a byproduct of rendering the lard. Every part of the pig was utilized except the oink!

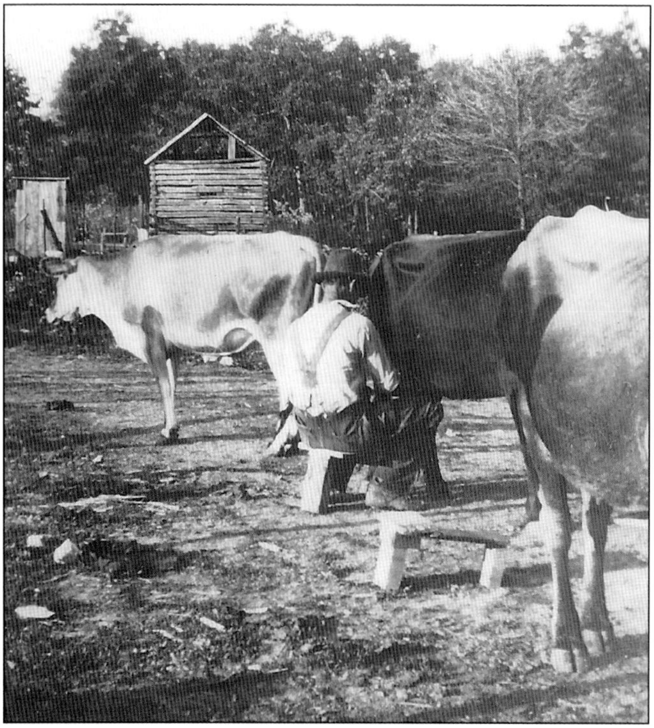

Milking by hand twice a day was a way of life for dairy farmers like Jim Wes Burris. Children as young as seven were responsible for milking cows. Jerseys were preferred as they were easy keepers; they did not eat much and produced high butter fat. The warm milk was strained, put into milk cans, and then stirred to "cool it out." It was then stored in spring houses and creeks or churned into butter.

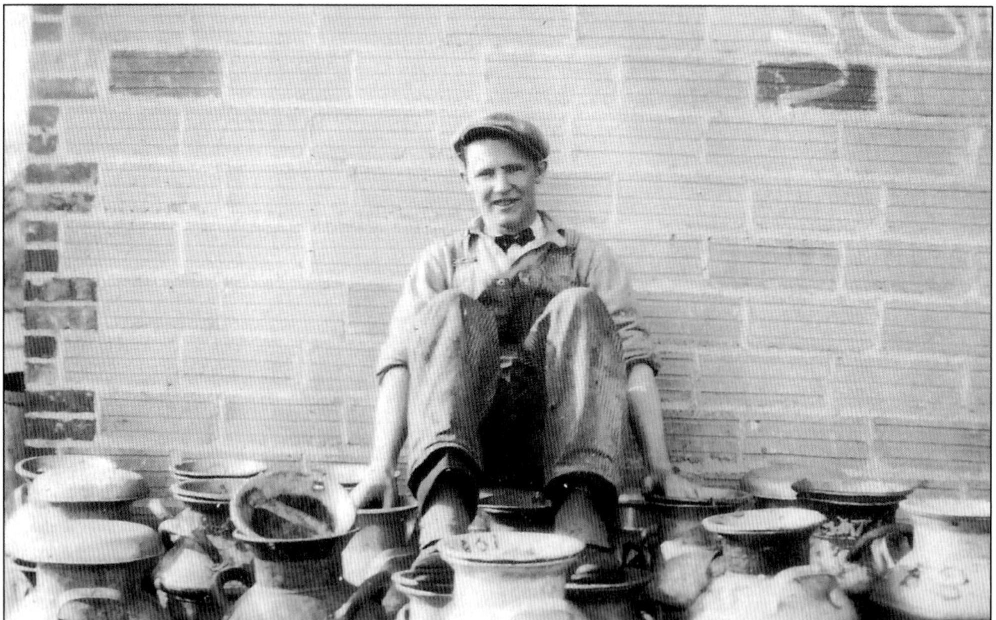

Dairying and Wright County are basically synonymous. In the 1920s, Elmer Strong (pictured) ran cheese plants in both Mansfield and Hartville. Milk cans were tagged with the farm's name or corresponding number and returned to the farm. Due to the volume of milk produced in the county, Mansfield supplied both the Sugar Creek Creamery and the Mansfield Cheese Plant. Wright County led the state in dairy production for many years.

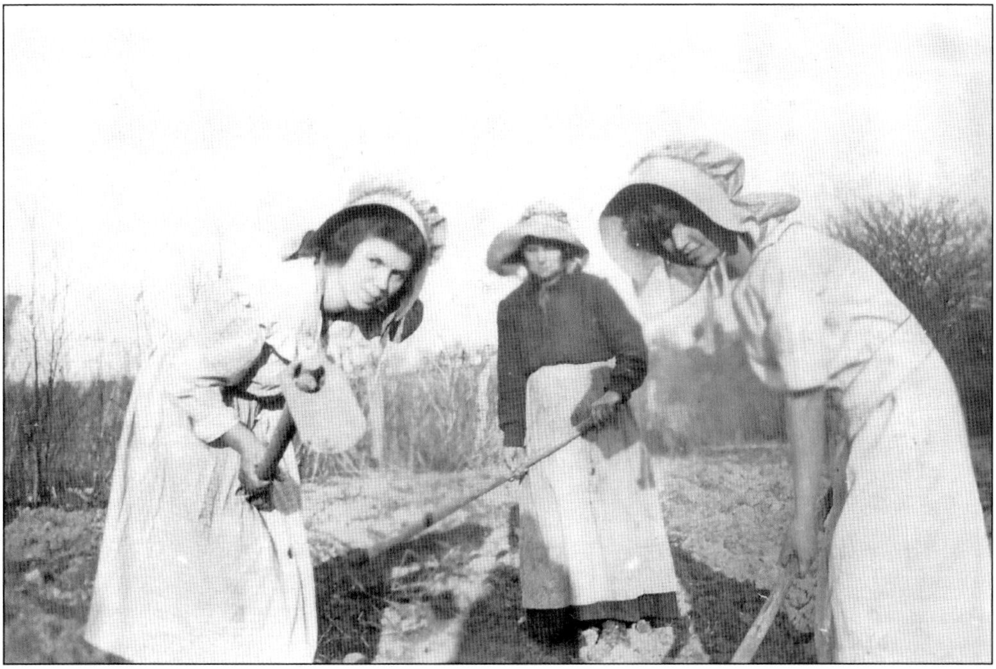

A garden was a must. Men prepared the spots using a plow and harrow, and women and children tended them. Early planting yielded lettuce, radishes, onions, peas, greens, and new potatoes. Green beans and corn were canned for year-round consumption. The fall harvest included squash, melons, sweet potatoes, pumpkins, and turnips. Because fresh vegetables were not available in the winter, the longest time of the year was "from turnips to greens."

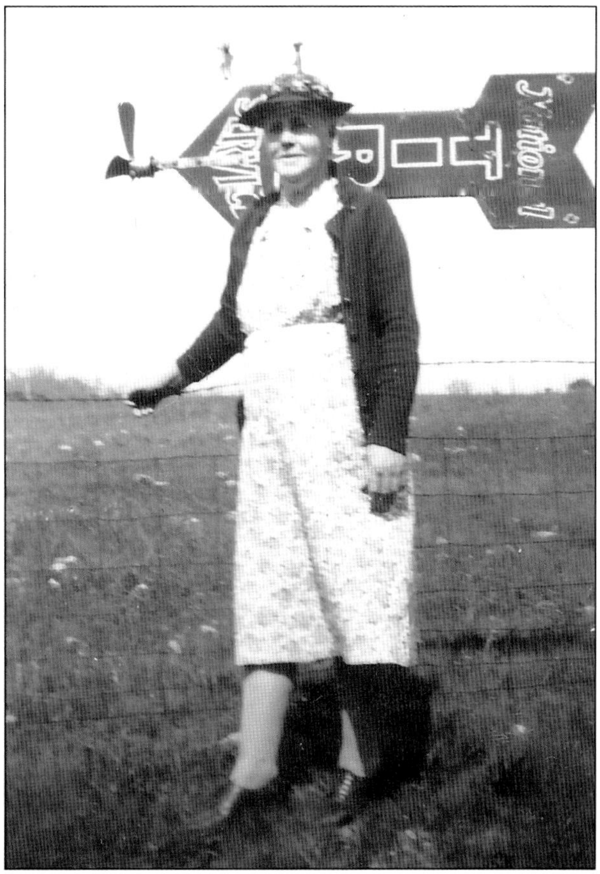

Mary Rush stands proudly alongside her whimsical, yet functional, whirling wind catcher. Whirligigs served to scare birds and varmints out of the fields. This whirligig, fashioned from an old metal sign advertising National Tire Service, stands as a testament to the ingenuity and creativity of Ozarkians. "Use it up, wear it out, make it do, or do without" was more than just an expression—it was a way of life.

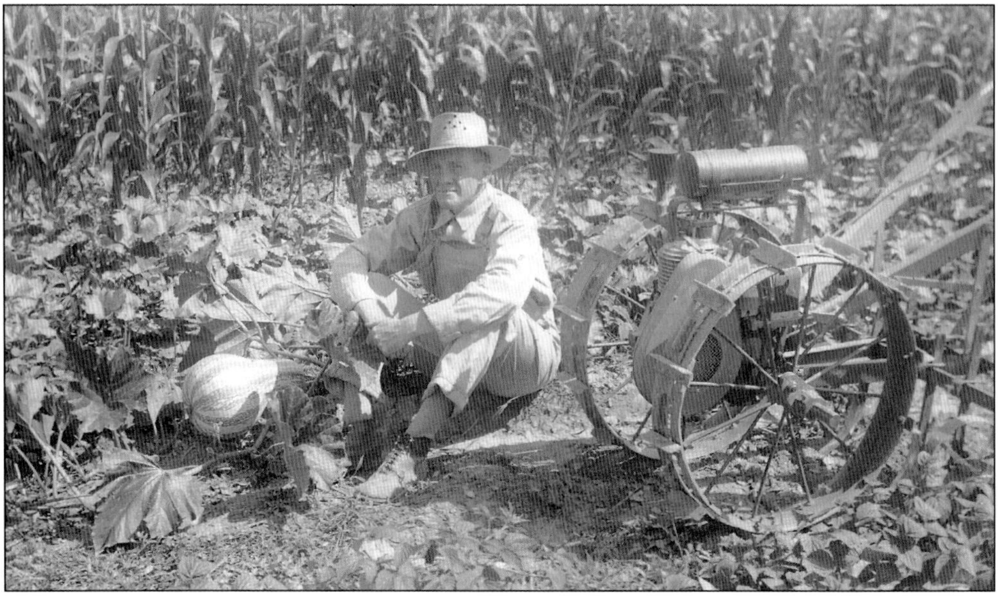

Mr. Samuels of Cedar Gap rests after using his David Bradley garden tractor. No respectable farmer considered planting without first consulting the *Farmer's Almanac*, which was also used to plan everything from weaning babies (barnyard and otherwise) to getting haircuts. Besides planting crops for personal consumption, some farmers planted another garden, or truck patch, for produce to sell. Leonard Samuels followed in his father's footsteps by planting large truck patches.

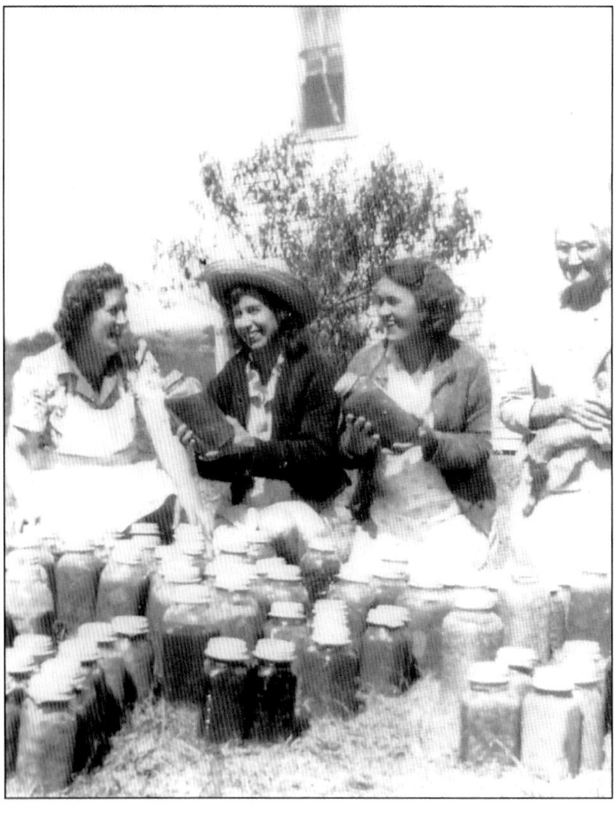

The canning of vegetables and fruits was a sweltering and tedious job but also a necessary process for farm women, especially those with large families. The jars could be stored in cellars for several years, and the preserved items were especially enjoyed during the winter when there was no fresh food. From left to right, Thelma Towe, Lilly Dixon, Cora Schlicher, and Lydia Towe (who raised 11 children of her own) enjoy a shared moment after a day of canning.

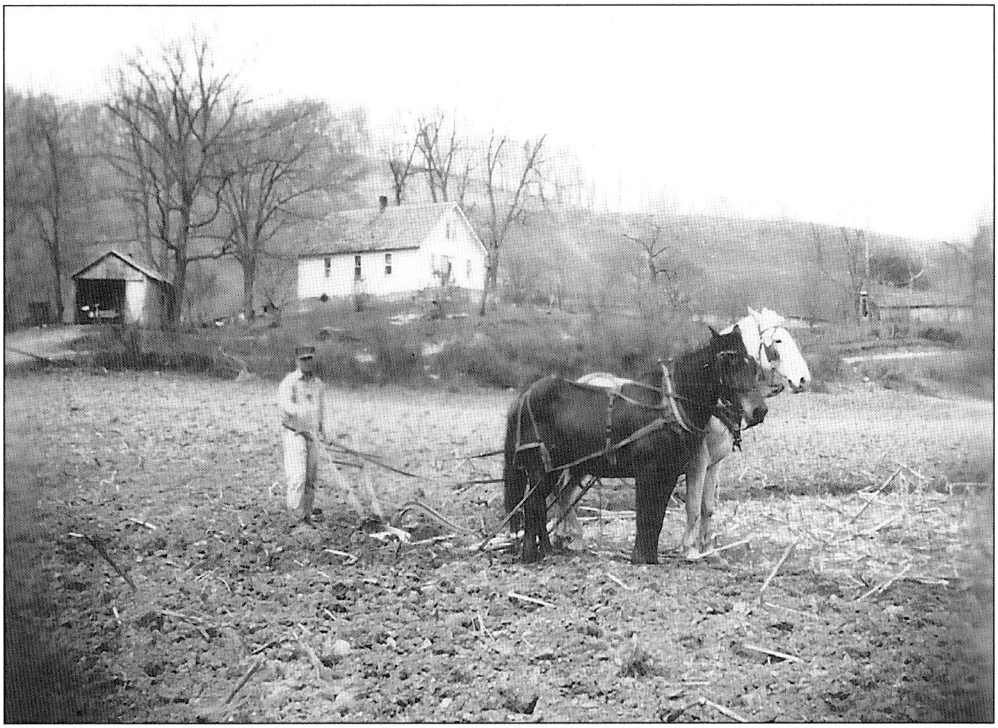

Before the introduction of tractors, plowing a field required much time and effort. For many years, the horse-drawn plow, an essential farming tool, was used to cultivate and prepare the soil for planting crops. Here, Floyd Blankenship works the field using a hand plow pulled by his two horses on his farm south of Mansfield.

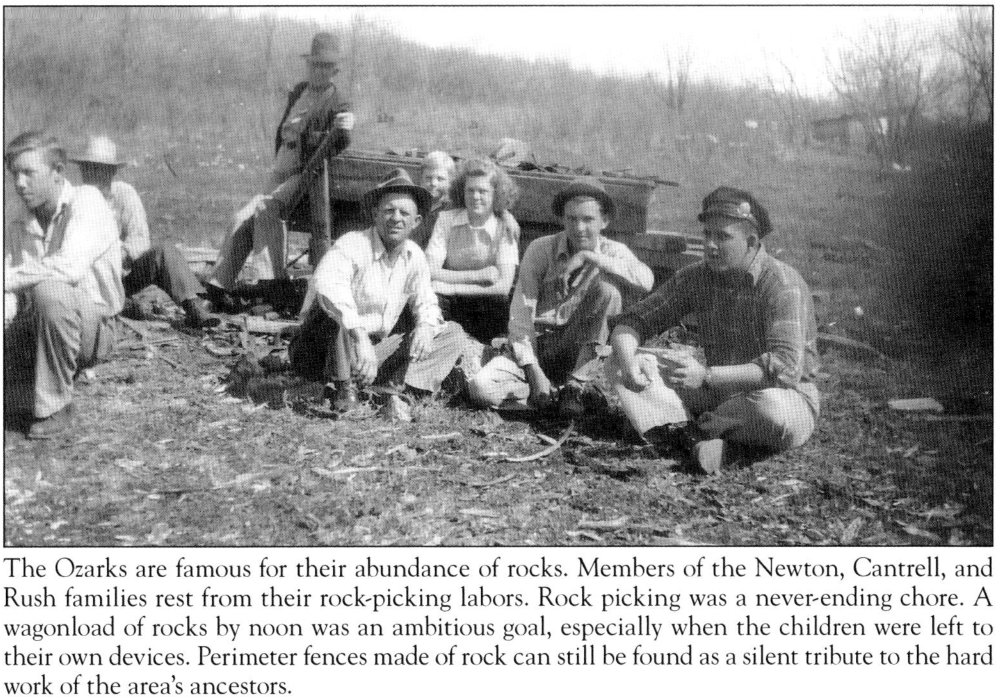

The Ozarks are famous for their abundance of rocks. Members of the Newton, Cantrell, and Rush families rest from their rock-picking labors. Rock picking was a never-ending chore. A wagonload of rocks by noon was an ambitious goal, especially when the children were left to their own devices. Perimeter fences made of rock can still be found as a silent tribute to the hard work of the area's ancestors.

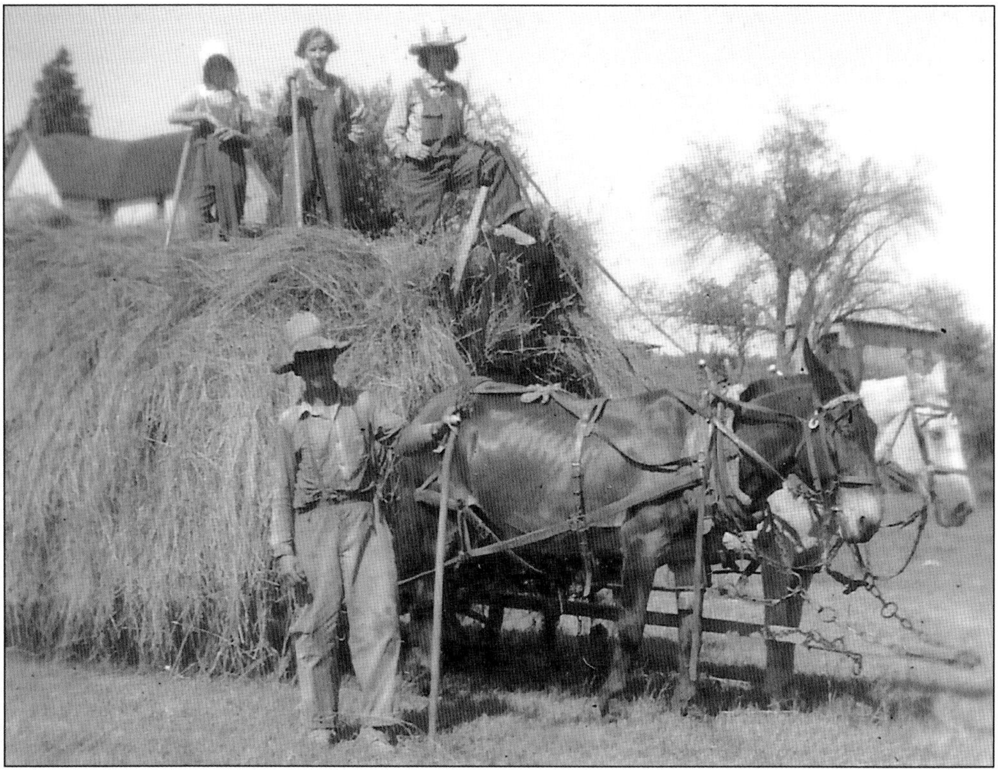

Prior to fescue, most hay consisted of orchard grass, red clover, and lespedeza. There was some alfalfa, but it was prone to weevils and had to be sprayed. The hay was cut with a horse-drawn sickle mower and then raked by a dump rake pulled by a team of horses or mules. Loose hay was stacked and then dressed down to shed water. Most haystacks remained in the field and were penned around to keep the animals out. Some farmers, like the Gaskills, seen above, loaded loose hay onto wagons to be put into haylofts, using a clam fork or harpoon fork. Ancil Dodson, pictured below, uses a hayfork to pitch his hay. Hay crews, assisted by neighbors, made their way from field to field. The women worked together to prepare a feast to feed the hungry hay hands.

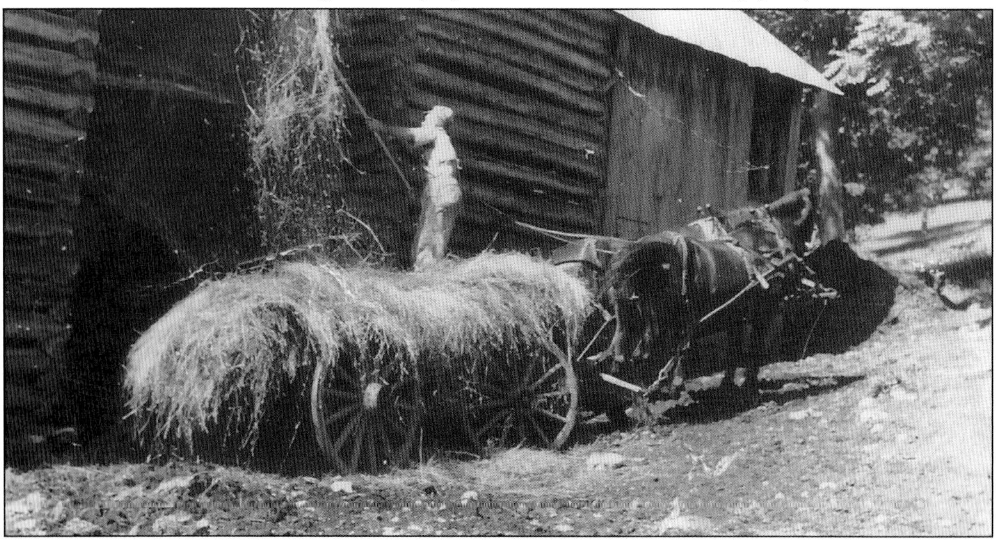

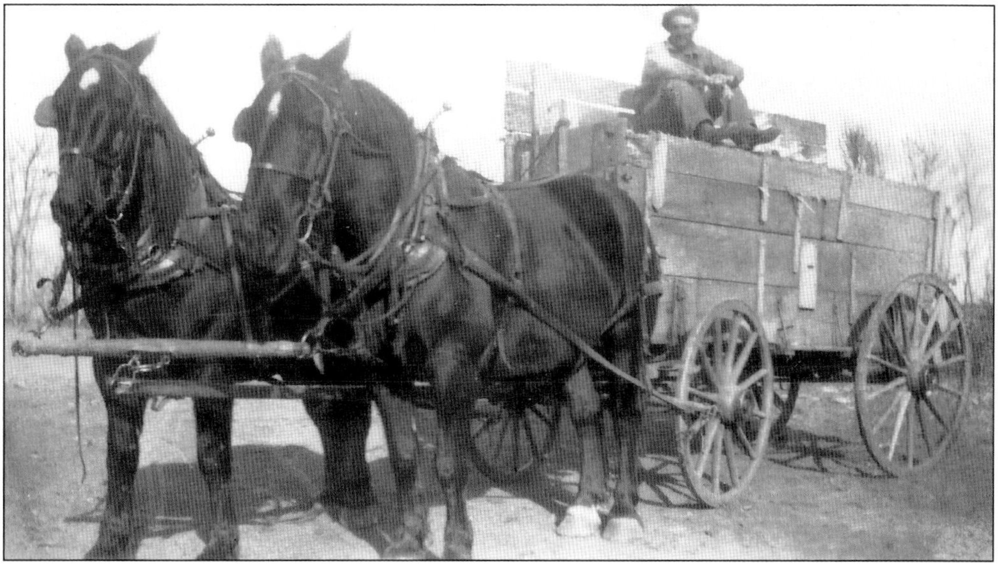

Corn was vital to the survival of families and their animals. Corn on the cob, also known as "roastin' ears," was a summertime treat. Dried ears, still in the shuck, were fed to hogs, the foliage was used in silage, and the cobs could be made into pipes. Cobs were also used in outhouses, as they were a necessity before magazines became popular and, later, the introduction of toilet paper.

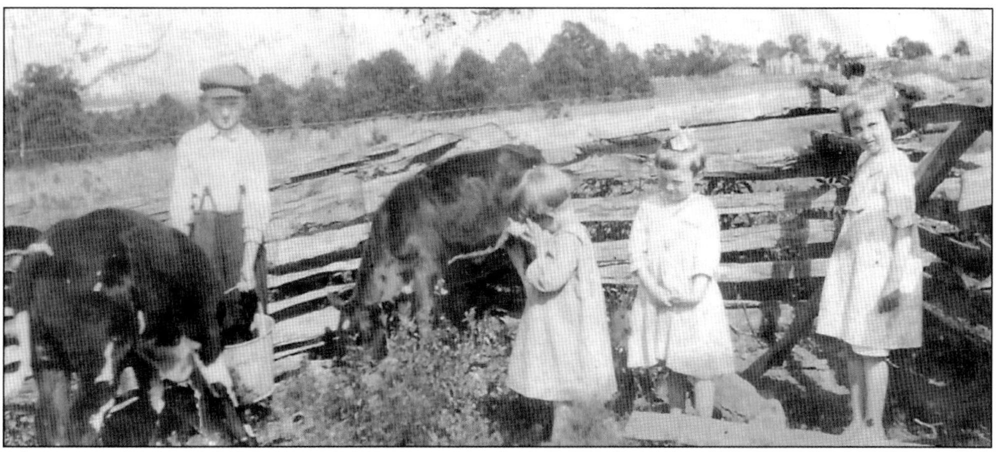

Many barns included a corncrib where whole ears of dried corn were stored. Children's chores often included shelling these ears by hand or running them through a hand-cranked sheller. The grain was used to feed calves and other small farm animals, but the best corn was saved for the workhorses to meet their nutritional needs.

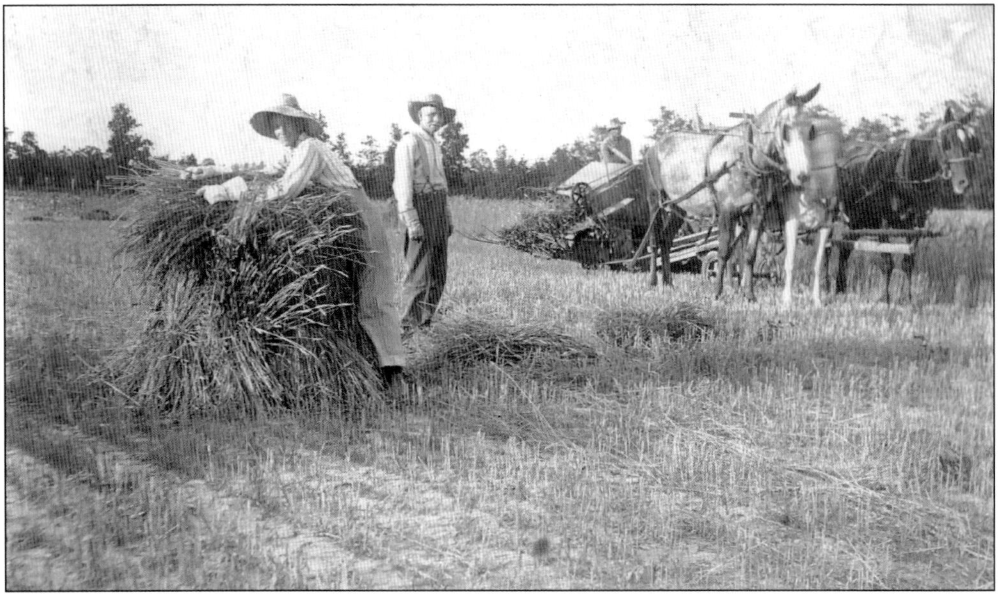

Various grains were grown to feed livestock. "Shocking" grains was a hot, dirty job. A triple hitch of horses was connected to a reaper, which cut the grain and bundled and tied it. The woman above, scandalously dressed in men's overalls, shocks bundles of grain, standing them on end to shed water. Local farmers then took turns helping each other with the threshing of their crops. Neighborhood men contacted the local thresher, and a specific day was set for the thresher to be at each farm. The men gathered the shocks from the fields, undid the bundles, and fed them into the thresher. Below, a thresher runs, channeling the grain out one side into a bag and blowing the chaff and straw out the other side into a pile to be used as bedding in the barns.

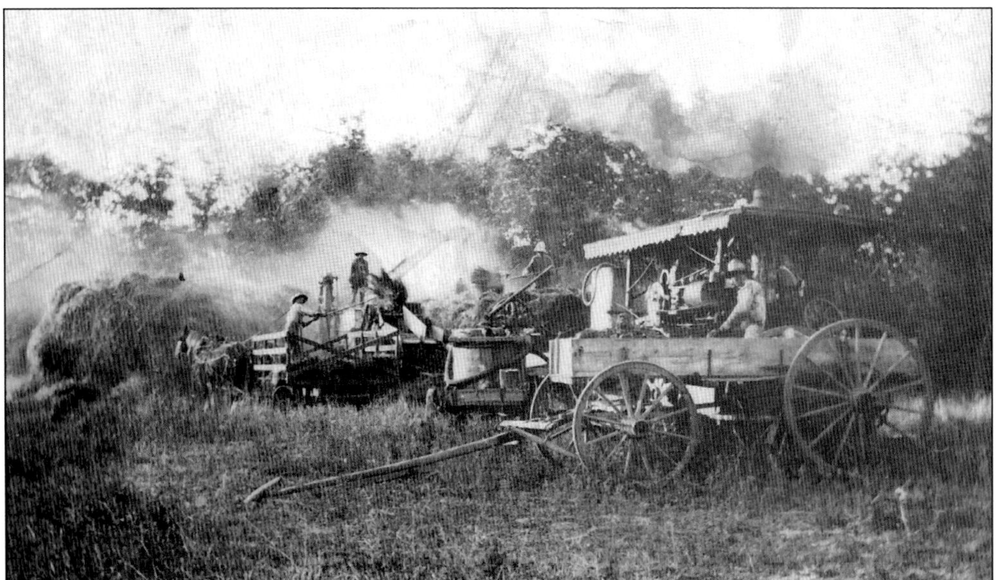

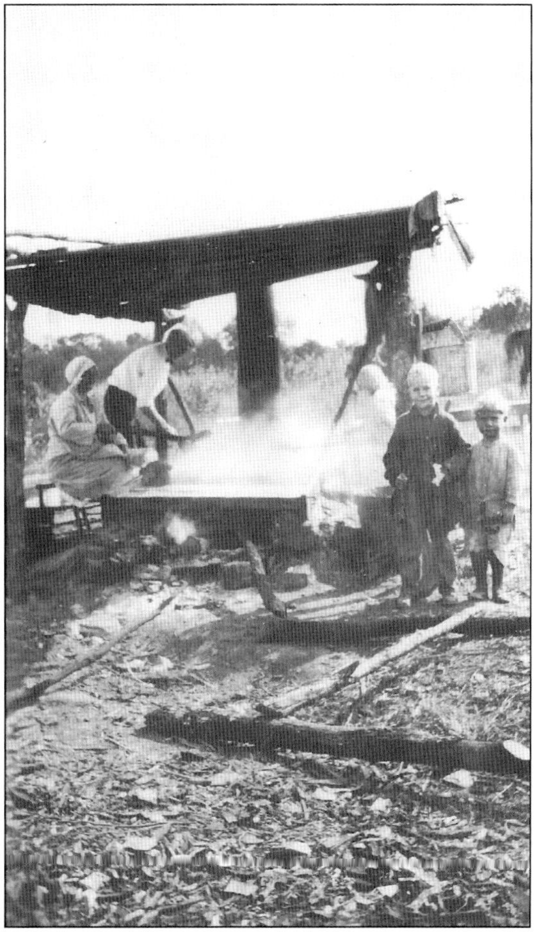

Every fall, the Pres and Louisa Newton family gathered to cook sorghum, a labor-intensive process. Before frost arrived, leaves were stripped, seed heads were removed, and stalks were loaded onto wagons and hauled to the mill. A horse or mule was harnessed to a pole connected to the gears of the mill, which squeezed the juice from the stalks into a trough. The dry stalks, or plummies, were heaped into a pile, a fine place for children to play. Next, the greenish-colored juice was strained and cooked slowly and carefully. Obviously, the acts of tending the fire, constantly stirring the syrup, and watching the pan required adult expertise. The golden-brown molasses syrup was then stored in jugs or crocks to be enjoyed later with biscuits. If the molasses scorched, it was called blackstrap. Eating blackstrap would turn a person's lips, teeth, and gums black.

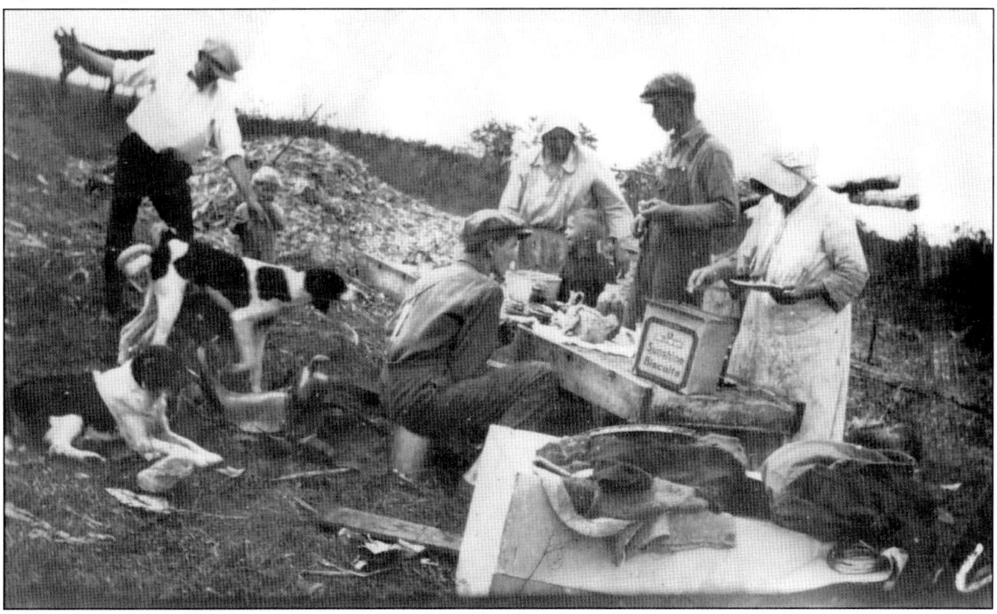

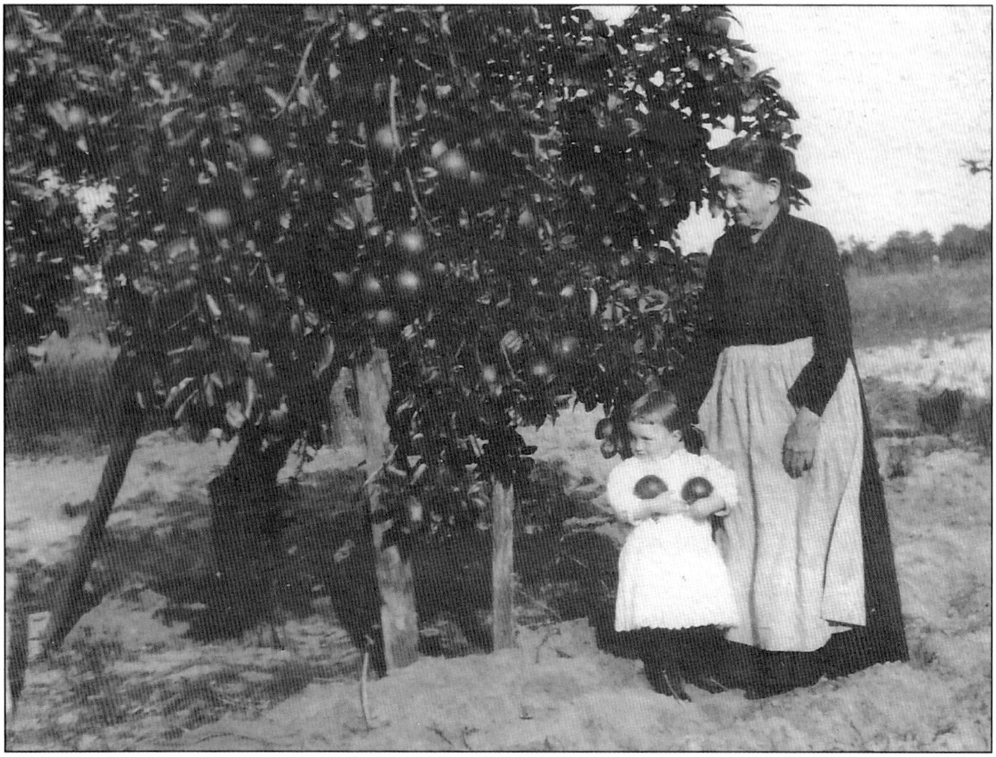

In the 1890s, several states bordering Missouri were experiencing a severe drought. Real estate companies published colorful brochures describing the Ozarks as the "Land of the Big Red Apple." One family drawn by these ads was the Wilders from DeSmet, South Dakota, who later moved to Mansfield. The intense labor required to harvest the orchards depended on the effort of everyone in the family, as seen above. Some families raised hundreds of acres of apples, pears, peaches, or plums, which they could market on the new Memphis Line. Many fruit companies sent buyers to the Ozarks to procure whole orchards of fruit. They then hired workers, like those pictured below, to pick the fruit, coopers to build barrels to pack it in, and haulers to transport it to the trains.

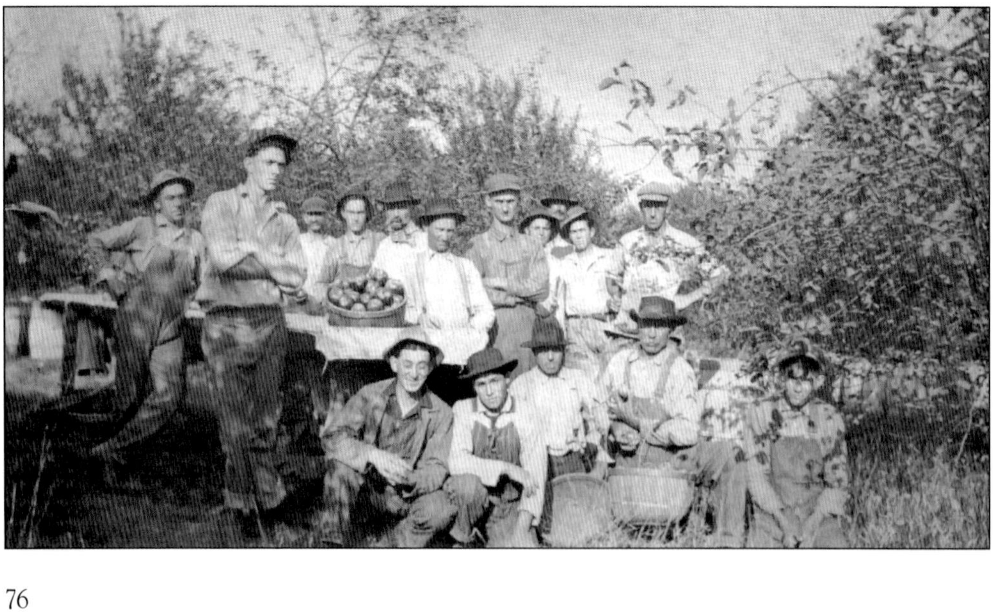

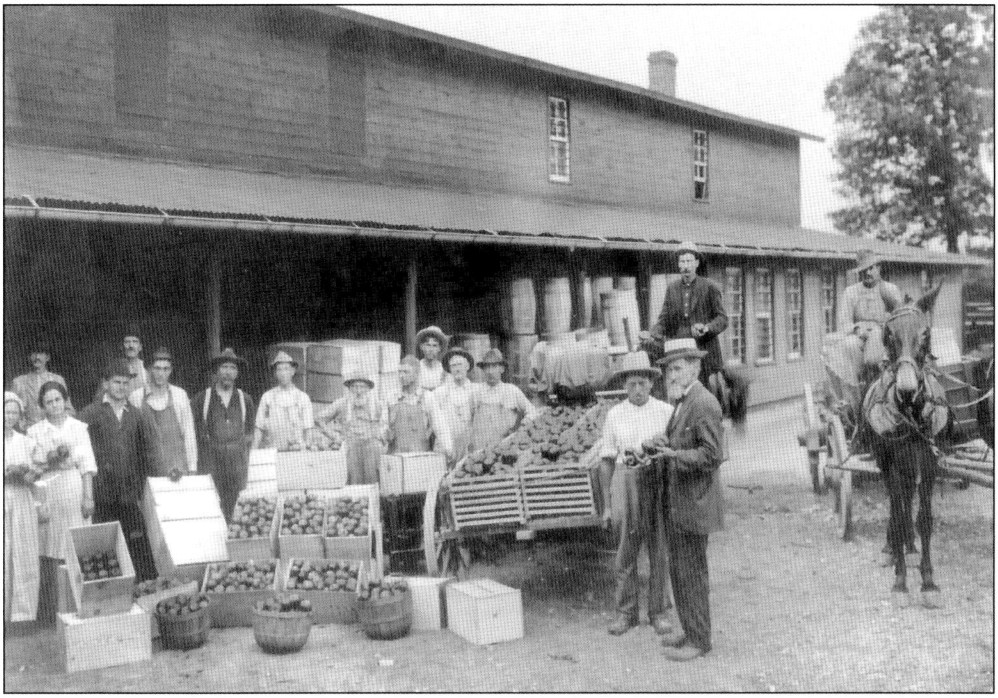

Railroad officials made an excursion from Memphis to Springfield to encourage businesses to build close to the line. The engine boiler burst at Cedar Gap. Passenger Col. Louis Erb, a produce wholesaler from Memphis, used the delay to walk around, envisioning the possibilities. He bought and leased over 1,000 acres for apple and peach orchards. He built a warehouse, cold-storage facility, cider mill, and an evaporating plant to produce dried apples. Erb hired as many as 200 pickers, who often set up make-shift tents, like the one below. Erb moved his family to Cedar Gap and founded the Memphis Summer Colony, where Memphis associates could rent cabins to escape muggy weather and yellow fever outbreaks. Above, Colonel Erb, the bearded man at center, buys apples from Jesse Van Ness. The man on horseback is Harry Kock, Erb's foreman.

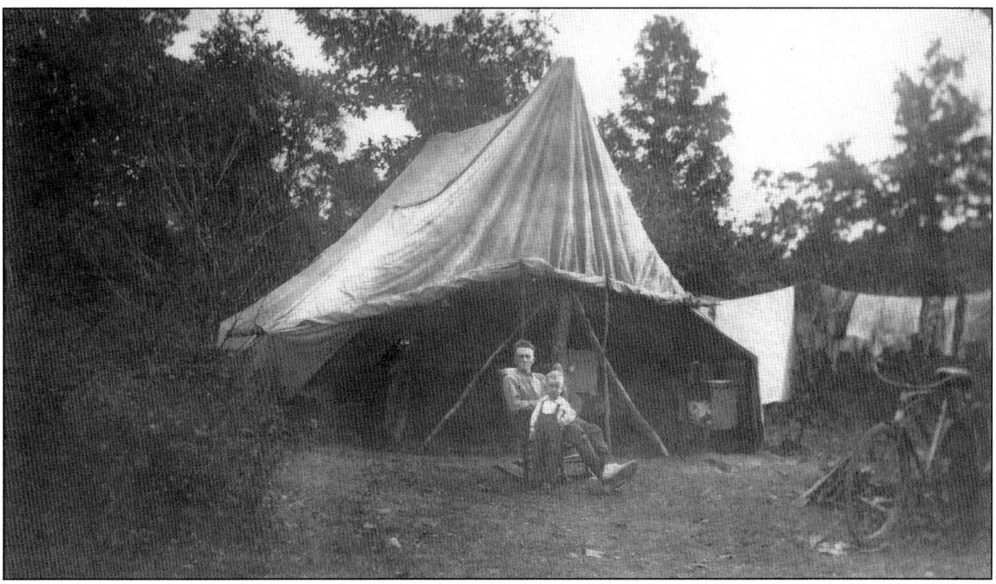

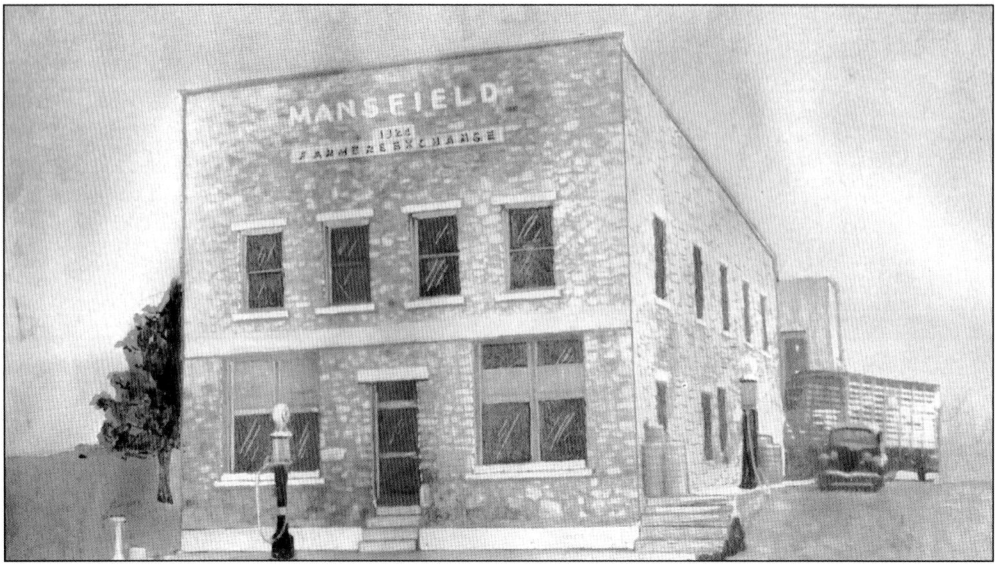

Crop prices were based solely on what buyers considered fair, so farmers decided to form a Missouri Farmers Association. Each town had its own association but paid a membership fee to be part of the county association, located in Mountain Grove. Farmers could market their produce through this association, which strived to do the best for its members. In 1924, the building seen here was constructed to handle the massive amount of goods being sold.

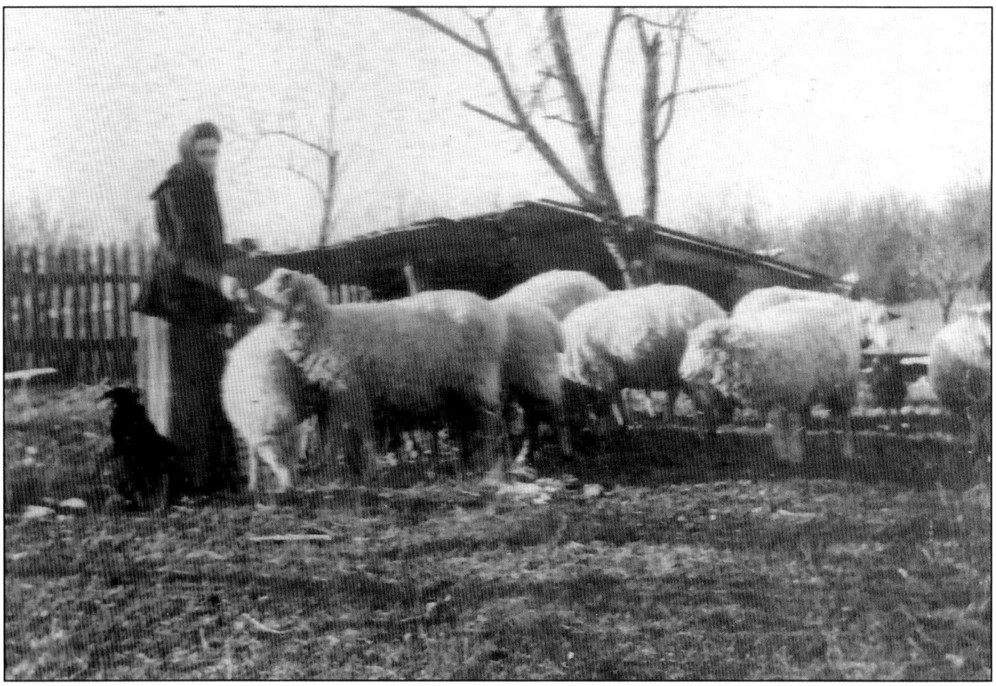

Sheep needed protection from predators, especially when they were lambing. Orphaned lambs often became children's pets. Selling sheep and lambs was basically a break-even proposition. The profit lay in the sale of wool. The fleece would bring a much higher price if it was sheared in one single piece. Some buyers noted for coming to local farms to buy wool were Kingsley Findley, Jason Box, Ward Mackey, and George Pryor.

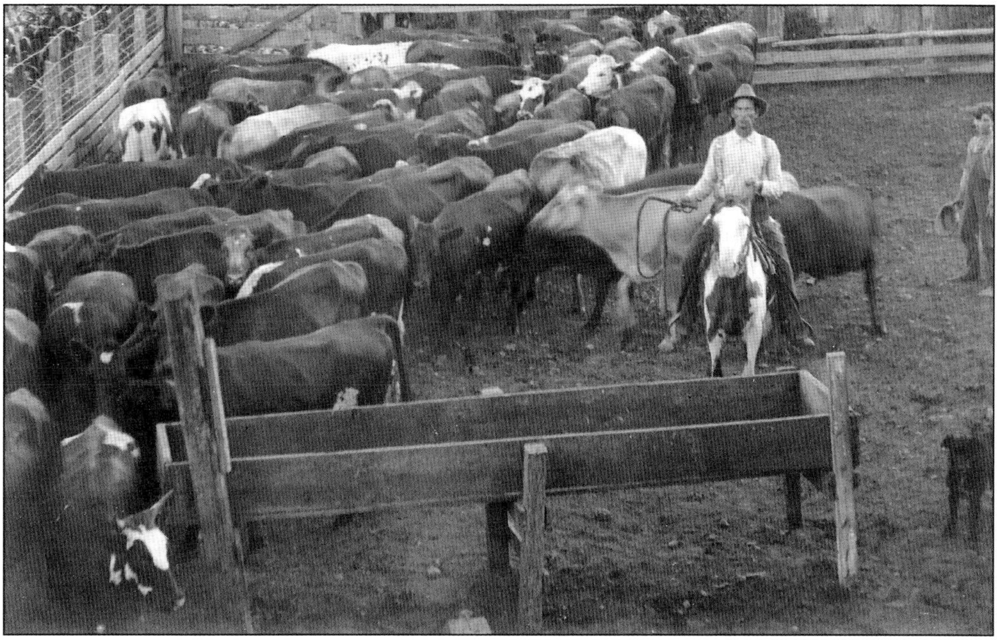

The railroad brought a new influx of livestock dealers. Early dealer George W. Miller was influential in the trading and raising of stock on his 1,040-acre ranch east of Mansfield. His success attracted the attention of firms in St. Louis, Kansas City, Omaha, and Chicago. Stock pens were constructed near the rails for local farmers to have easier access in loading and shipping their cattle.

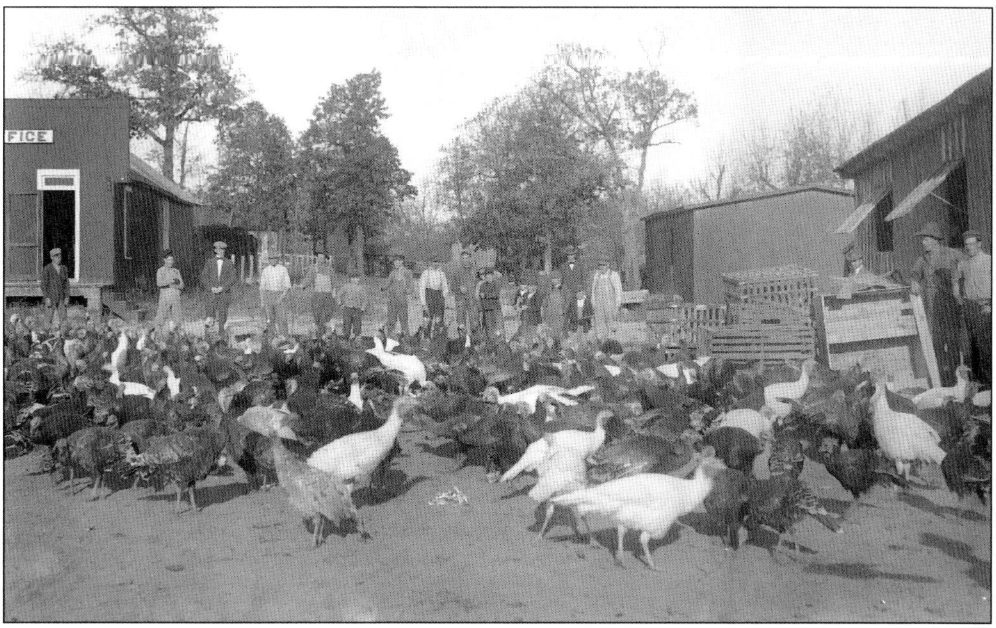

Flocks of turkeys were walked to the rail at Mansfield. A man with a bucket of corn led the way, while boys herded the turkeys from the rear. The lead turkey often wore a bell around its neck and was known as the "Judas" turkey. Wherever they were when the sun set was where they would spend the night; many stopped overnight at Jordan Bogart's place, south of London Store.

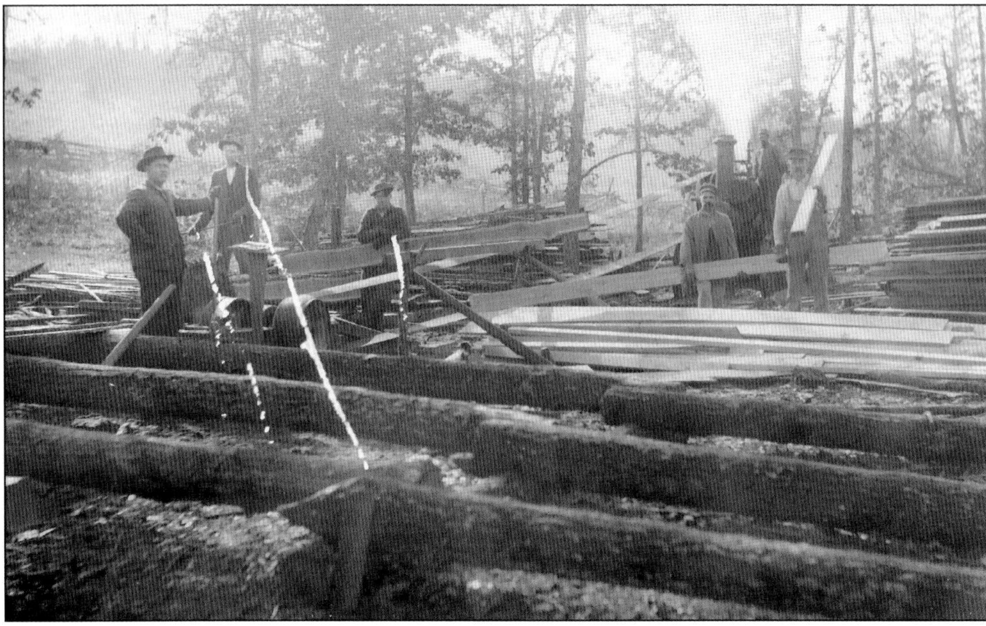

Early settlers in the Ozarks were drawn by the vast amount of natural resources, one of which was virgin trees including oak, elm, walnut, and sycamore. One of the first uses for this timber was making railroad ties. Ties were hacked by hand from the trees, preferably white oak, and hauled to the local tie buyer where the seller received 25¢ per tie. In the above image, a sawmill rips timber into lumber for building. With the invention of portable sawmills, the lumber industry exploded and moved into areas never dreamed of before. These portable sawmills allowed people to build homes using their own trees. Sawmill owners brought in their mills, and the cut trees were made into lumber to be sold or used to construct buildings on the farm. Below, the Bruce and Sadie Hensley family poses in front of their newly constructed home.

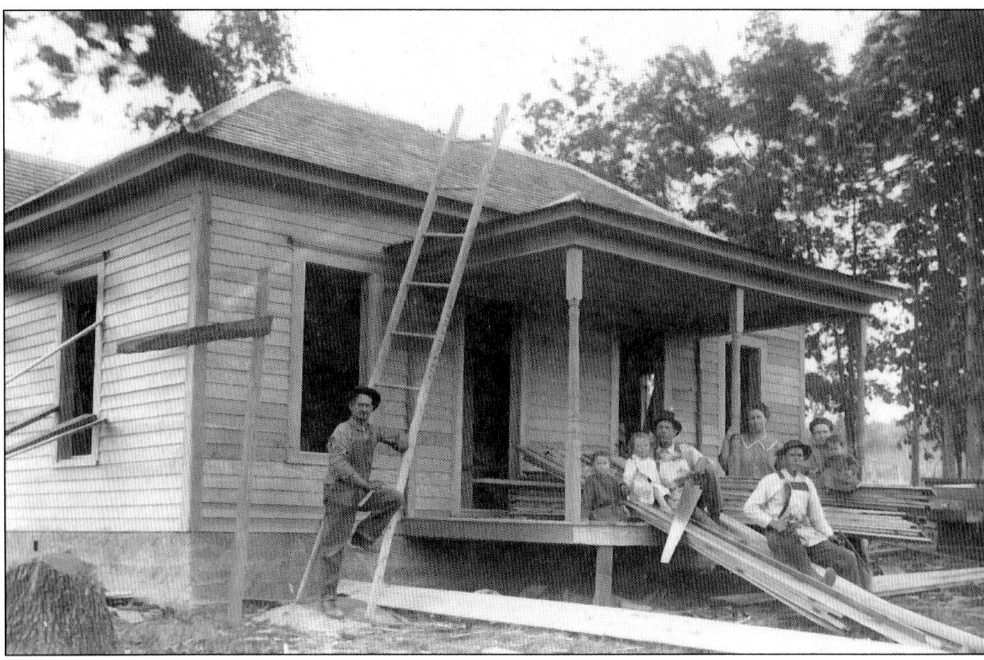

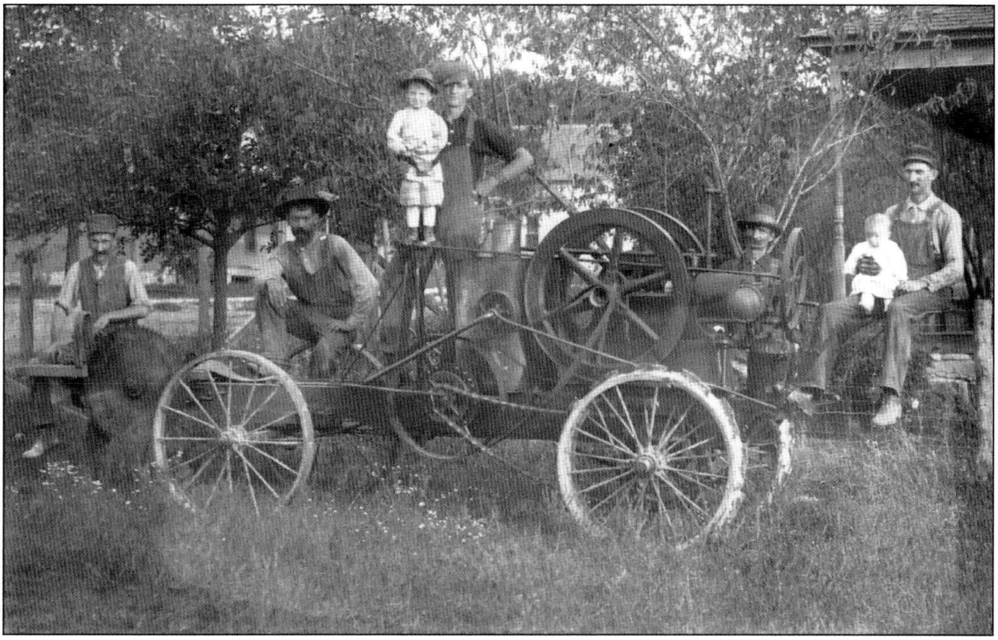

The timber covering the Ozark Mountains made life easier for the people who lived there. They used the wood to heat their homes and fuel their cooking stoves. Throughout the year, families cut down trees; using horses, they then skidded the logs, referred to as pole wood, to their wood lot. When they felt that they had enough, they contacted someone with a pole saw to cut it into sections. Then they pitched the split wood into piles. These photographs show two different families who owned pole saws. The one above was owned by the Short family, while the one below was owned by the Gilley family. The huge blades on the front of the saws were dangerous. Arthur Gilley lost two of his fingers while sawing pole wood at the Jordan Bogart farm. The men were relatives, so the family put the fingers in a Mason jar and buried them in the wood lot.

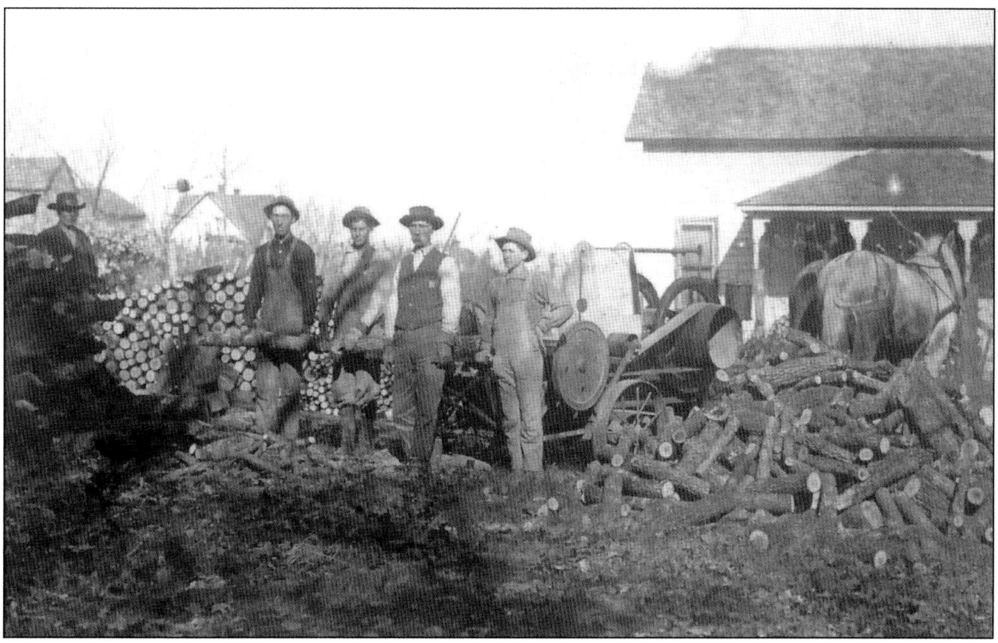

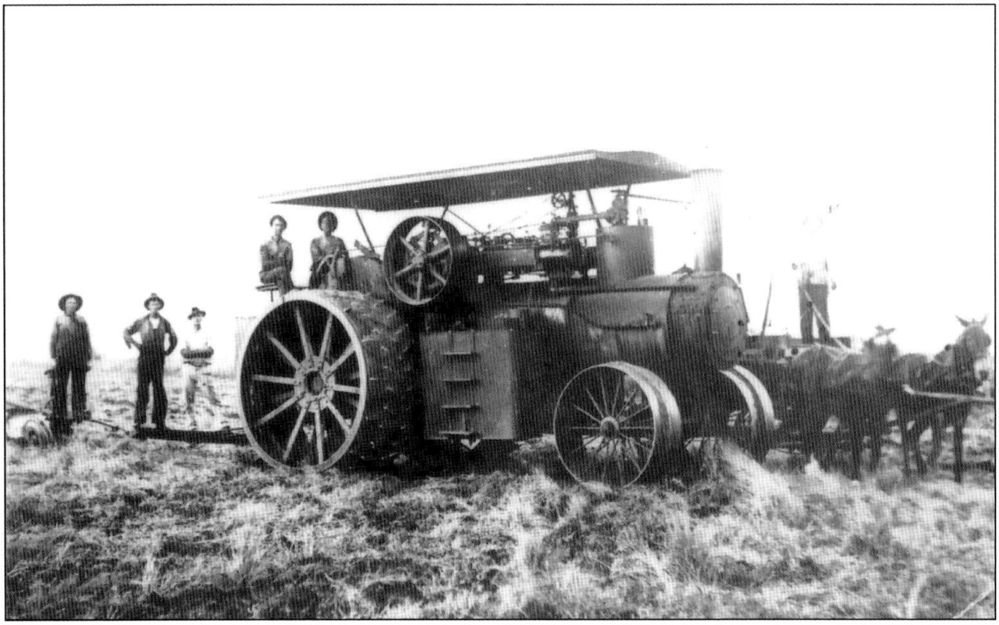

One of the easiest ways to make extra money was to work the harvests in the western states. Men who did not have enough money to pay train fare jumped the train. This meant that they hid in the brush along the tracks, usually at a watering stop, and waited for the train to either begin to leave the station or slow down on an uphill grade. They then ran alongside the train and jumped into a boxcar. The main consideration was to not get caught by the bull, or railroad police, because the offenders would receive a severe beating. Once workers reached the harvest fields, they sought work with a harvesting crew and began sending money back home. These photographs, taken by a local resident working in the harvest, show typical western Kansas harvesting crews.

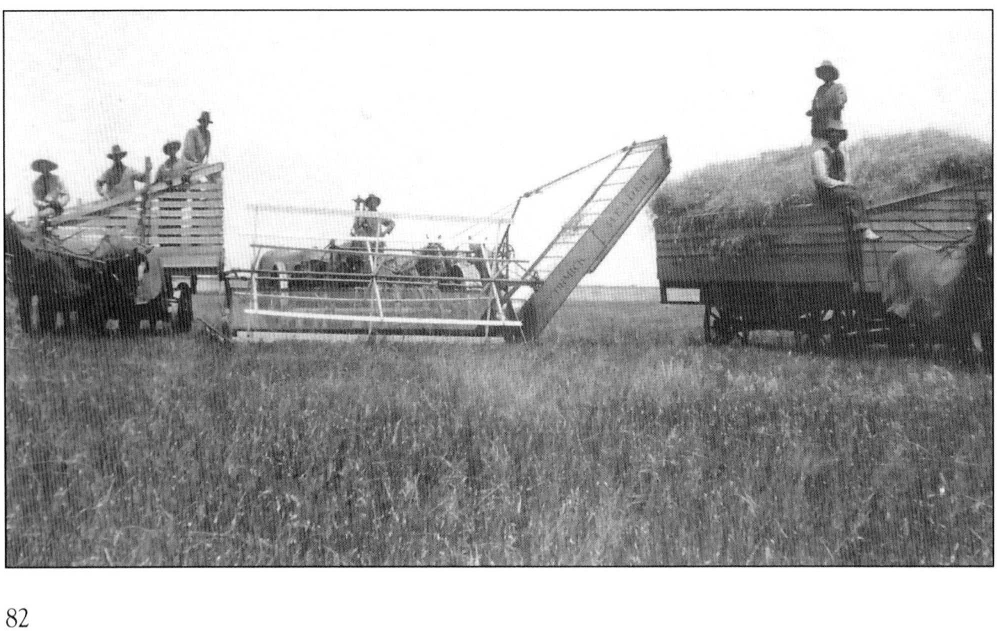

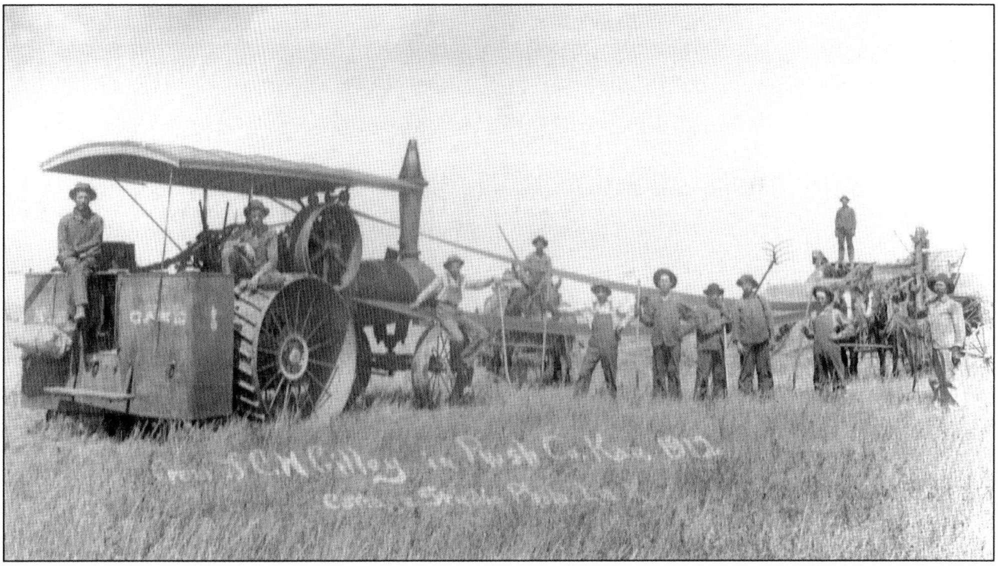

Grain harvest time in Kansas was moneymaking time for threshers in Mansfield. Both photographs show the Arthur Gilley threshing crew working the harvest in western Kansas. Local threshers would either take their crews to Kansas and rent a threshing rig or just take their own rig with them. Arthur Gilley always loaded his rig, which included his equipment, teams, and crew, onto the train in Mansfield. Once in Kansas, they went from farm to farm, threshing the grain crops. Working the harvest could take many months, which meant that these men were away from home and their families for long periods of time. Two members of Charles Woodson Gilley's threshing crew, Jordan Bogart (fifth from the left) and Walter Bogart (ninth from the left), are pictured above.

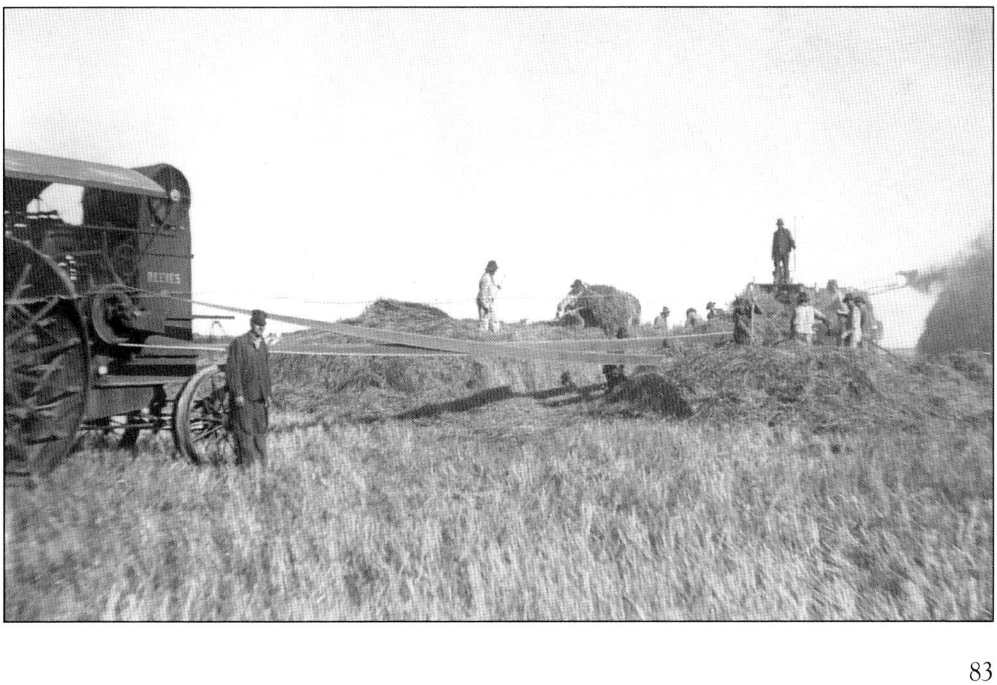

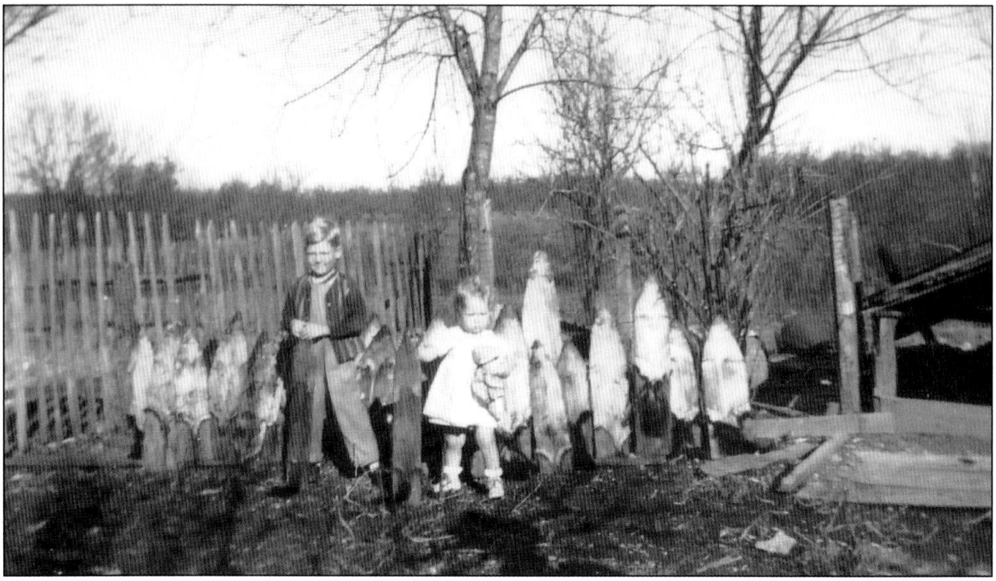

Hunting and trapping provided income for families to supplement the bottom line. Gutted rabbits were sold whole for 10¢. Skunks, rabbits, possums, and coons were skinned, and their hides salted down and stretched to dry before being sold. Area farmers often sold their hides to local merchants Dave Ellis and Henry Moore. Gorman and Margaret, children of Mart Newton, stand in front of hides prepared by their father.

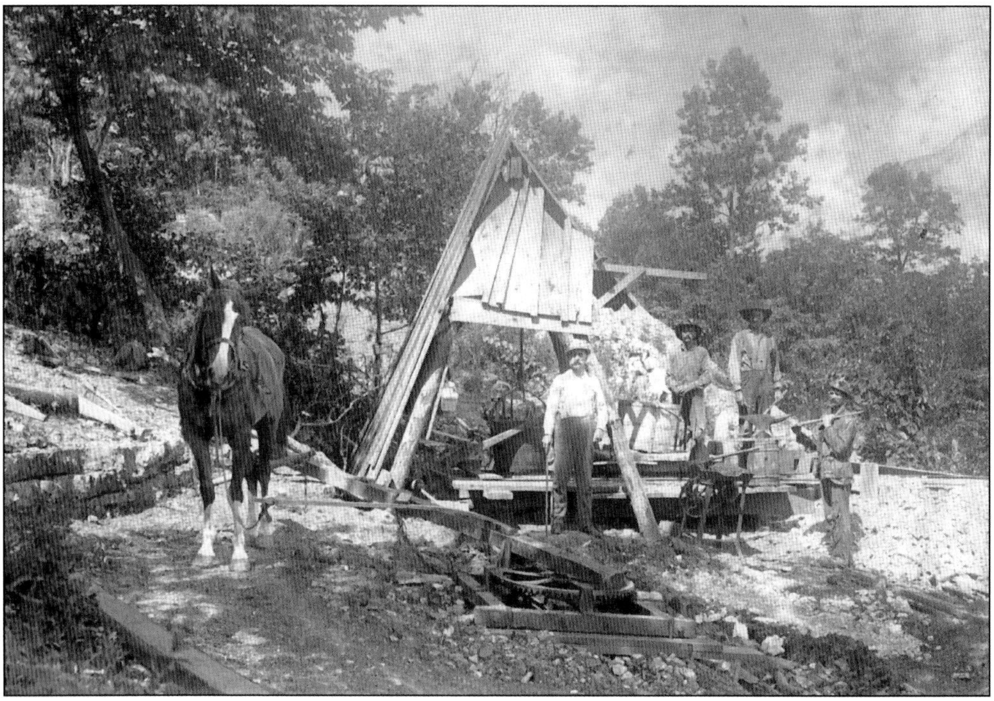

In the late 1890s, the Dodson Lead and Zinc Company of Bethlehem, Pennsylvania, was mining both lead and zinc at the Lead Hill Mine west of Mansfield. The ore was then transported to the mill at Crusher Pond. Mr. Kendrick, the boss at the mine, is shown supervising local residents Marion Lovall, Fred Morris, and John Davis.

Six

Gone but Not Forgotten

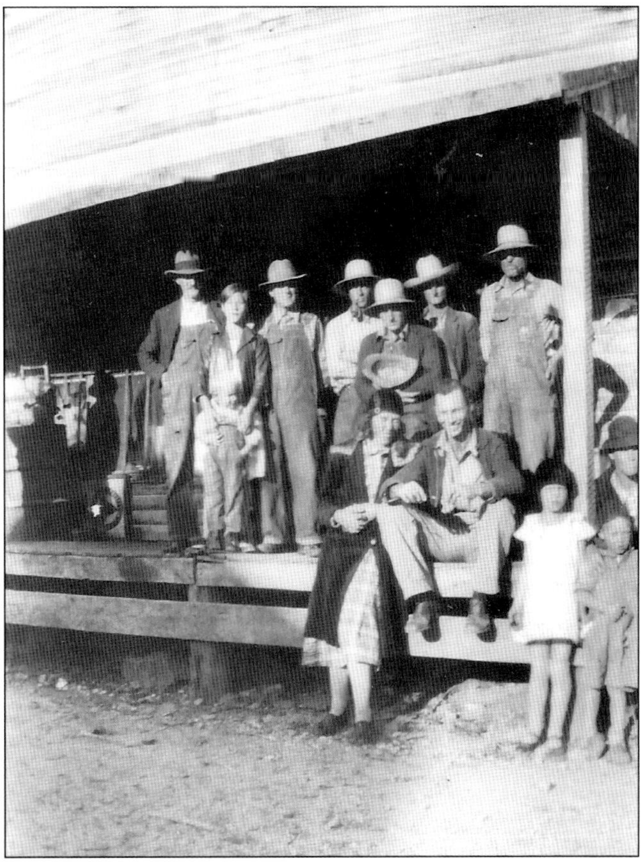

Before Mansfield was founded, the area was surrounded by small trading communities where local people could purchase staples needed for survival, such as salt, flour, sugar, feed, and kerosene. Farmers could also take such items as eggs, butter, produce, and chickens to barter for goods that they needed. The front porch of a general store, such as this one at London, was an ideal place to spend the afternoon visiting.

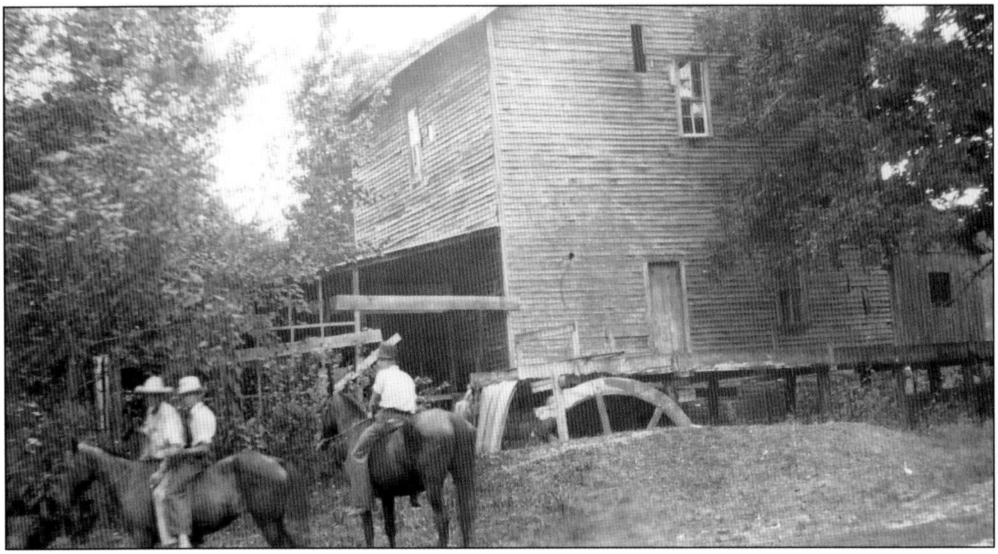

As farmers began to grow grain crops, men of an enterprising mindset saw a way to make money. When crops were harvested, farmers needed a place to grind the grain, so these entrepreneurs began to construct mills for that purpose. A constant supply of water turned the mill's water wheel, which then turned the grinding stones. Mills like this one at Bryant began popping up near available water sources.

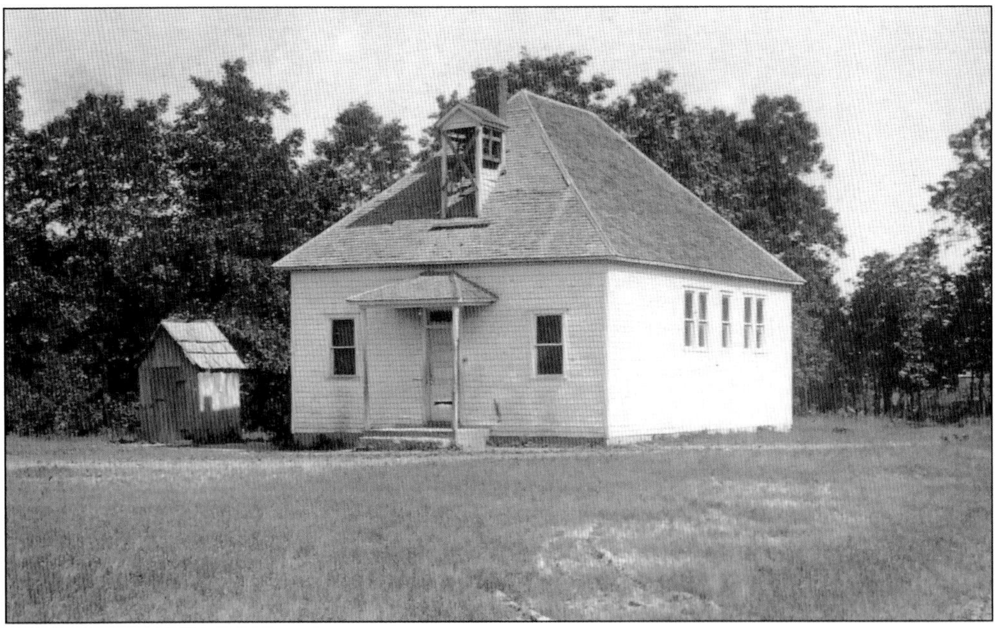

One-room schoolhouses, like this one, were important components of rural communities. By the 1900s, most schoolhouses were similarly constructed with white clapboard siding, belfries with cast-iron yoke bells, rows of evenly numbered windows on two sides, cast-iron water pumps, and usually two outhouses for the boys and girls. Pie suppers, music parties, and lodge meetings were often held at the schools.

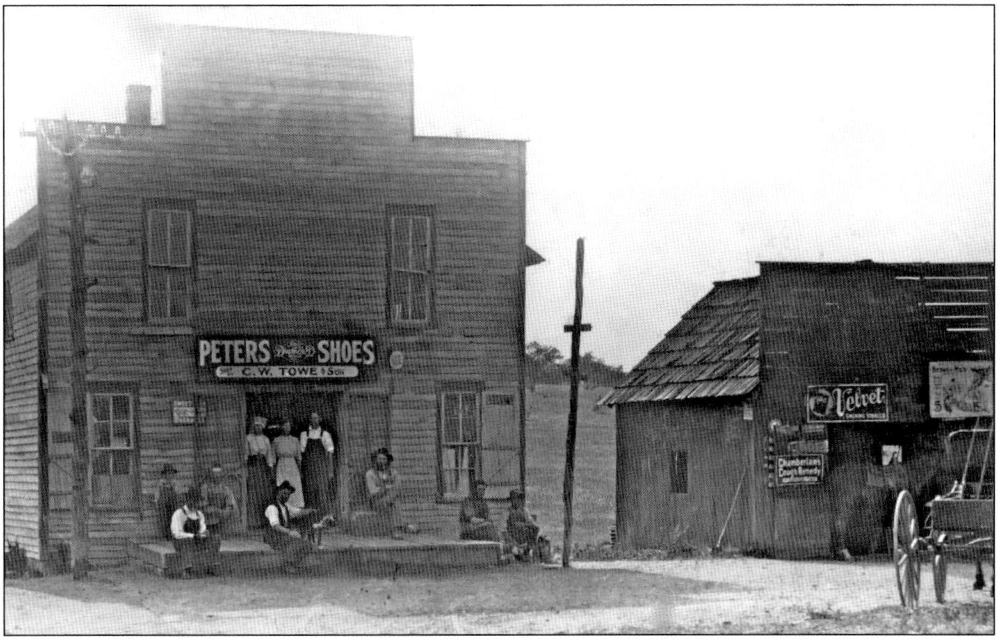

Land homesteaded by Charley Walter Towe and his wife, Lydia, when they arrived from Virginia around 1894 became the town of Olathe, located approximately eight miles southeast of Mansfield. Customers from miles around purchased necessities at the C.W. Towe & Son general store, often on credit since cash was hard to come by. Charley also owned and operated the telephone switchboard and was postmaster for a brief time.

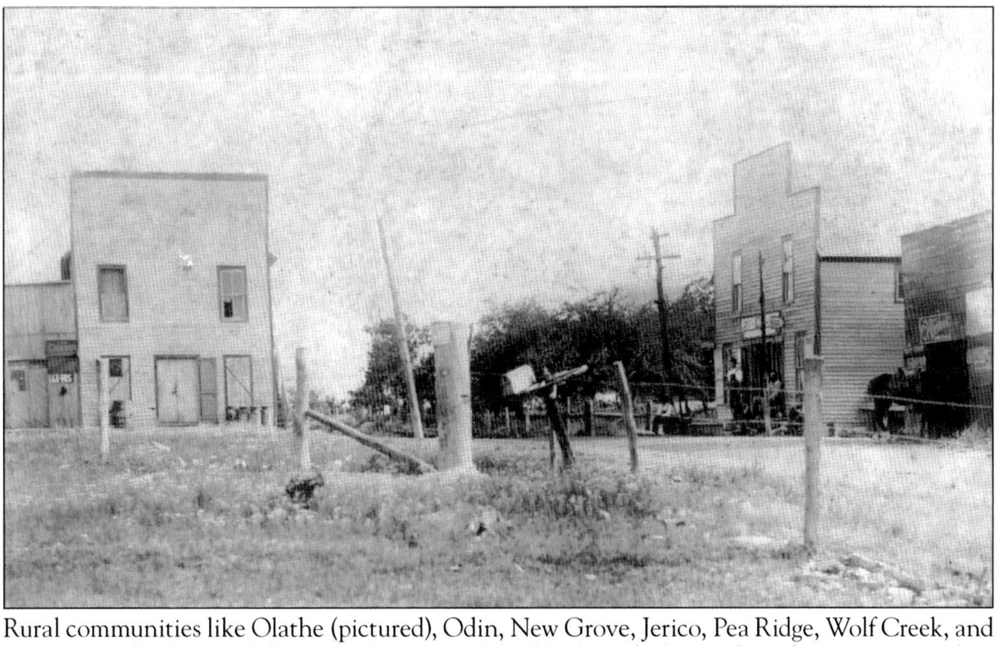

Rural communities like Olathe (pictured), Odin, New Grove, Jerico, Pea Ridge, Wolf Creek, and Dennis revolved around the general stores and the blacksmith shops where farmers came to buy supplies and have their horses shod. Carl Mays and his brother Wesley rode horseback to Olathe to sell their mother's eggs for 7¢ per dozen. One brother held the reins while the other one held the eggs.

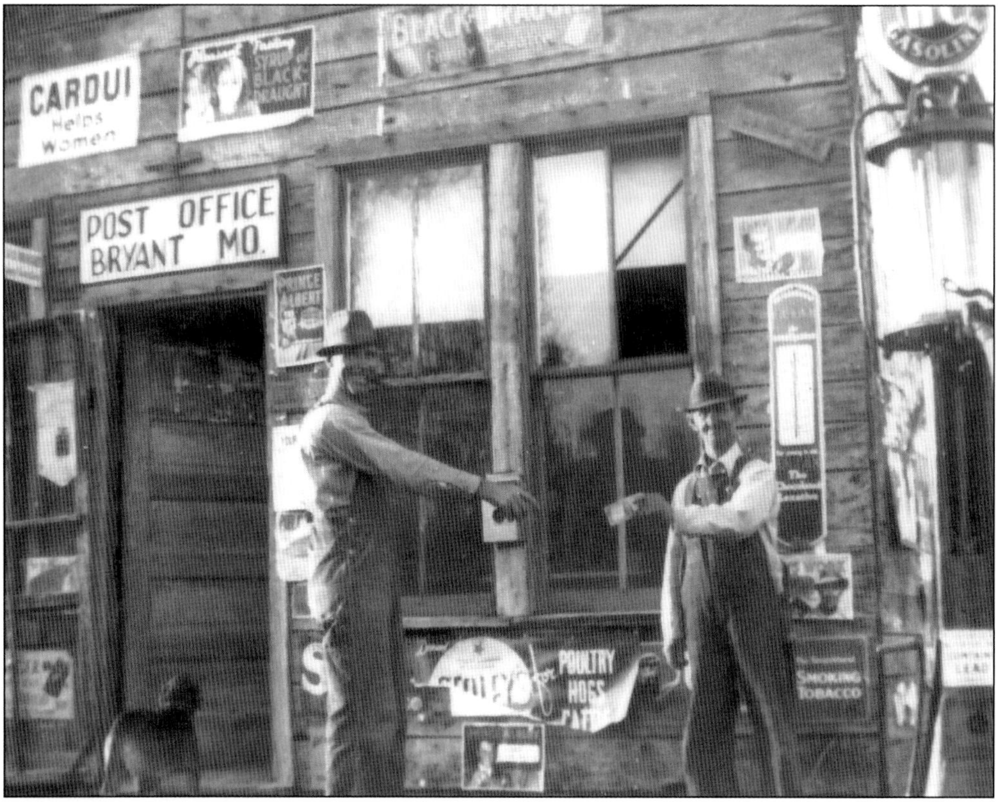

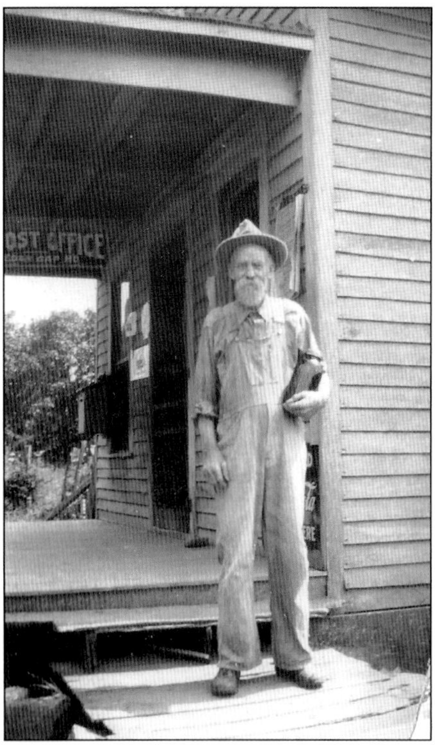

General stores, like this one at Bryant, often advertised the products they sold by covering the outside walls with brightly colored, beautifully lithographed, and porcelain-covered metal signs. With the invention of automobiles, some of the stores also served as gas stations, with tall glass-topped pumps appearing in the early 1900s.

Mail was delivered and picked up on a regular schedule at the general stores where the post office was usually located in the back. For many years, John Preston Newton was postmaster for Cedar Gap. He was well-known around the Cedar Gap community for his many beehives. His bees helped pollinate the orchards, and he kept the area supplied with honey.

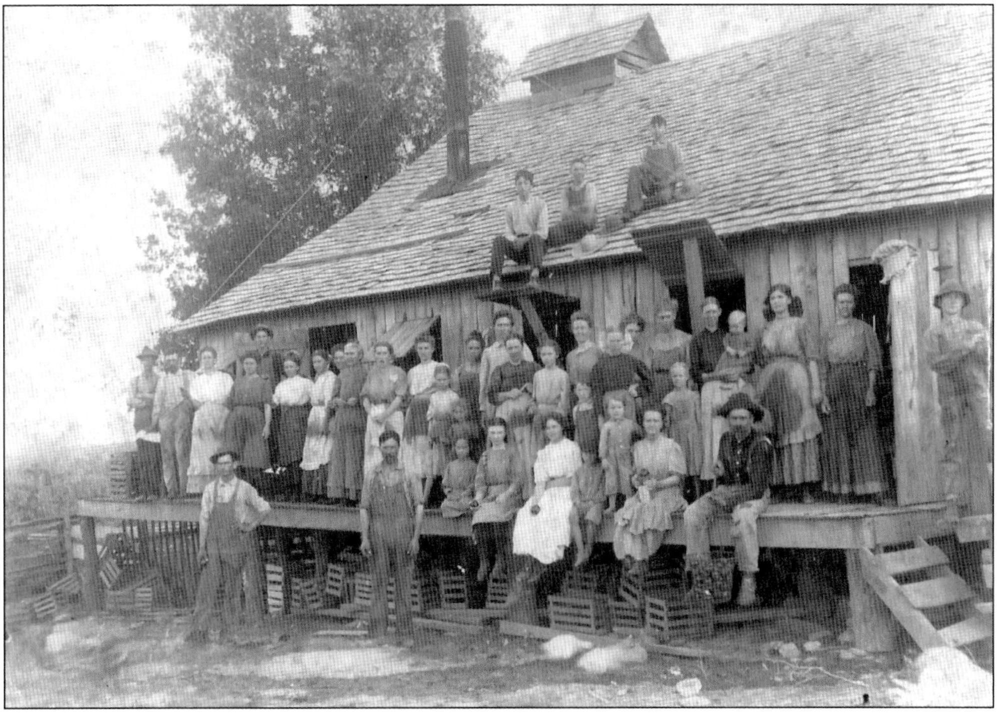

During the late 1800s, people found that the soil of the Ozark Hills was ideal for growing Red Gold tomatoes. Since canneries, such as the Jerico Cannery, pictured above, required a large amount of water, they needed to be close to a spring. As tomato canneries began opening throughout the countryside, the owners needed assurance that they would receive tomatoes. They provided local farmers with seeds in return for the tomatoes being brought to their canneries after picking. Families raised and tended the plants, picking the produce in the summer's burning heat and packing it in wooden tomato crates. Workers like Sara Bogart and Julia Cantrell, pictured below in the London Canning Factory, scalded, cored, peeled, and packed tomatoes before putting labels on the cans. Work in the canneries, which were sometimes hotter than the fields, provided with extra money.

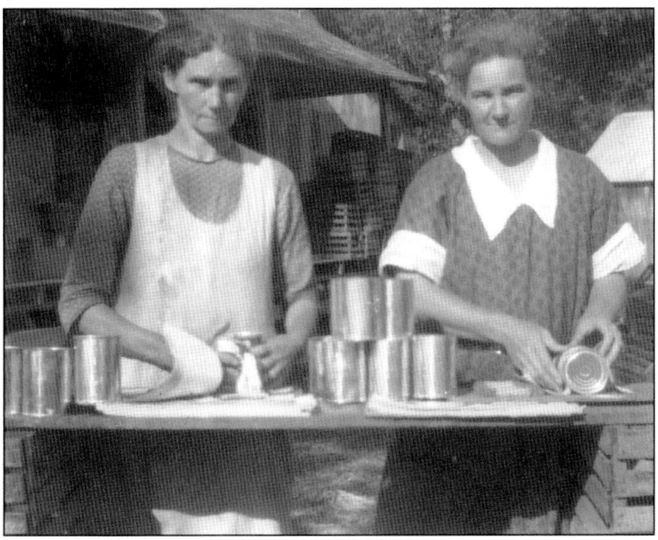

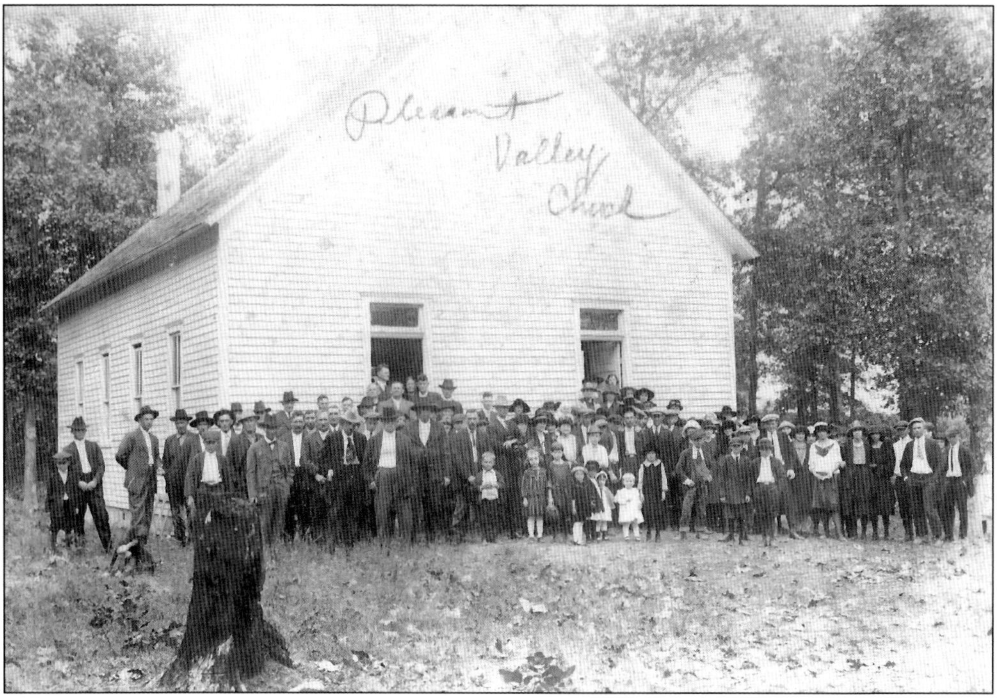

Churches were an integral part of any community. The earliest house of worship in the Mansfield area was Pleasant Valley Cumberland Presbyterian Church, established in 1841 by families with ties to Tennessee and Kentucky, where the denomination was founded. This church boasted a pre–Civil War membership roll of over 125 people. The building shown above was the third one for this church. It had two doors for the men and women to enter separately. Men sat on the left, and women were on the right. The first few pews on the left side were shorter to accommodate the area known as the amen corner, where the deacons sat. The building was heated by a potbelly stove and cooled by raising the six-foot windows on the sides. Below, Rev. John Russell stands at the front of the church on Mother's Day.

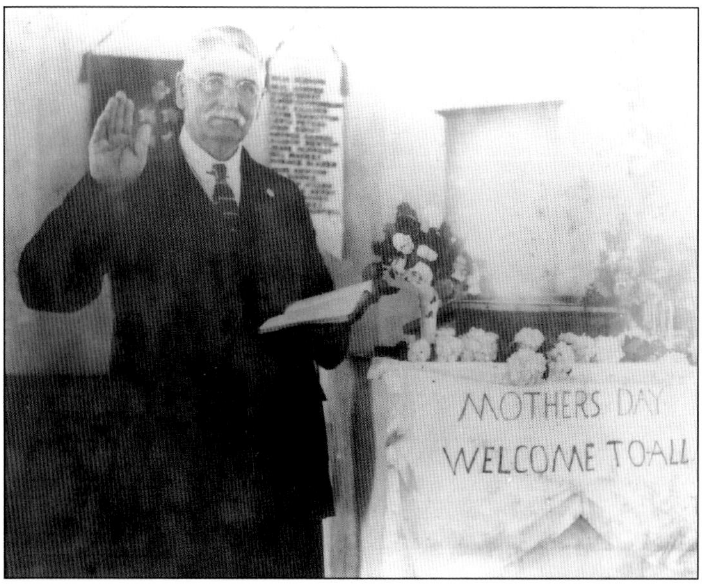

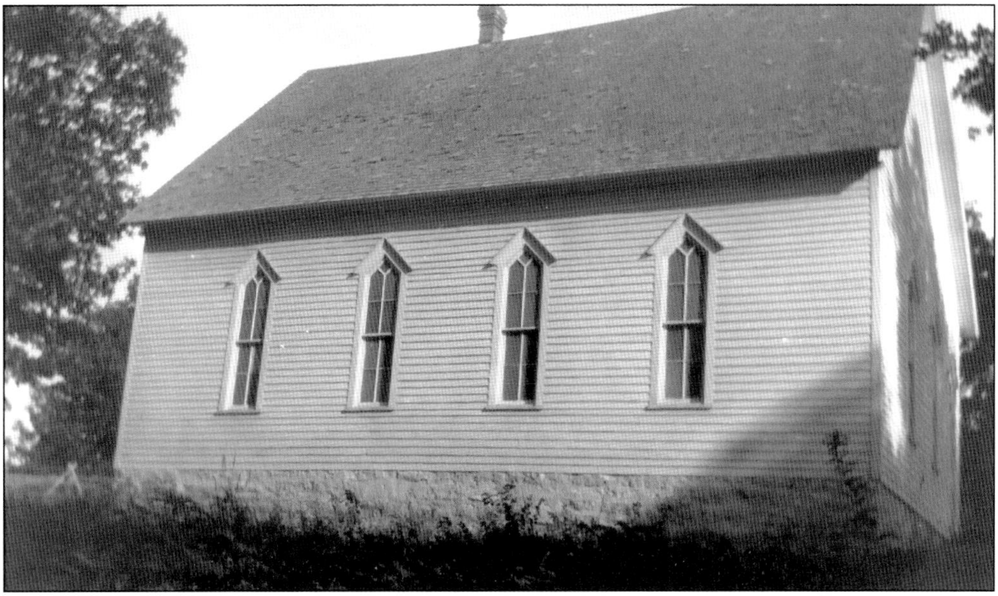

Many country churches, such as Mission Temple Baptist Church pictured above, held services only once a month. Established in 1891, it was built on land donated by James D. Newton. Members arrived early on the appointed day, usually Saturday, to do their trading at the London General Store. They would then, in the late afternoon, travel down the road in time for the preaching, which was followed by a business meeting.

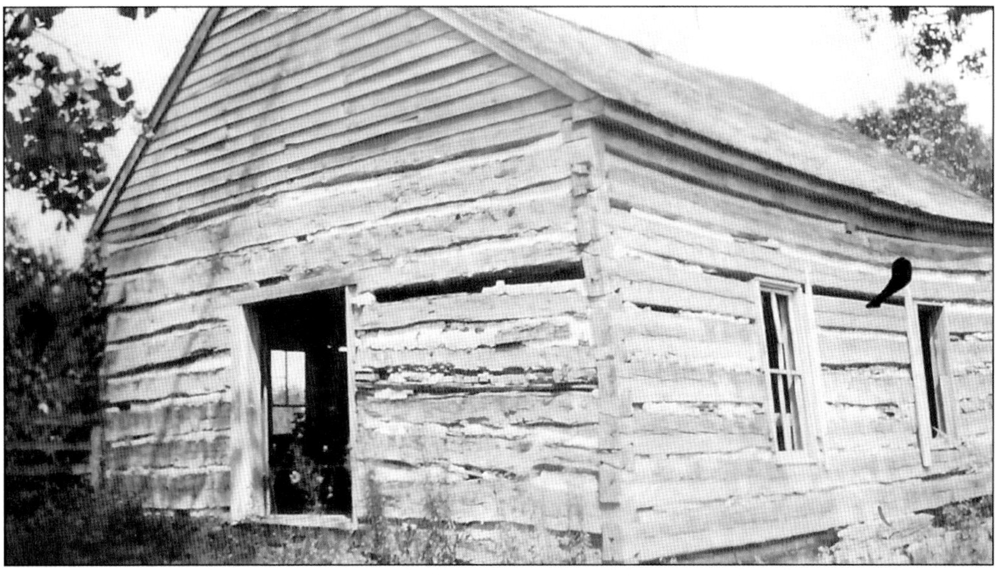

Many of the early church houses were built of logs. The Old Dennis Church, pictured here, is a typical example of the appearance of these buildings. It was built in 1867 by members who donated their time and effort to the construction. Members also donated the logs, sometimes pledging enough for either half a wall or a whole wall. The pews were made from logs split in half.

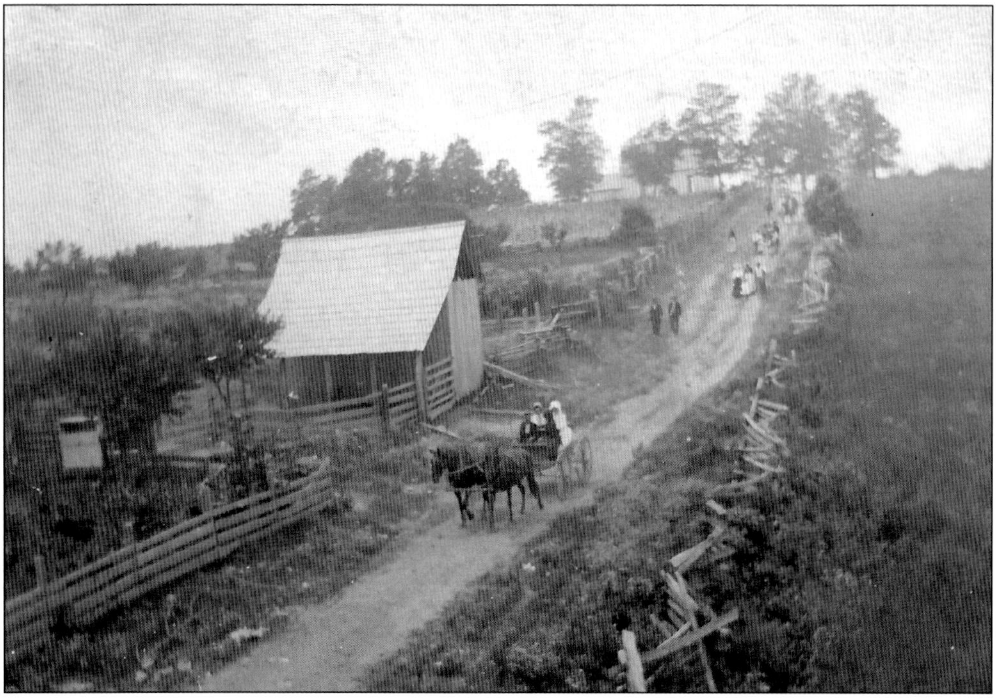

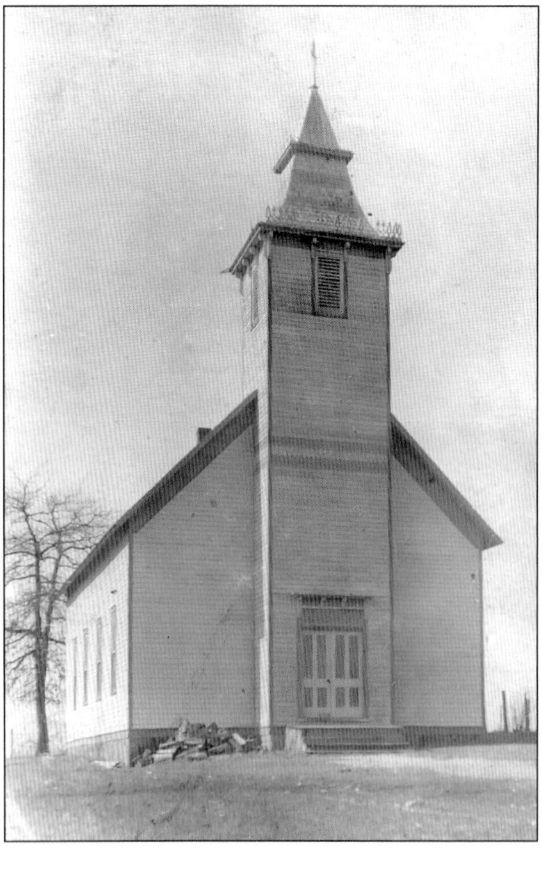

Fairview Church of the Brethren was located near what used to be the town of Olathe, southeast of Mansfield. The original church is pictured here with people returning home following the services. At this time, the dirt road ended at the church, and many of the congregation simply walked up the hill to it.

The Mansfield congregation of the Cumberland Presbyterian Church formed on Sunday, October 28, 1883. J.C. Spence, Margaret Spence, J.J. McMullin, M.H. Rippee, G.W. Freeman, Sophia Freeman, and A. Moore constituted the founding members. The Reverend J.C. Shepard was named the first minister; his annual salary was $100. The church building, the first in town, was completed in December 1884 and continues to serve the present congregation.

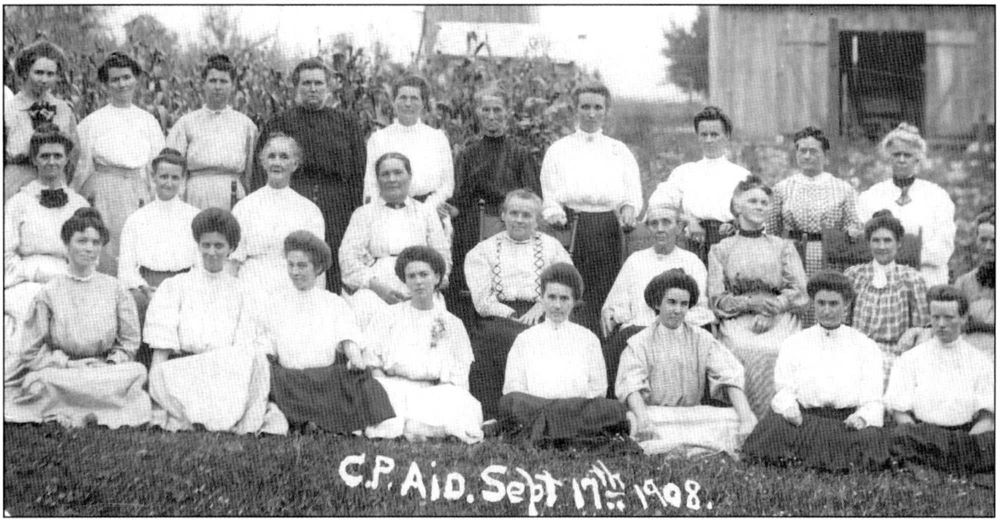

Members of the Mansfield Cumberland Presbyterian Church's Ladies Aid Society were, from left to right, (first row) Myrtle Tripp, Verba Turner, Rebecca Bell, Verdie Moore, Emily James, Mamie O'Harren, Ora Rippee, and Nora Riley; (second row) Eliza Peters, Carrie Rogers, Sophia Headley, Mrs. Moore, Mrs. James, Sophia Freeman, Elizabeth Tripp, Laura Beach, and Margaret Riley; (third row) unidentified, Maude Williams, Mollie Freeman, Ann Rippee, Mary Dennis, Margaret Bell, Ida Strong, Rinda Brazeal, Mrs. Andrews, and Jane Rippee.

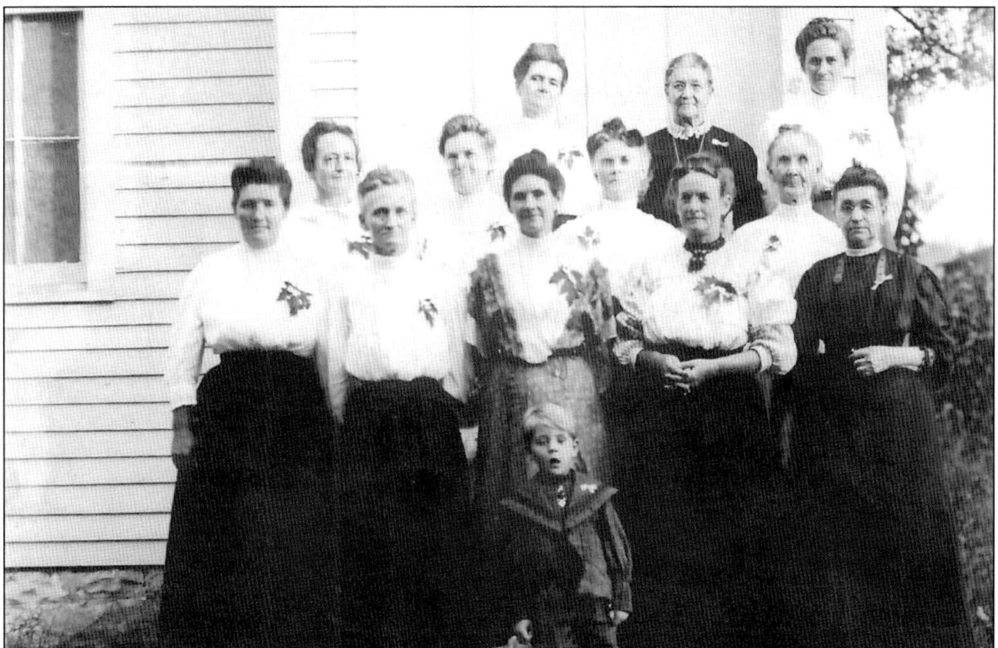

In 1909, Mansfield's chapter of the Women's Confederated Temperance Union included, from left to right, (first row) Mollie Hoover, Carrie Rogers, Laura Beach, Margaret Riley, and Clara Comstock, with Alton Coday in front; (second row) Susan Burney, Maggie Reynolds, Elizabeth Tripp, and Sophia Headley; (third row) Eliza Peters, Mrs. Smith, and Mary Coday. Originating in 1874, it is America's oldest continuing women's organization.

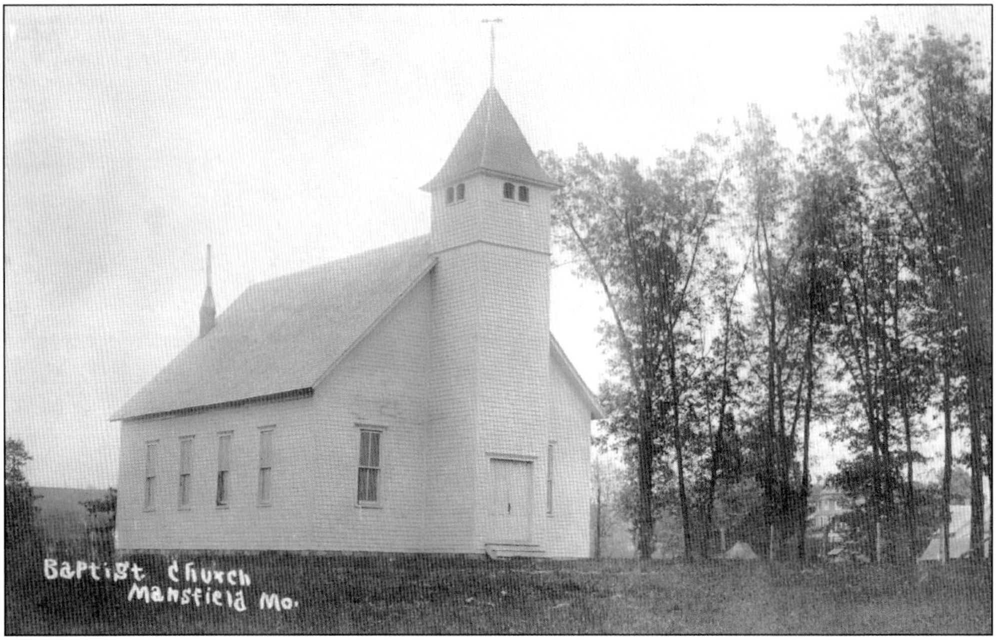

By the early 1900s, many townsfolk felt it was time to permanently establish a Baptist church in town. Some Baptists had been attending the Old Dennis Log Church, which was called Mount Pleasant. Others had been meeting in the upstairs of the Grand Army of the Republic building, located on the square in Mansfield. In October 1909, the Baptist church, shown here, was completed and dedicated.

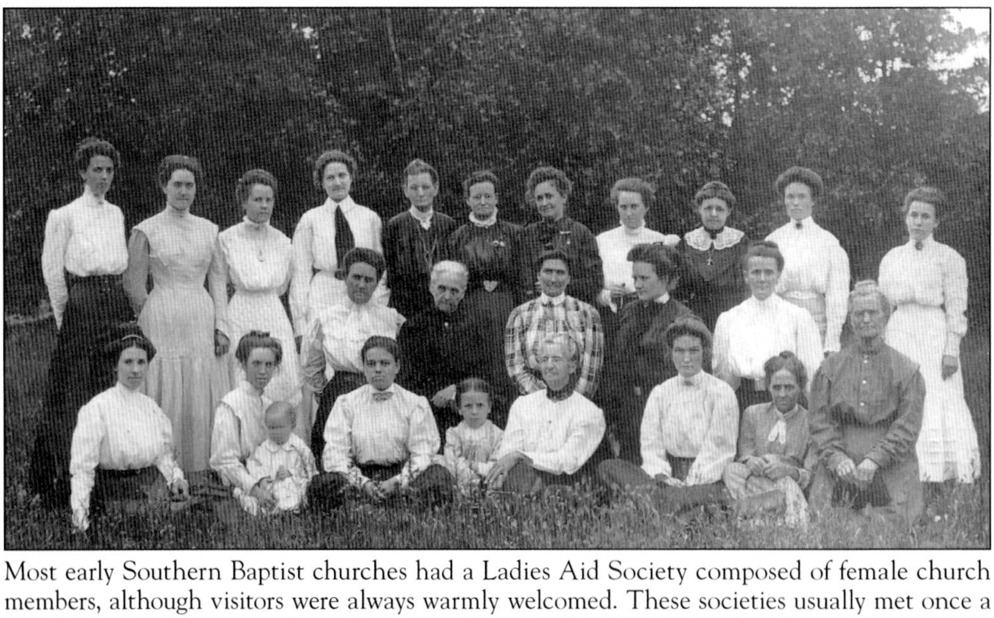

Most early Southern Baptist churches had a Ladies Aid Society composed of female church members, although visitors were always warmly welcomed. These societies usually met once a month. During the get-togethers, there was a devotional or inspirational reading, prayer, singing, a business meeting, a collection, and visiting over refreshments. The main goal of the society was to support the church, the pastor and his family, and the members.

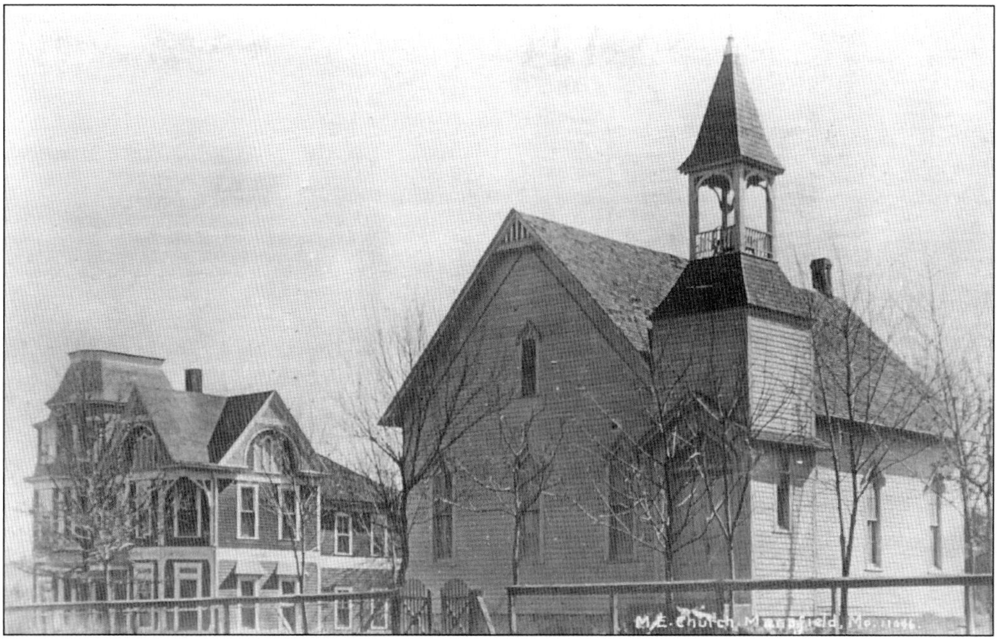

When the Wilders arrived here in 1894, there were only two houses of worship: the Presbyterian and the Methodist. They chose the Methodist, feeling it was more like the Congregational Church they had attended in DeSmet. However, the Methodists did not have their own building until 1899. Almanzo and Laura Wilder faithfully attended church as long as their health allowed. Their funerals were held in the original church house.

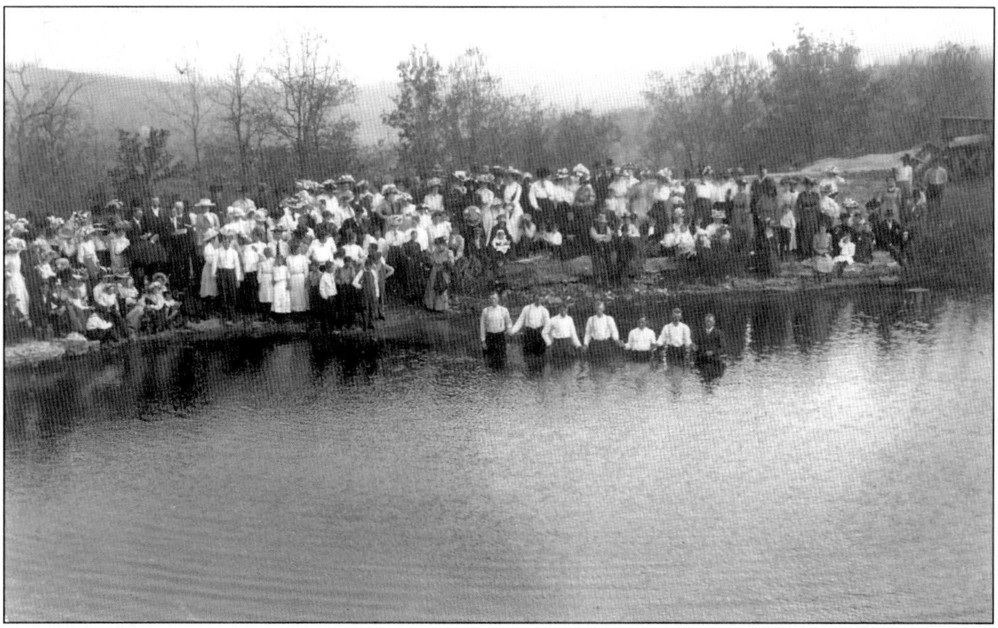

Baptizing is an integral part of many Christian faiths. It is a symbol of rebirth after the salvation experience. Since there was no baptistery in the original First Baptist Church, baptisms were held at Crusher Pond, on the southwest edge of Mansfield. This was also the site to which all the mined ore was brought to be crushed before being loaded onto trains.

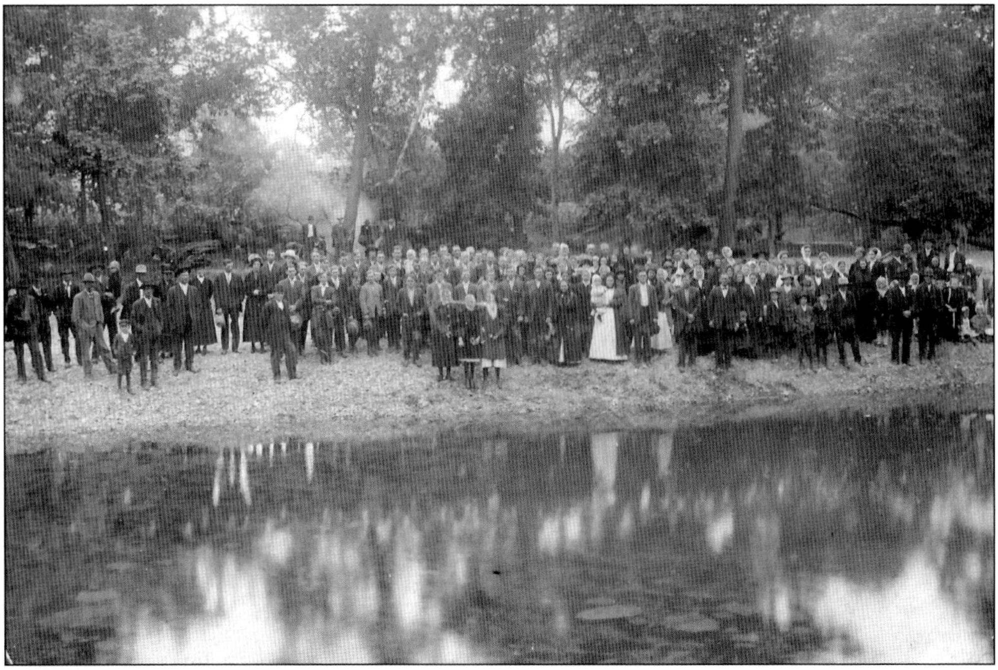

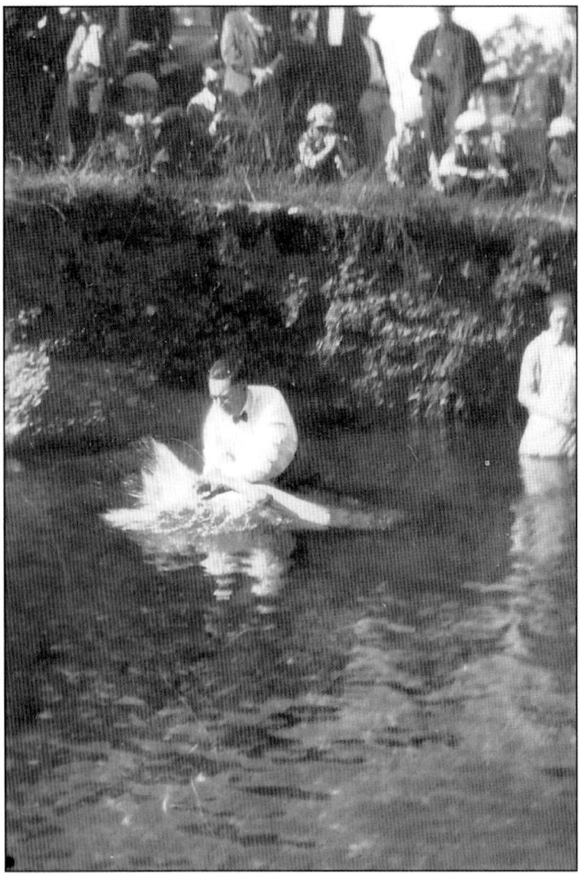

Country baptisms were performed in creeks or swimming holes. After a person was saved, the congregation gathered at one of the local creeks, such as Gasconade, Wolf, Baker, Rippee, Spence, or Bryant. Baptisms were performed in the heat of summer and the dead of winter. At times, ice was anywhere from eight to twelve inches thick and had to be cut for the baptism. Often people sang "Shall We Gather at the River" before the candidates, who were often wearing their Sunday best, were led into the water. The preacher would place the person's hand over their nose and mouth and say a few appropriate words; then the candidate was laid under the water. After a few seconds, the person was raised up to shouts of "Hallelujah" and "Praise the Lord."

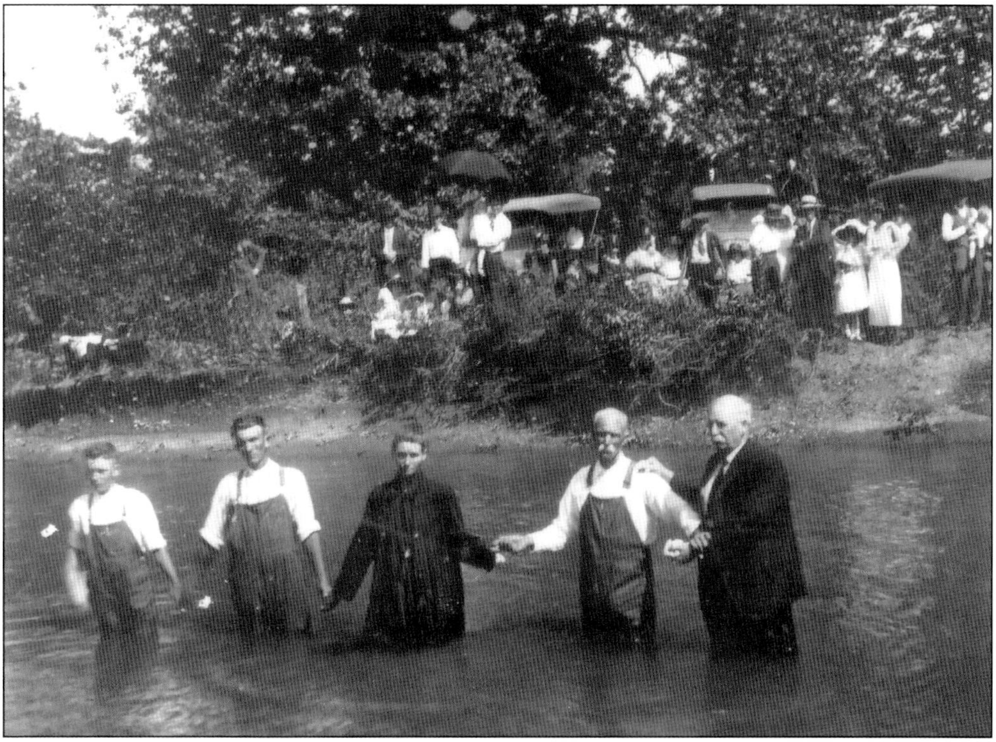

It was a common practice for families to be baptized together. The Elwood Bogart family were all saved together at Mission Temple on June 5, 1921. The congregation dismissed services and went to the Clay Bank swimming hole. Members of the Bogart family being baptized are, from left to right, Marvin, Jordan, Sarah, and Elwood. Mission Temple performed all their baptisms at Clay Bank.

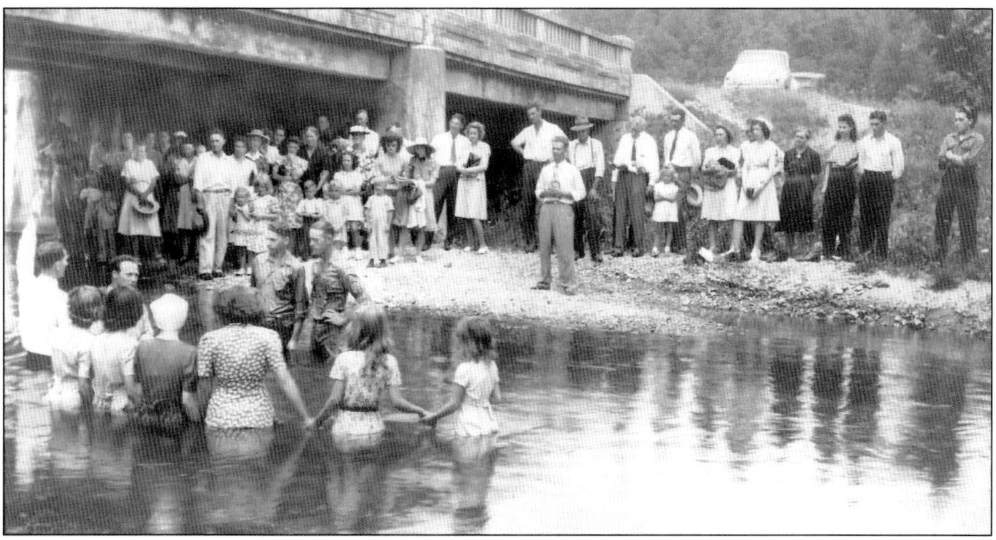

The congregation of the Lead Hill Baptist Church gathers at a local creek in 1946 for a group baptism. At this time, it was common to hold creek baptisms during which the people were completely submerged or immersed in the water. The three men in the creek waiting to be baptized are, from left to right, Leonard Samuels, James Cameron, and Judd Corder.

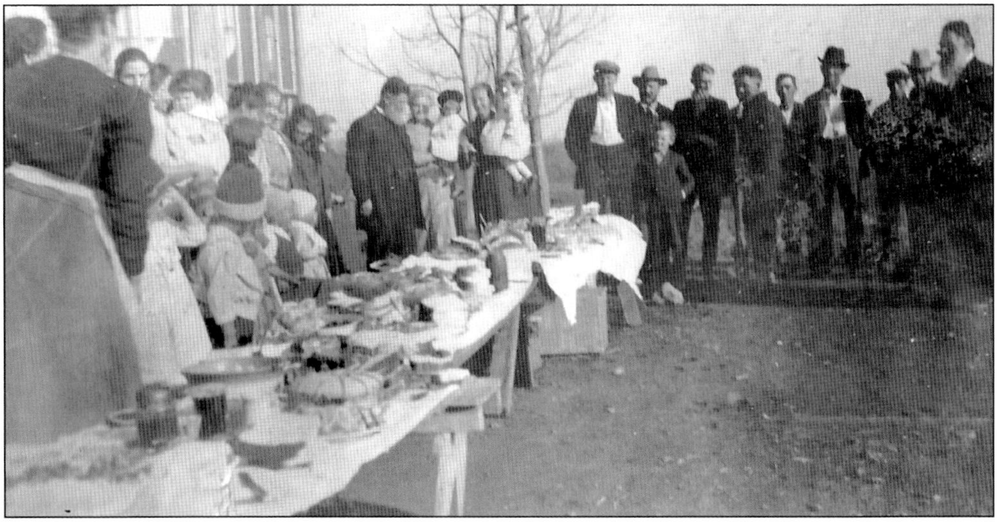

Often, dinners were held after church services. Fairview Church of the Brethren, located near Olathe, was no exception. Church pews were taken outside and flipped upside down to be used as the legs of the table. Large sheets of wood were laid across the pews for a table top. The women distributed their dishes around the tables. Grace was said by the minister, and then the eating began.

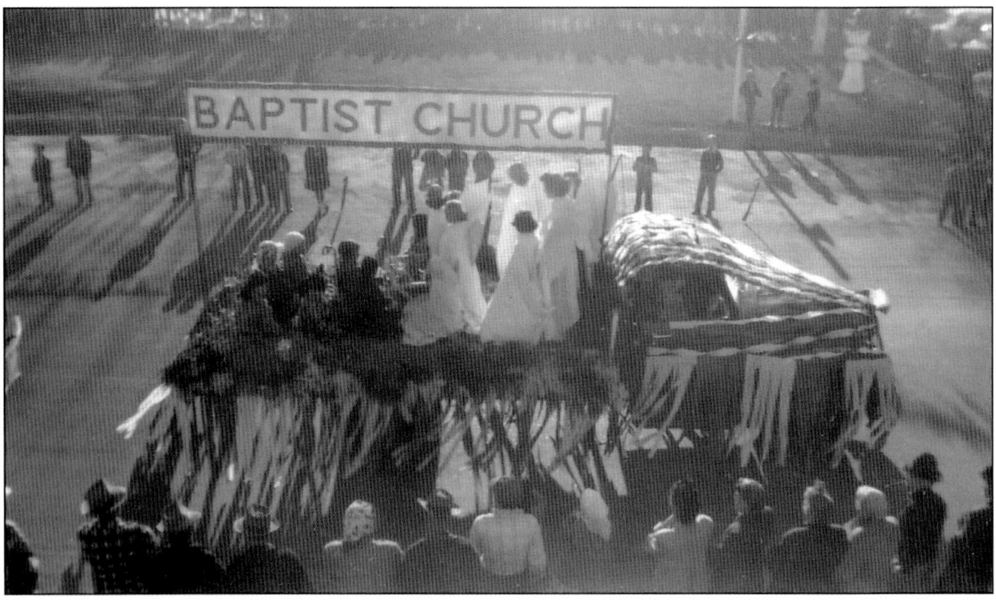

For many years, a Christmas parade was held during the early part of December. Generally, local merchants planned this event to bring people into town to shop for their presents. In this photograph, the Baptist Church has entered a float displayed on a flatbed hay truck. Children from the church, dressed as angels, wise men, and shepherds, pay homage to baby Jesus in a nativity scene.

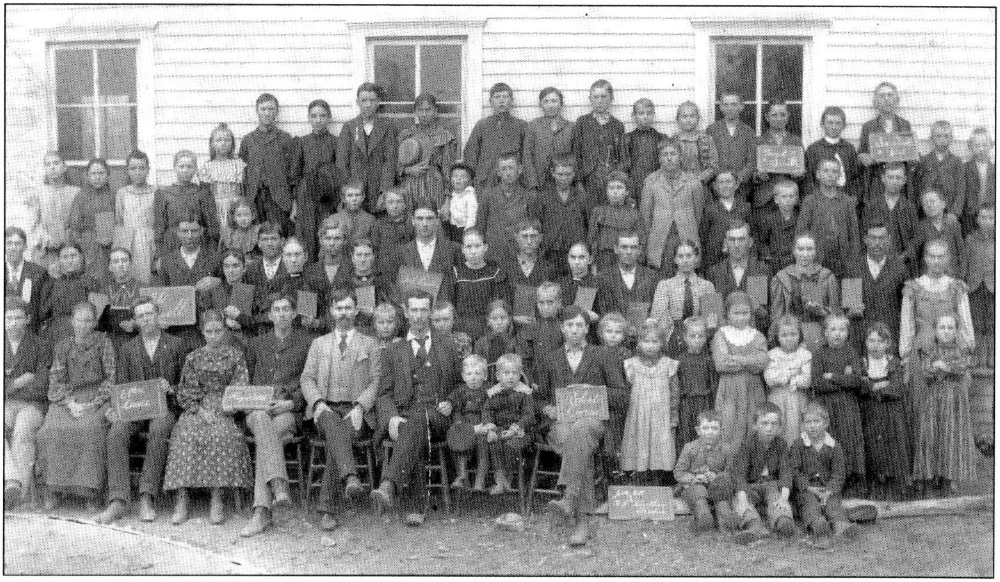

Singing schools made the Ozark hills ring. People of all ages attended these schools to learn to sing or to sharpen their singing skills. Singing schools were held in either the local schoolhouse or church, such as Pleasant Valley. Students learned to sing using the shaped-note technique. Each note stood for a different tone that the singer made. The class learned to pick the correct pitch by ear.

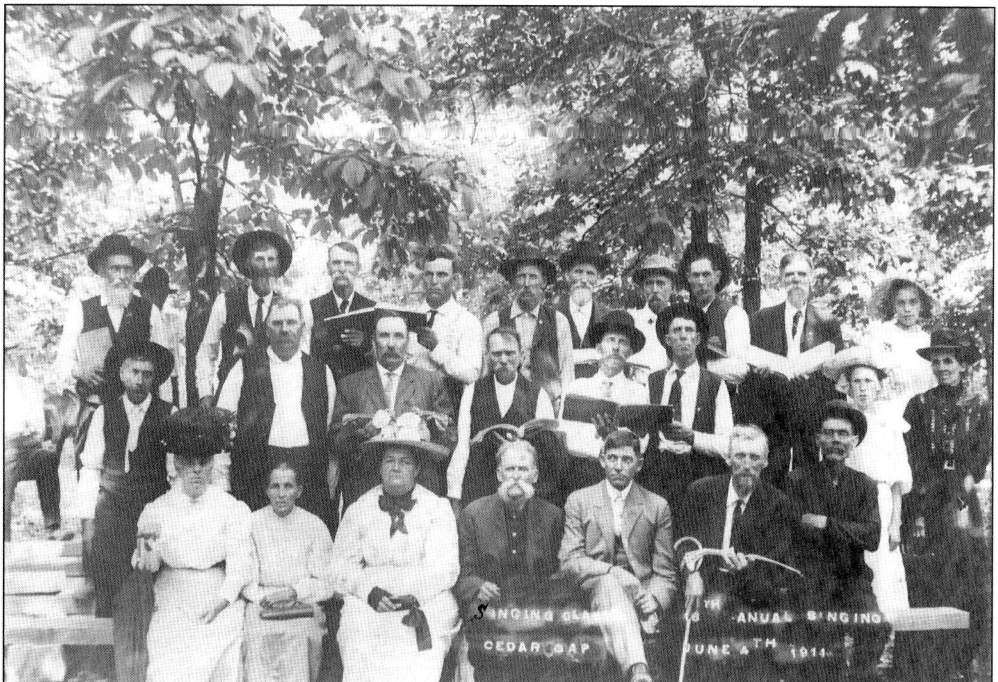

In 1895, the first Cedar Gap June Singing Convention was held. Since then, the annual, all-day event is held on the first Sunday in June. In the early years, Frisco ran special trains from Springfield to Cedar Gap just for this occasion. A service was conducted in the Cedar Gap Church, followed by a dinner; then the singing began. This group is the Cedar Gap singing class of 1914.

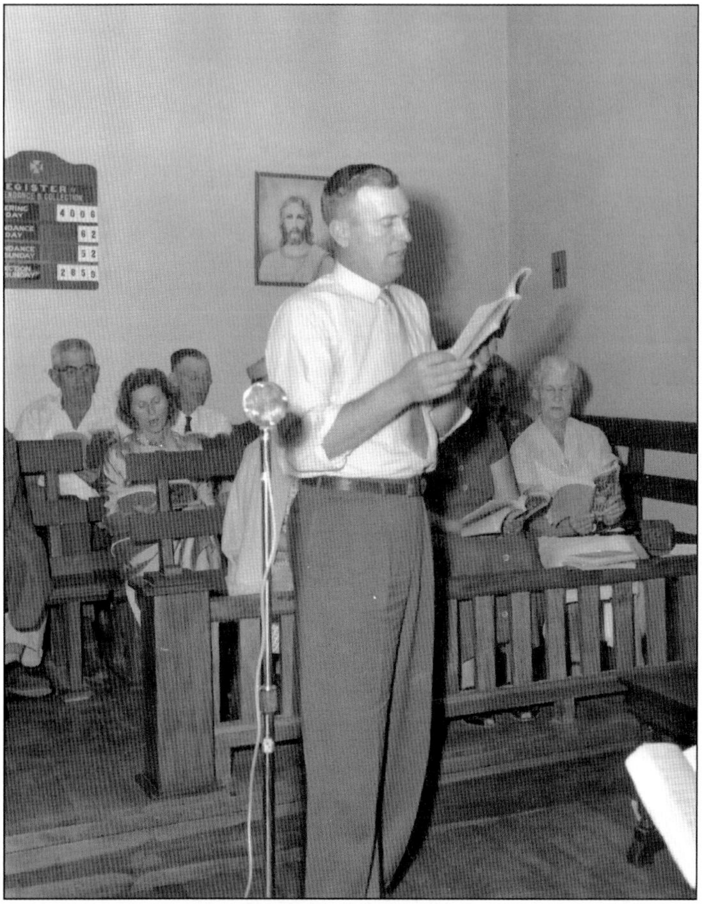

Gorman Short leads the singing at Wolf Creek Freewill Baptist Church. Seated behind him is the choir, made up of church members and guests. *World Wide Songs*, a shaped-note songbook, is being used. Special singing days like this included congregational singing, but also special solos, duets, and quartets performing praises to God. Each group had its own signature song and sound.

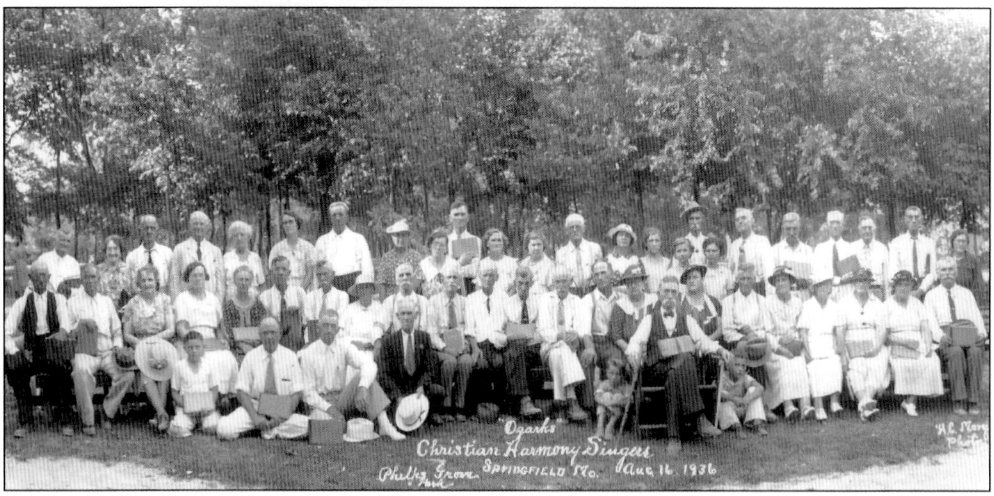

Members of the Christian Harmony Singers were immortalized in a poem by area resident Lon Dennis, who wrote a verse describing each person. Members of the singing group included Henry Brazeal, Ada and Della Claxton, Jim Coday, Joe and Laura Dennis, Lon Dennis, Isaac Edwards, Trace Hume, David and Myrtle Janzen, Albert and Sarah Latimer, Jim and Ellen Odle, Cora Selby, Herbert Shelton, Barney and Mary Smith, Veena Thomas, and Docia Whittaker.

Seven

Ozarkiana

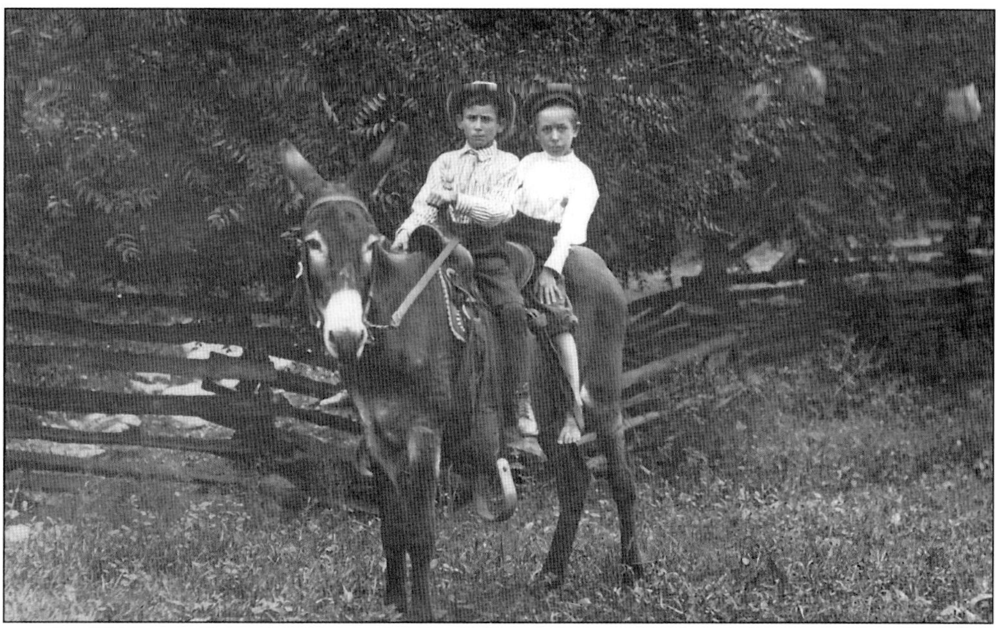

Crossing a male donkey, or jack, with a mare produces a good old-fashioned Missouri mule. This handsome specimen is ready to carry its two young companions off on an adventure. Mules were good utility animals and not as expensive as horses. The split rail fence behind them is a perfect example of Missouri ingenuity. Wood was plentiful, and these were easy to put up and take down when moving livestock.

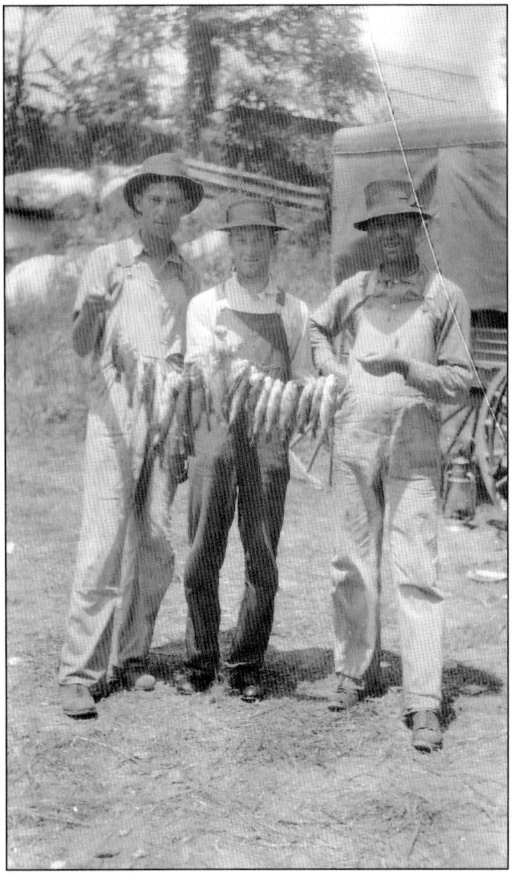

Fish are abundant in the Ozarks, and fishing is a mainstay to the Missouri lifestyle. Walter Coday (center) and friends display a good day's catch. The locals still have a tradition of sucker-gigging at night using a light and a forged metal gig to spear the suckers. A fire and a pot of hot oil are the only tools needed for a sucker fry on the river banks.

Members of the Rippee family prepare for a fox hunt. The art of running dogs was often passed down from father to son. Fox hunting was considered a man's sport, but here in Mansfield, Rose Wilder, daughter of Laura and Almanzo Wilder, hunted with the men. She would stay up all night and run the dogs with the best of them. Herb Short made Rose a special horn for calling the dogs.

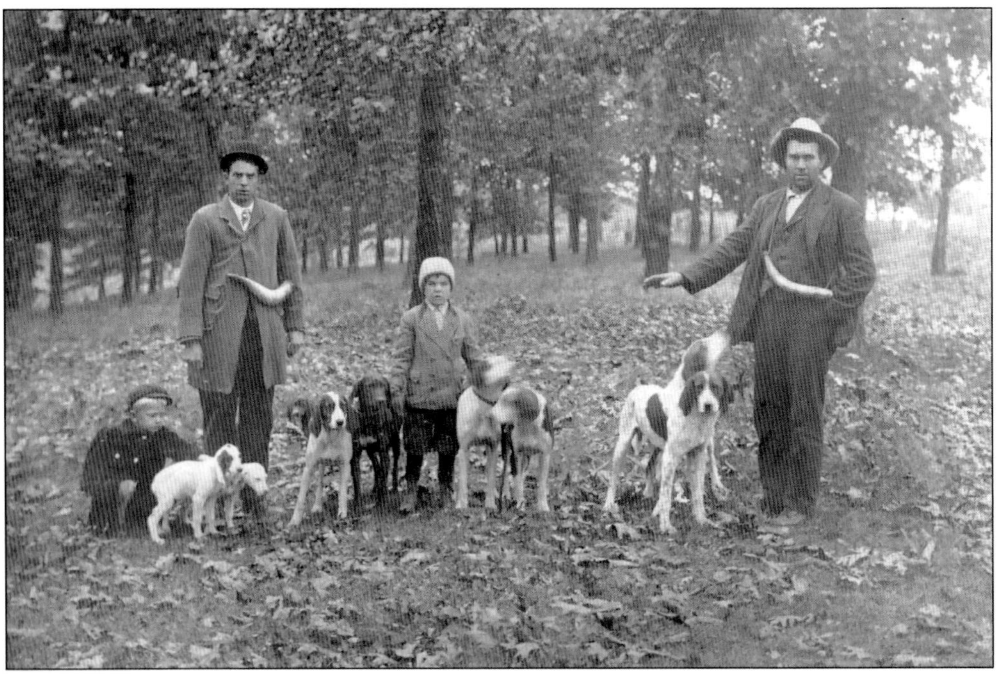

Socializing and smoking behind the haystack seems a rather risky business. In this era, it was not considered ladylike for women to smoke although many used snuff. If they did smoke, it was usually in secret, late at night, or in this type of situation, a shared puff behind the stack. However, families do tell stories of grannies chewing tobacco and smoking their corncob pipes down home on the farm.

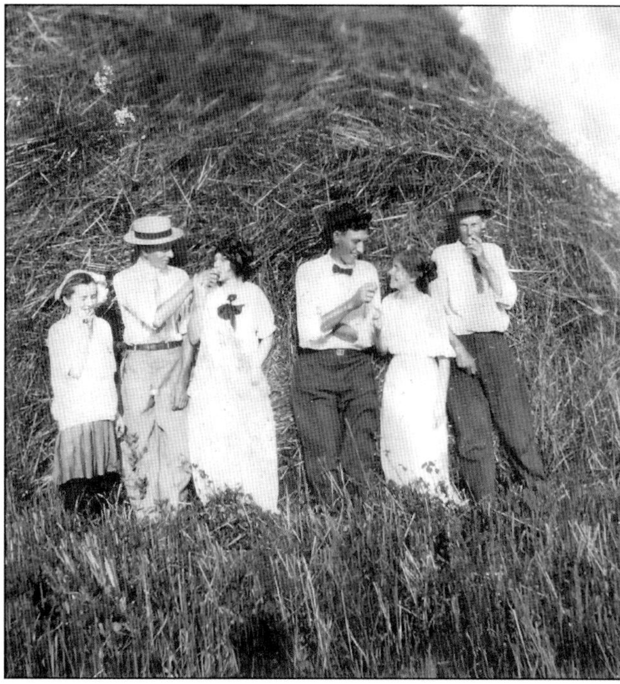

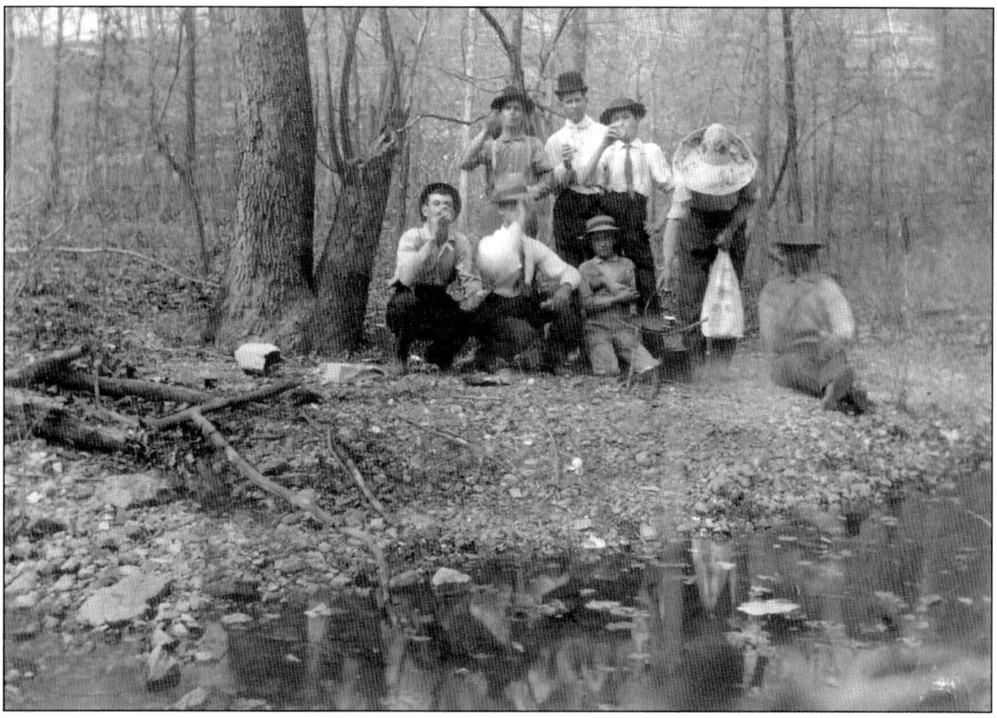

This afternoon of relaxation includes a little moonshine. Stills producing liquor were hidden in the creeks and "hollers" (valleys) of the Ozarks. Farmers could supplement their income with the sale of moonshine to locals. Because there was a tax on liquor, federal agents, called "revenuers," were sent to destroy these stills. This was risky business as many of them were booby-trapped. Stills were frequently moved to hide them from these agents.

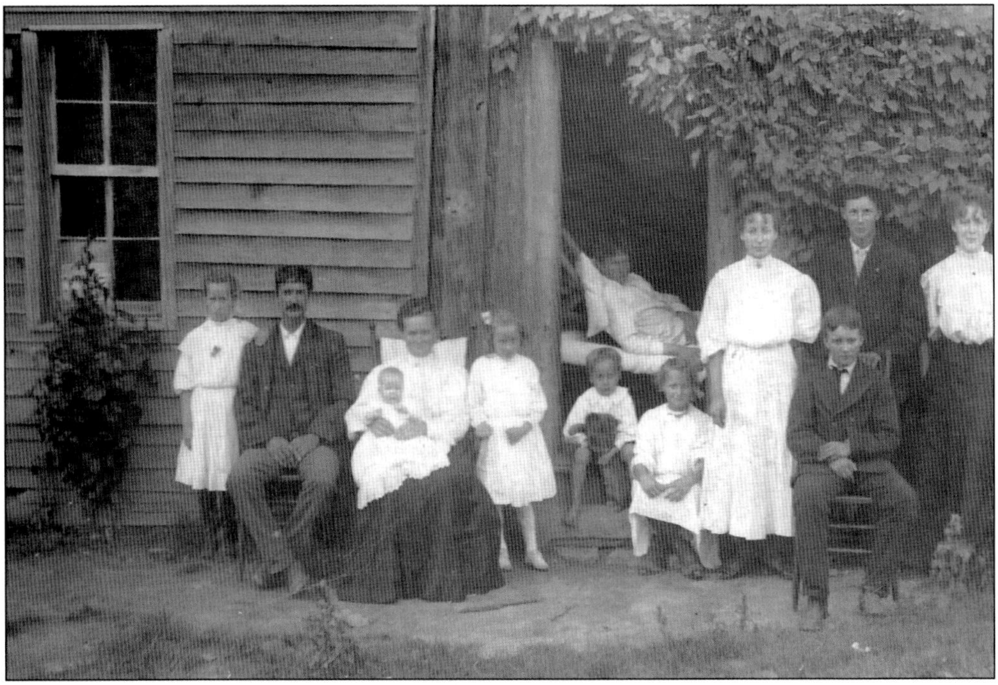

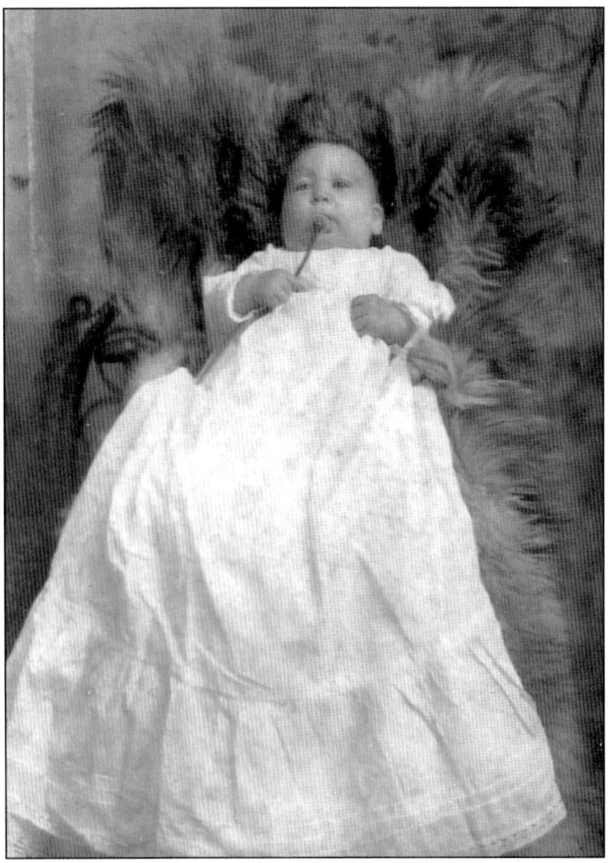

Members of the Short family are, from left to right, Opal, George, Mollie, Agnes, Geneva, Glen, Mary Ann, John (in bed), Bessie Lou, Luther, Effie, Fred, and Teddy Bear. In rural America, traveling photographers crisscrossed back roads to capture the essence and lifestyles of families. Blood was always thicker than water, and families took care of their own. This family photograph was carefully structured to include John, who was ailing.

Irene Newton uses a unique baby bottle in this c. 1909 photograph. This type of bottle, introduced in 1864 in England, consisted of a rubber tube with a nipple-shaped mouthpiece attached to a glass tube inserted through a cork and into a glass bottle at the baby's side. This invention helped free up a woman for her household duties and helped ensure the health of a child whose mother had died in childbirth.

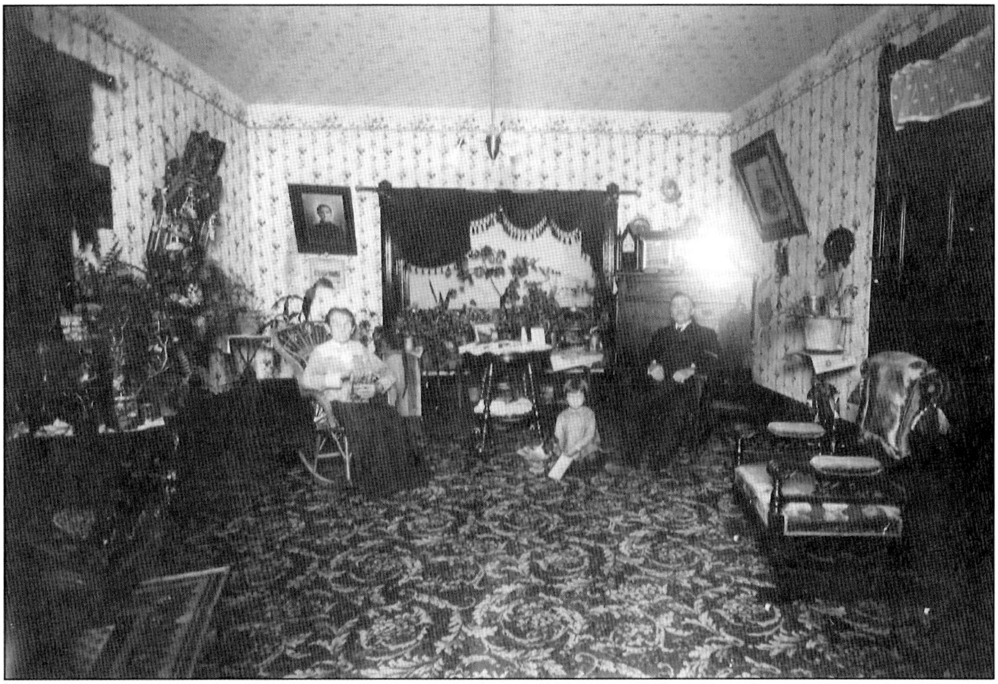

Aunt Sophie and Uncle George Freeman enjoy quiet time in their parlor. In *Farmer Boy*, Laura Ingalls Wilder explained that parlors were special places in people's homes. They were large, open sitting rooms furnished with the family's best and reserved for receiving special guests. They were also used for receptions following a loved one's funeral. Parlors were used mostly on Sundays and closed off the rest of the week.

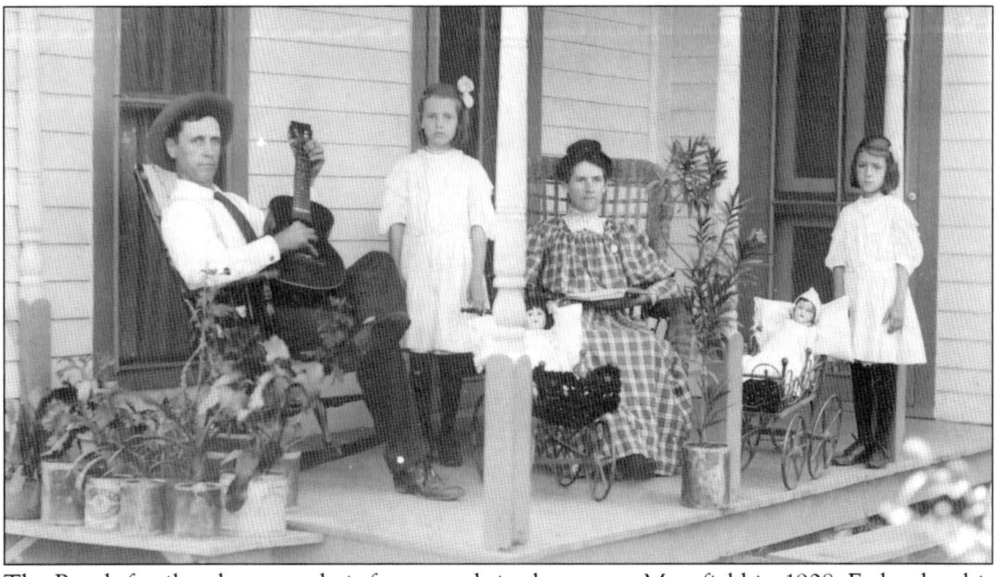

The Beach family relaxes on their front porch in downtown Mansfield in 1908. Father has his guitar, Mother has her sewing, and the girls have their dolls. Sitting on the porch as a family was a way to communicate, relax, and watch the neighbors and the world go by. Some porches also served a functional purpose. Screened-in porches were often used as sleeping quarters during the hot nights of summer.

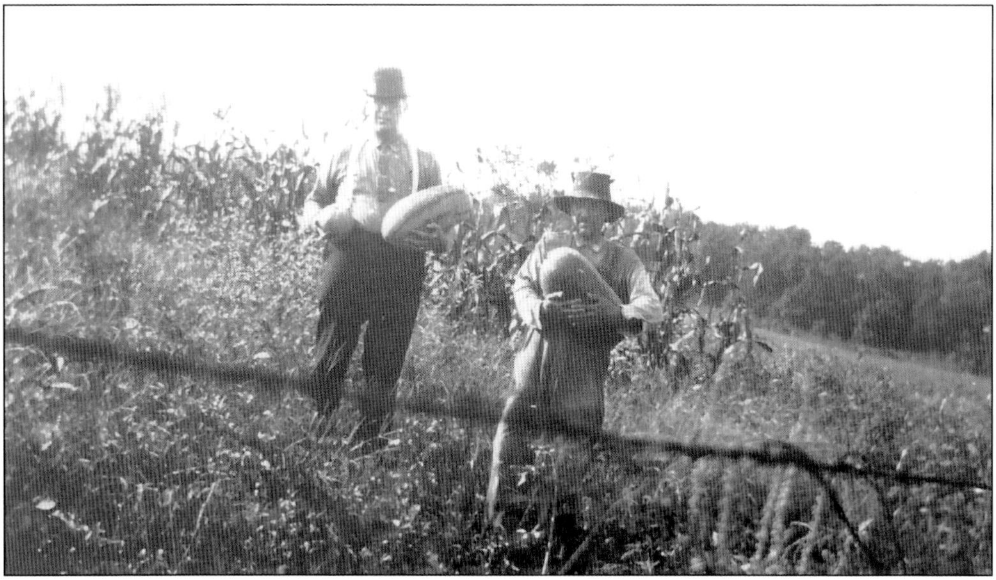

Watermelons cooled in an Ozark stream have always been a favorite delicacy, and mischievous teenagers have always loved to steal them. Some farmers stayed up all night with buckshot ready to scare off the watermelon villains. Many farmers cultivated a side garden of watermelons to take to market for extra cash. Gardening was a necessity for large families.

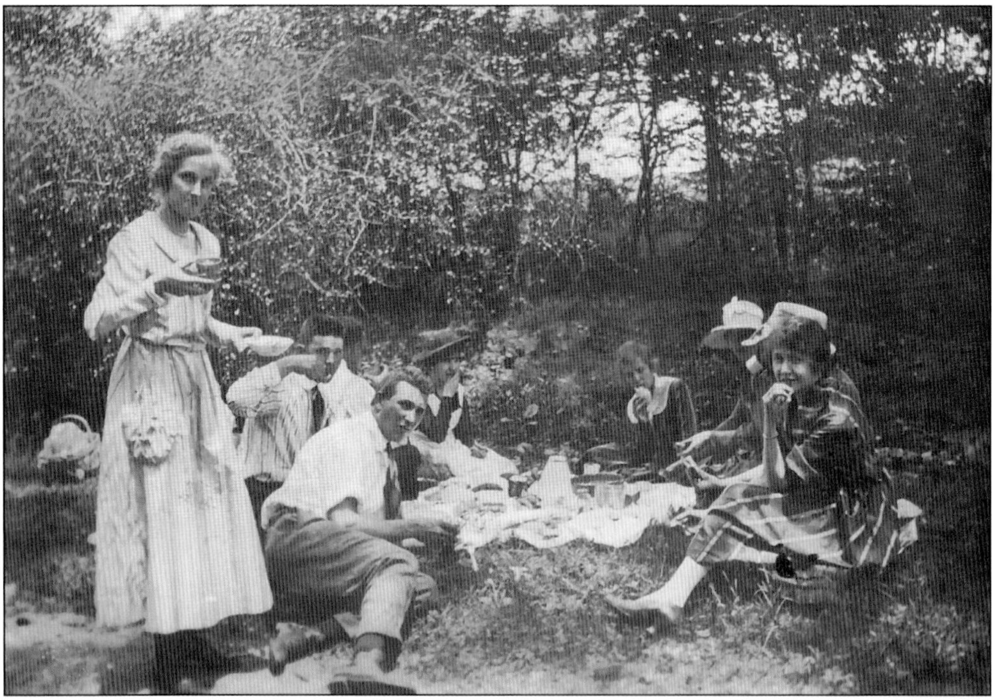

Picnics were a wonderful way to relax. The backdrop of beautiful, rolling hills and rambling creeks in the Ozarks was the perfect setting. Fried chicken, potato salad, homemade biscuits, pies, and watermelons were staples of a good down-home picnic. At church socials, picnic boxes were auctioned off to the highest bidder, and the reward for the young men with the highest bids was lunch with the young ladies who made the boxes.

Leisure time was rare in the small communities around Mansfield, but almost every farm had a pond or a creek that provided cool relief on a hot day. The best swimming holes were known by all the locals. Taking a cool dip after a long day's work was a relaxing reward. Many hardworking farm boys jumped in and swam with their overalls on before heading home to supper.

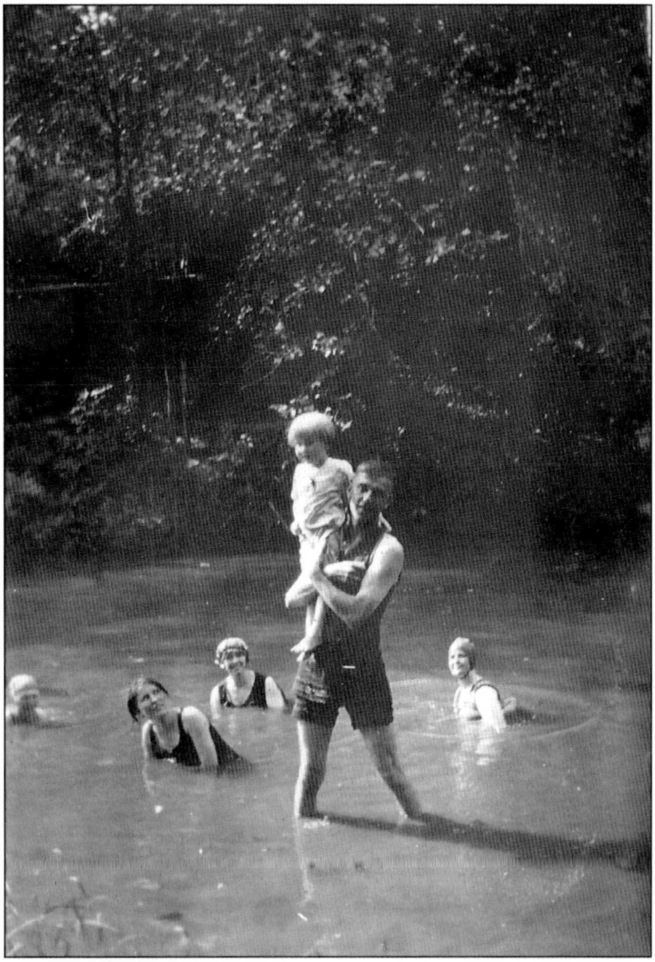

Locals say that a farmer lost one of his prize pigs; searching his neighbor's property, he discovered a 60-foot sinkhole leading to the entrance of a cave. He shook his head and said, "If that pig fell in that hole, he is halfway to China by now!" Lewis Moody climbs out of China Pig Hole on August 28, 1940. The cave's walls have inscriptions dating back to the 1800s.

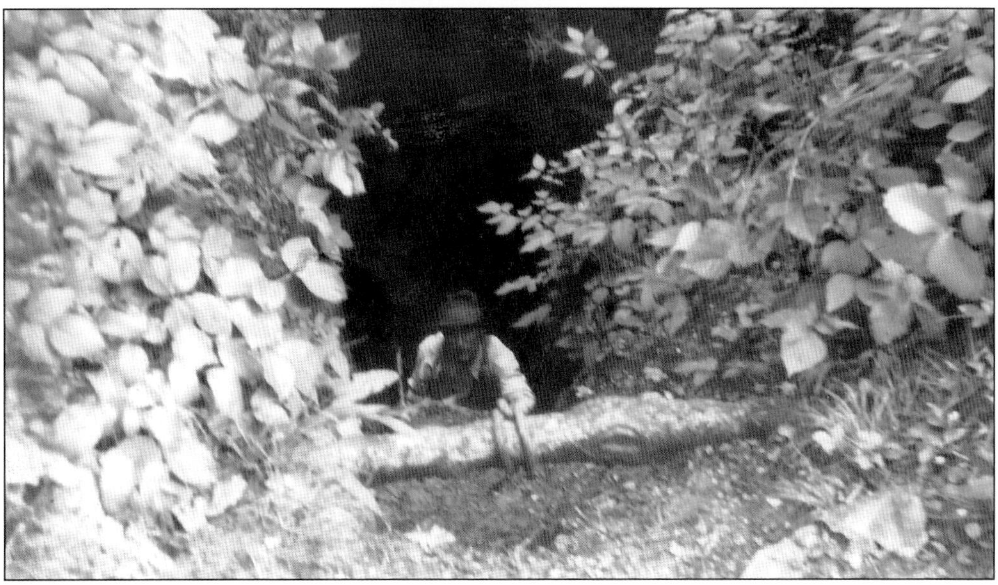

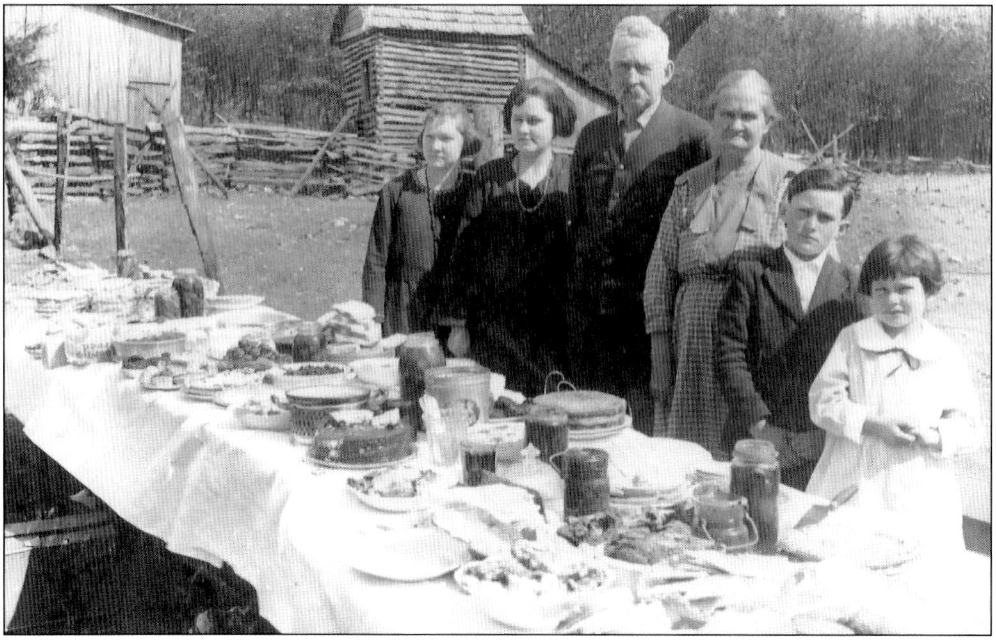

John and Eliza Hensley celebrate their 50th wedding anniversary with grandchildren Marie Gilley and Doris, Floyd, and Lois Hensley. Celebrations like these often consisted of a dinner for family and friends served in the yard. Tables were loaded with a variety of food brought by guests. In this case, canned goods rest next to a silver casserole and a lard bucket in the center of the table.

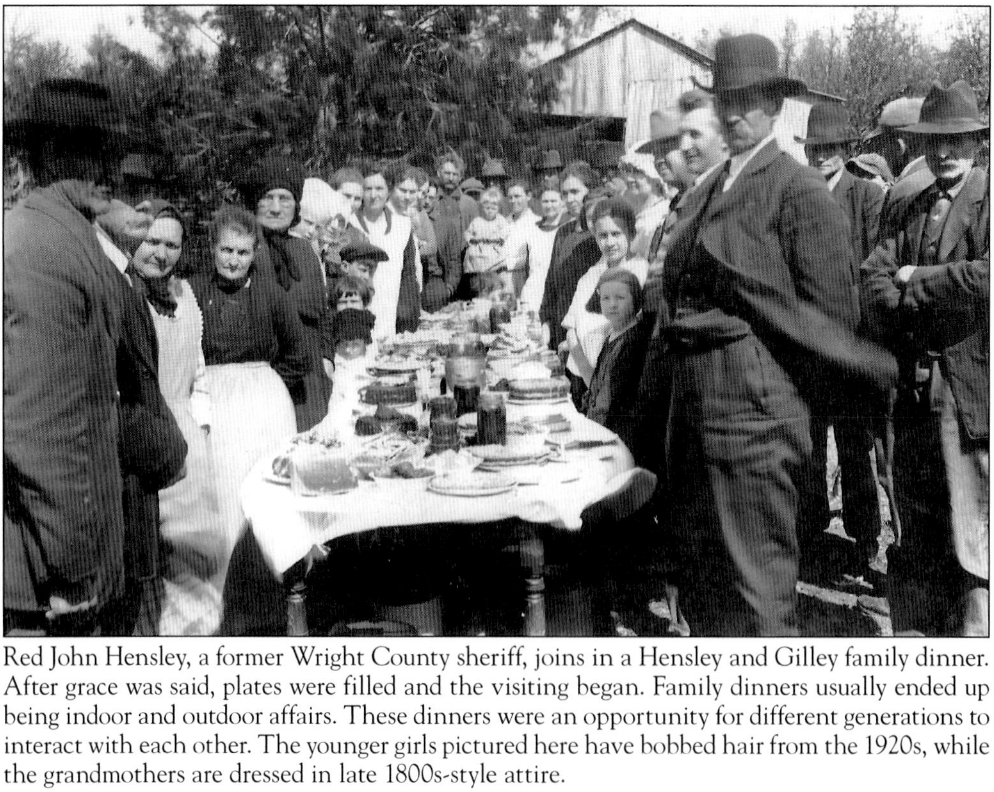

Red John Hensley, a former Wright County sheriff, joins in a Hensley and Gilley family dinner. After grace was said, plates were filled and the visiting began. Family dinners usually ended up being indoor and outdoor affairs. These dinners were an opportunity for different generations to interact with each other. The younger girls pictured here have bobbed hair from the 1920s, while the grandmothers are dressed in late 1800s-style attire.

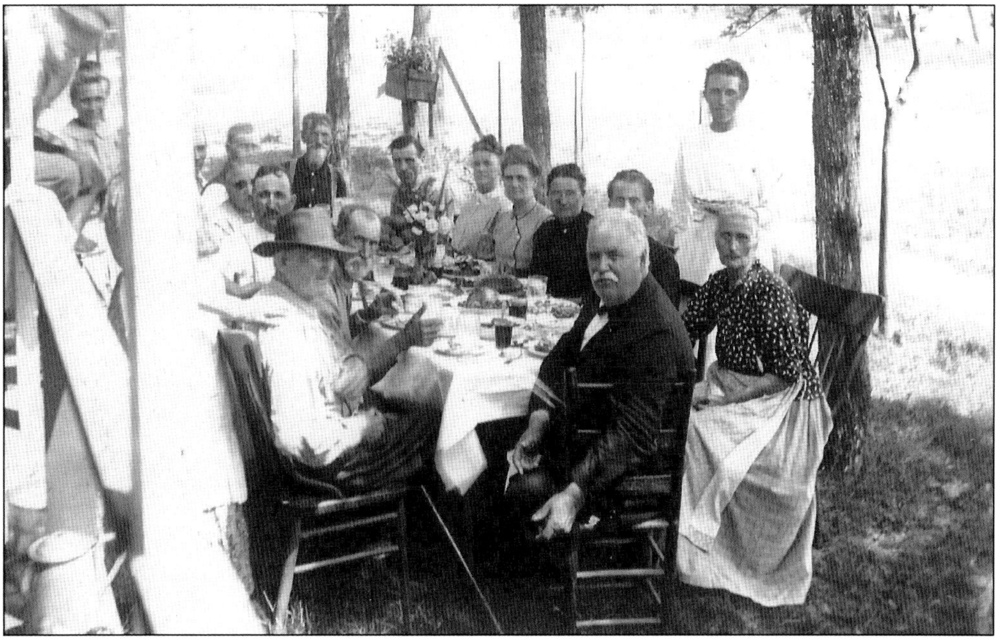

After-church dinners offered families and friends an opportunity to stay connected through socializing. Teenagers were given the chance to form friendships that sometimes led to courtship and marriage. Guests joined each other at the appointed home after church services. Tables were brought outside and put in the shade of the trees. They were covered with the hostess's finest linens, which were freshly starched and ironed, and her best glassware and dishes. Women brought side dishes or desserts for which they were locally known. Either a visiting minister or the eldest man usually asked the blessing. The older members ate first and then the table was cleared and reset for the younger ones. In these pictures, members of the Gilley, Newton, Cunningham, Rippee, and King families have gathered for lunch after attending services at Pleasant Valley Church and Mission Temple Church.

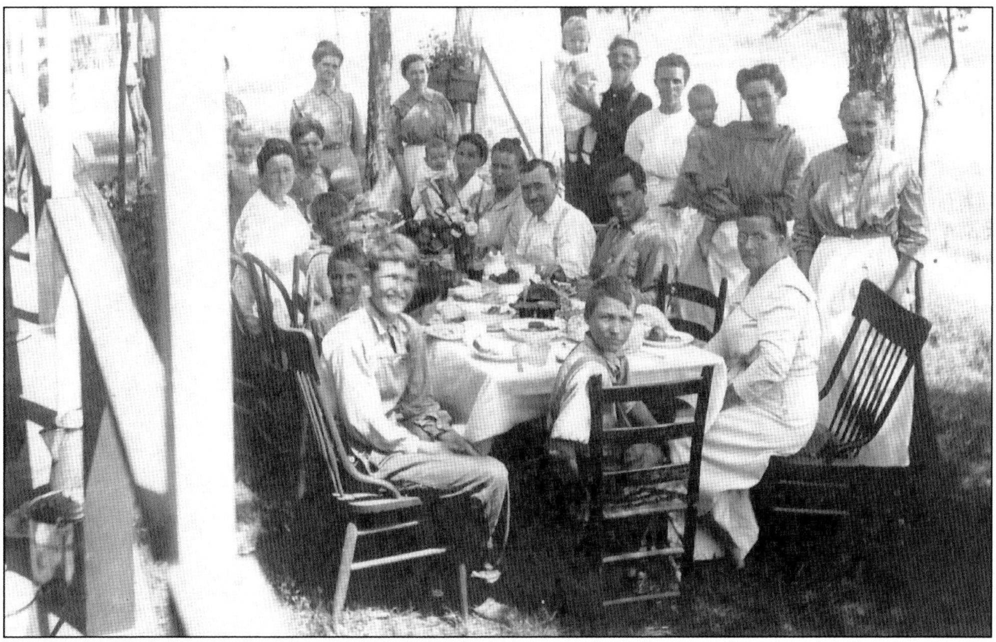

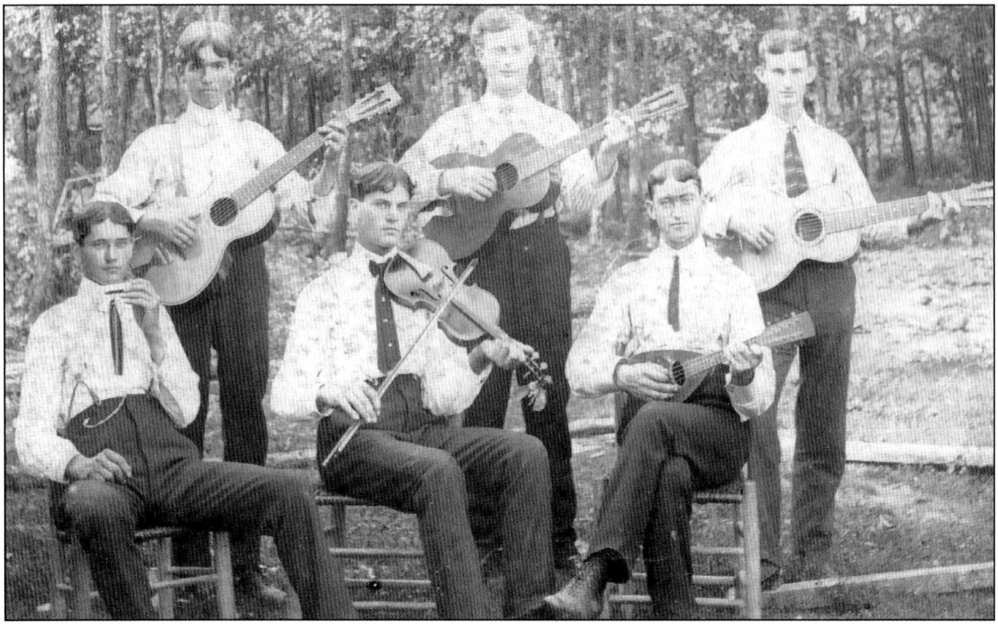

Music has always been an important ingredient to communities. It lifts the spirits, praises God, and echoes through the churches, schools, and community halls. Local musicians were always ready to play for a barn dance or a music party at a private home where guests rolled up the rugs and danced. Many of these incredible musicians were self-taught and could play up to 100 songs by ear.

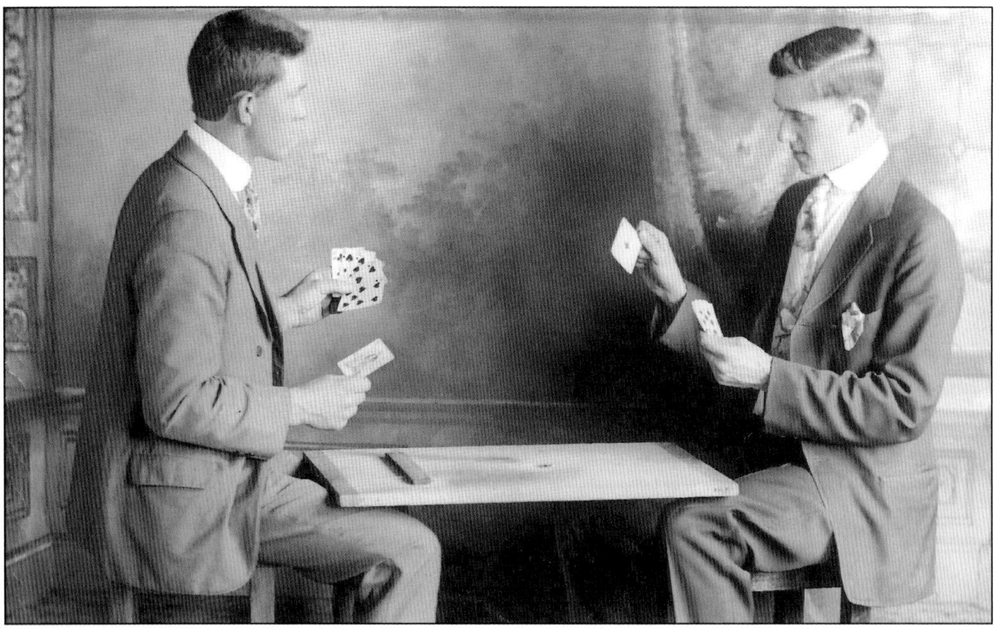

Dorthea Long once said, "Photography takes an instant out of time, altering life by holding it still." Until George Eastman created the first commercial camera in 1888, photography was an art that only the wealthy could afford. Traveling photographers helped document the lives of many rural communities. Studios also staged photographs of interest, such as this one of Verner Rippee (left) and John Baker, taken by Carl Mackey inside a photography studio in Mansfield.

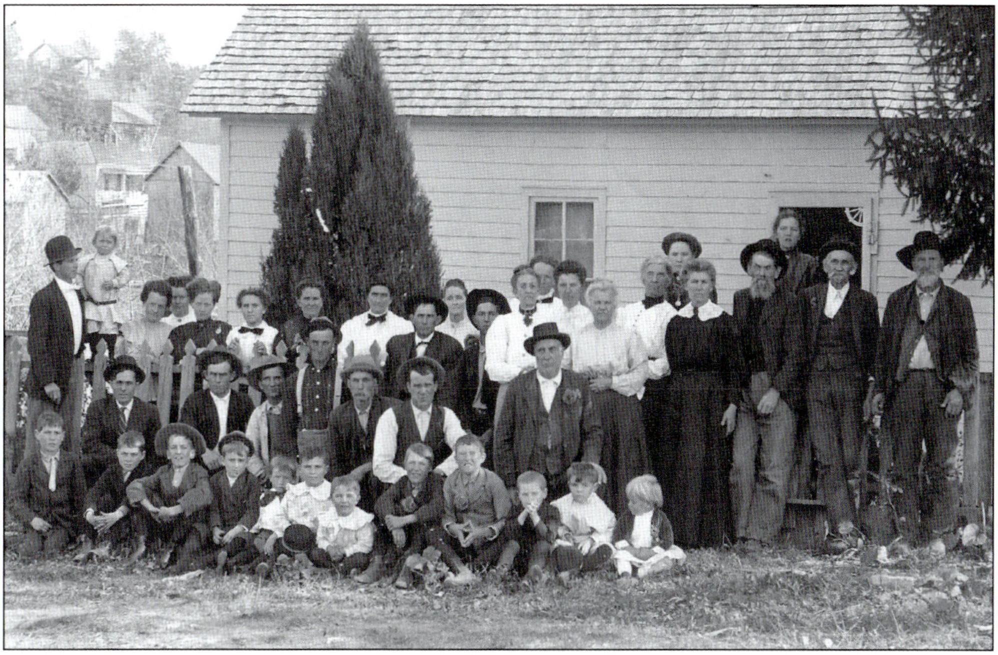

One tradition characteristic of the Ozark culture is the family gathering held on Sunday afternoons. The White family is assembled at their home on Rock Road just south of town. In the background on the left are some of the buildings in town. The man kneeling down, second from the left, is Walter White. His wife, Julia, is the third woman from the left, standing behind the fence.

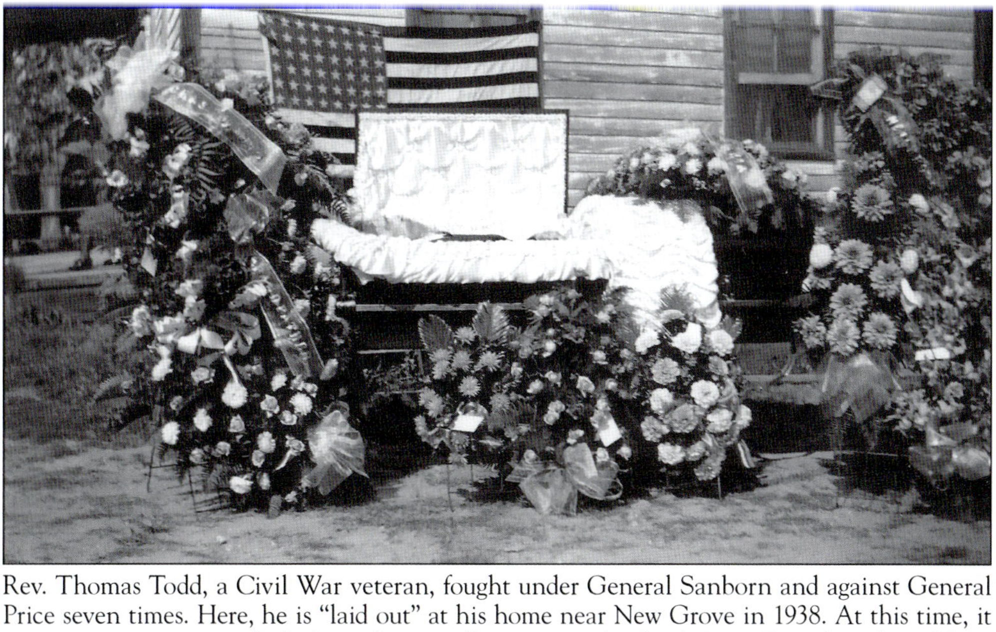

Rev. Thomas Todd, a Civil War veteran, fought under General Sanborn and against General Price seven times. Here, he is "laid out" at his home near New Grove in 1938. At this time, it was customary to stop all clocks and cover all mirrors at the death hour. Friends and neighbors would then call on the family to show their respect and to "sit up with the dead."

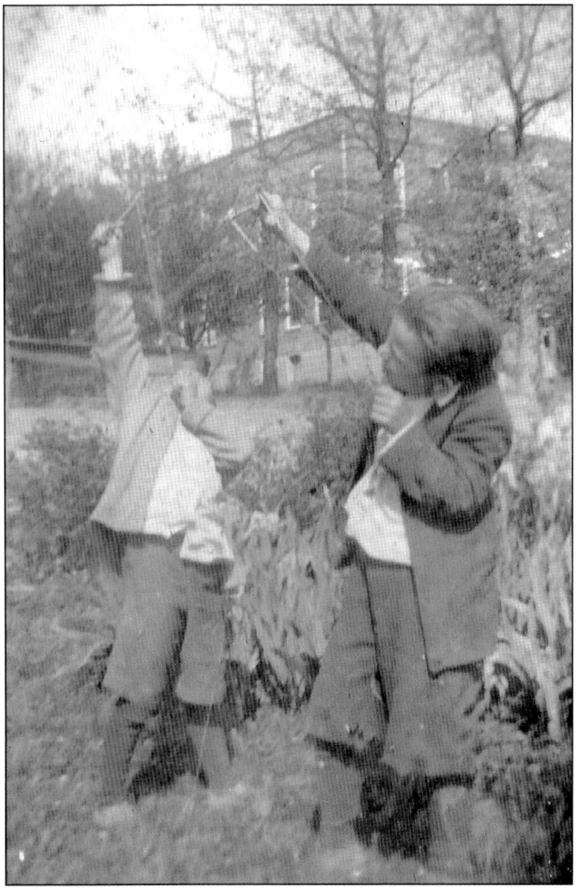

Slingshots, made from forked branches and strips of inner tube, were used by young boys primarily for fun but also for hunting. However, instead of using a slingshot, Missouri Sports Hall of Famer Carl Mays threw rocks to kill game. His arm and aim were such that, even as a young boy, he consistently brought rabbits and squirrels home to feed his struggling family.

The patriarch of the Dennis family, Joseph Harrison Dennis, is on the left beside his sons, from left to right, Marve, Ural, Roy, Dwight, and A.B. "Bill" Dennis in this c. 1918 photograph. Joseph had given each of his sons a colt out of his favorite mare. Here, they pose with the mare and her offspring on the square during the Mansfield Carnival and Stock Show.

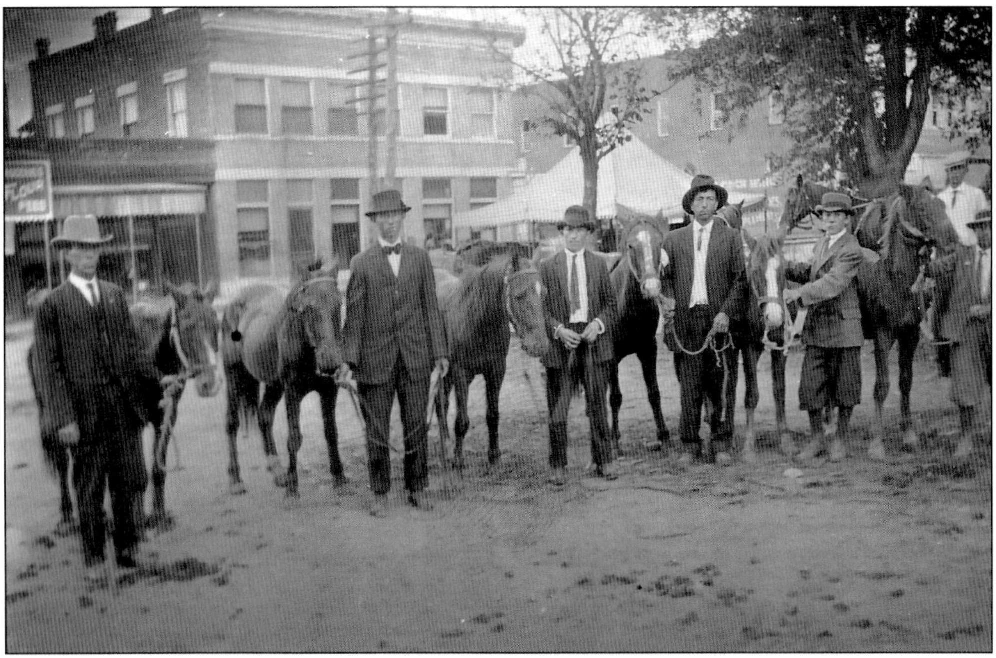

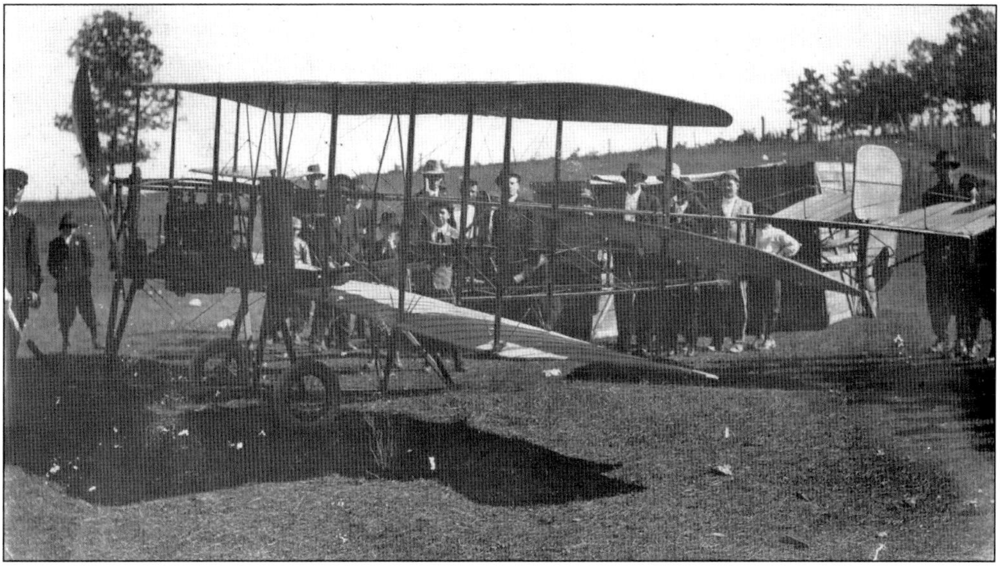

During street fairs and carnivals, death-defying activities attracted huge crowds. This airplane was brought in by train and then assembled in town. People were charged 15¢ to be strapped down to the wings and taken for a ride. The plane was then taken apart, put in a wagon, and hauled to Hartville for another celebration. Afterwards, it was hauled back to Mansfield to be put on the train again.

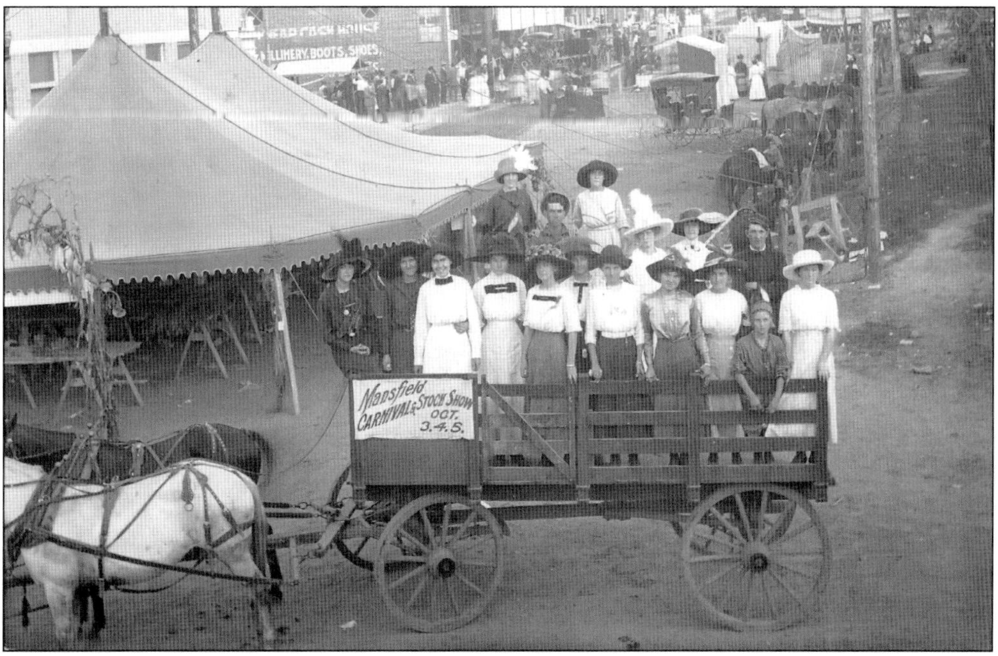

Mansfield became famous for its street fairs, with people coming from as far away as northern Arkansas to enter contests for livestock, produce, and baked goods. In this 1912 photograph are, from left to right, (first row) unidentified, Bess Turner, Gertrude Stone, Lula Carter, Zella Coday, Jewell Hoover, Eula Tripp, Mable Hoover, Leona Hoover, and unidentified; (second row) Maude Coday, Lester Stone, Mable Coday, Blanche Moore, Vada Coday, and Elmer Strong.

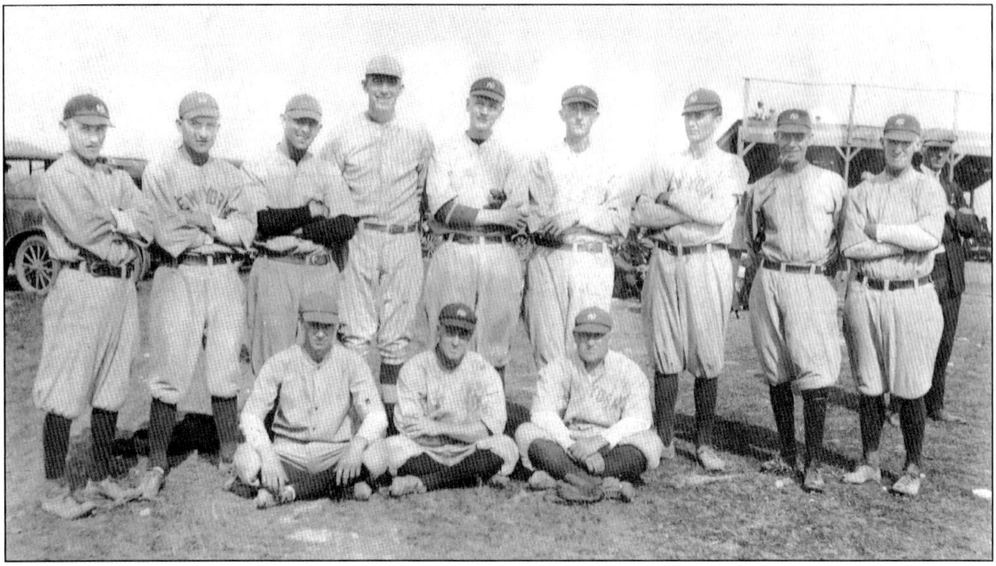

Mansfield's answer to the barnstorming teams of the 1920s was the Grays. They won 90 percent of their games, proudly wearing Yankee uniforms donated by Carl Mays. Pictured above, from left to right, are (first row) Jack Rippee, Walter "Speedy" Coday (second base), and Ural "Hip Pocket" Dennis (left field); (second row) Pete "Fleetfoot" Freeman (center field), Donnie Stone, Cotton Strong (pitcher), Slim Owens, Doc McGinnis (third base), Guy Pool (catcher), Herb "Banty" Short (right field), Dee "Old Lefty" Gaskill (pitcher), and Orel "Lippy" Dennis (first base). Below, the 1927 Grays are, from left to right, (front row) Coday, Frank White (shortstop), U. Dennis, and Raymond "the Arm" Brasher (catcher); (second row) Doc Clark, Freeman, Strong, O. Dennis, Fred Raby, Short, Henry Nichols, McGinnis, and Gaskill. Other team members were Bull Carter, China Carter, Glen Craig, Dwight Dennis, Frank Dennis, Marve Dennis, Roy Dennis, Smith Fry, Wes Fry, Slim Harris, Ernie Roy, Silas Seal, and Alva Turner.

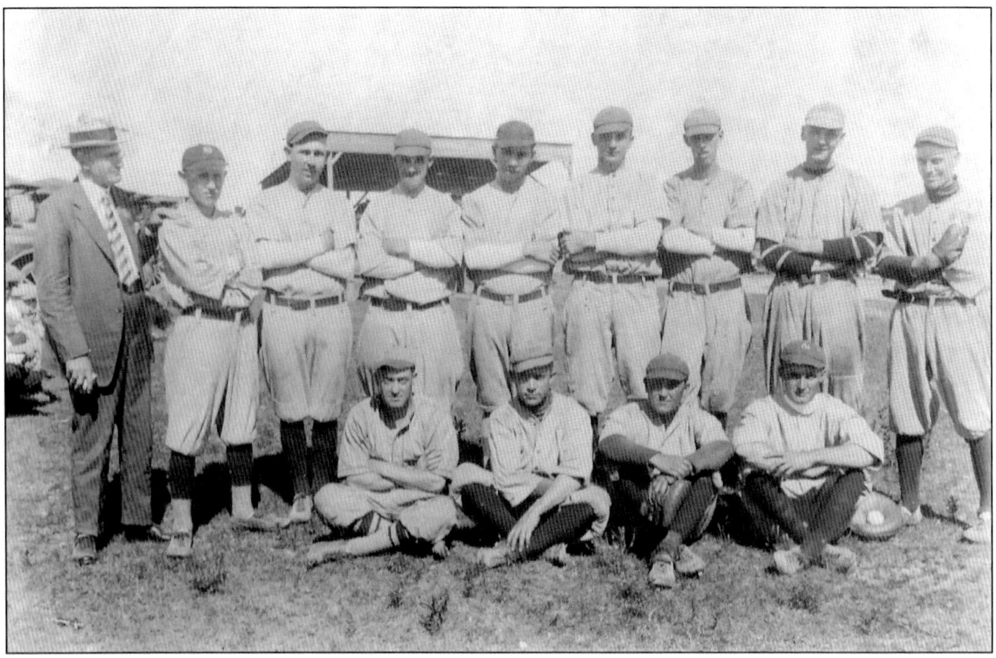

Eight

LEAVING A LEGACY

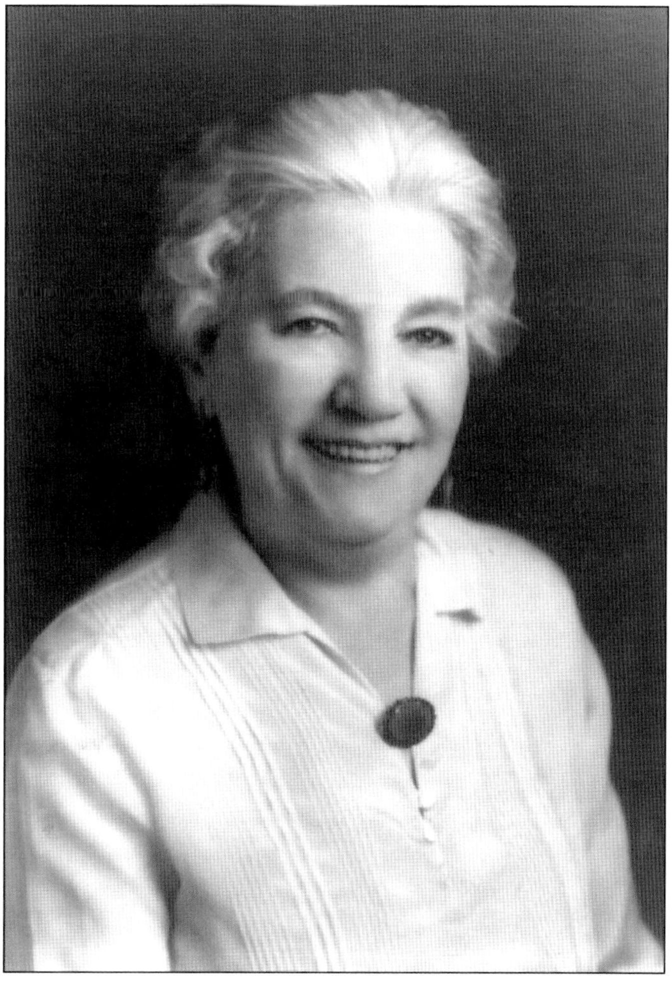

Laura Elizabeth Ingalls, America's frontier girl, was born February 7, 1867, in Pepin County, Wisconsin. Laura, daughter of Charles and Caroline Quiner Ingalls, came from pioneer stock. "Pa" had itchy feet, always looking for a better life for his family. Consequently, Laura spent her childhood traveling back and forth between Missouri, Indian Territory (Kansas), Wisconsin, Minnesota, and Iowa before settling in South Dakota; "Ma" decided they would not move again.

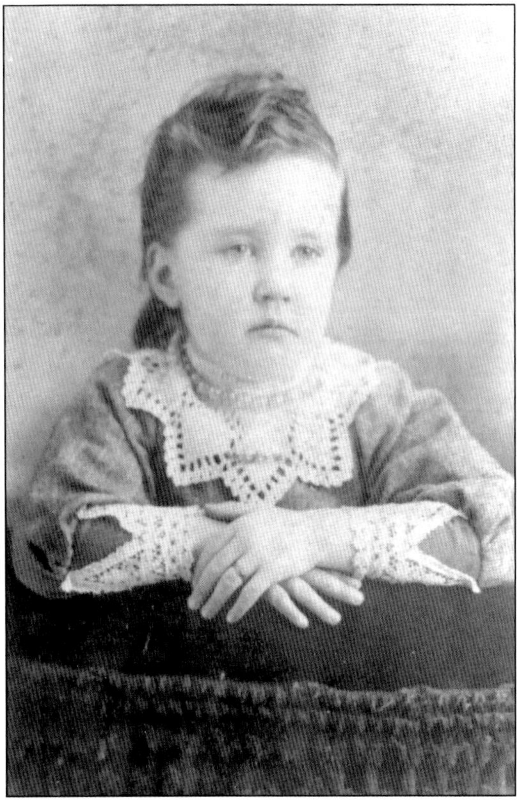

While living in DeSmet, South Dakota, Laura caught the eye of local farmer Almanzo Wilder. They married August 25, 1885, and began wheat farming. Their daughter Rose, pictured here, was born December 5, 1886. After four years of misfortune, including the loss of three crops, Almanzo suffering a stroke from diphtheria, the loss of an infant son, and their house burning down, the Wilders joined Almanzo's family in Spring Valley, Minnesota.

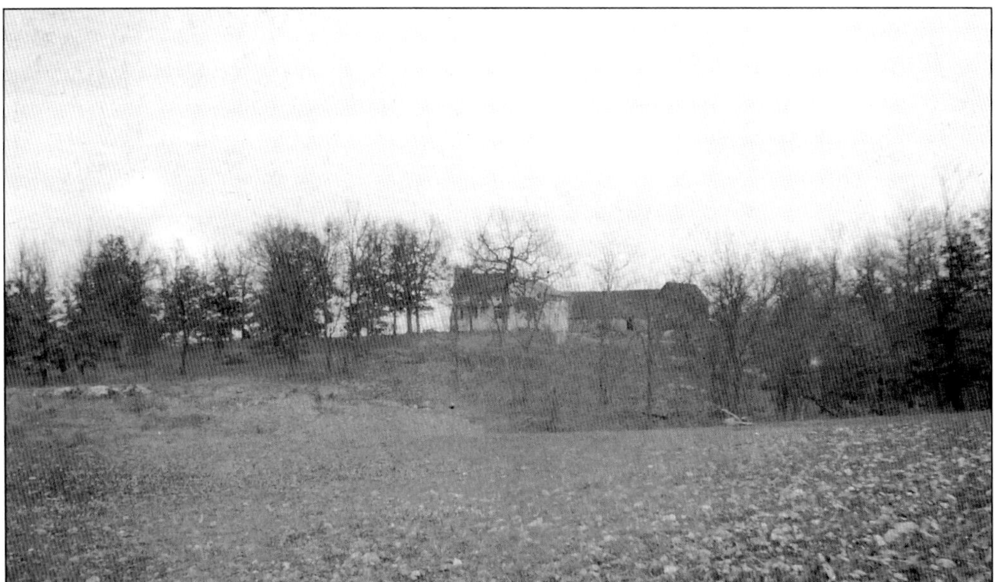

Because of Almanzo's health, the Wilders traveled to Westville, Florida. Seeing no improvements in his wellbeing, they returned to DeSmet in 1892. While there, they heard of land development in the Ozarks. Some friends scouted the area and brought Laura the biggest, reddest apple she had ever seen. In 1894, they moved to Mansfield, Missouri, where they purchased Rocky Ridge Farm, seen here. This is the only known picture showing the barn.

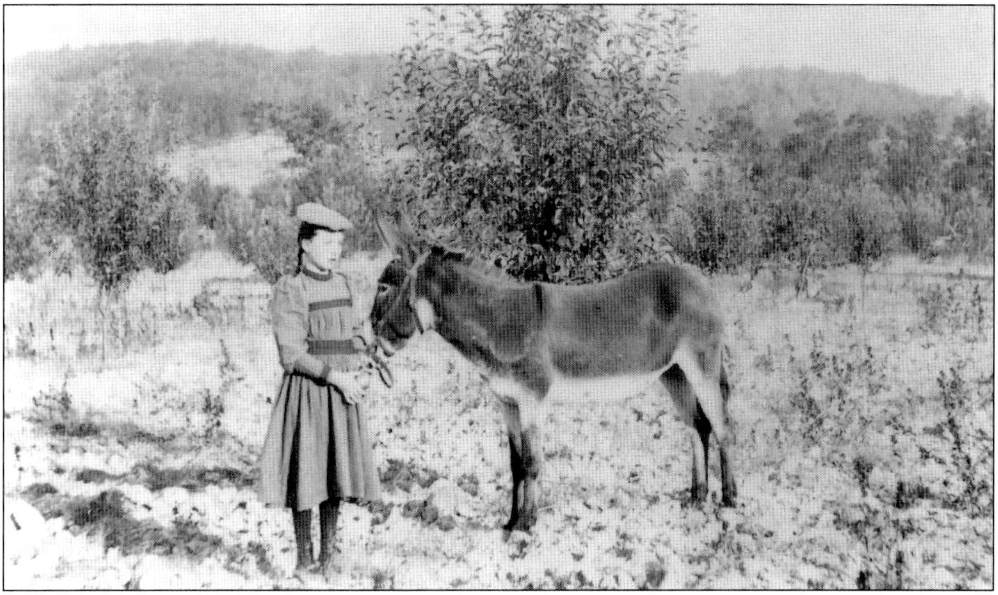

When the Wilders first moved to Rocky Ridge, they lived in a log cabin, but later built a two-room house. Times were tough. Almanzo sold stove wood in town for 75¢ a load. Laura sold eggs, and Rose picked berries to sell for 10¢ a gallon. Rose is shown with her donkey Spookendyke, a gift from her father. Rose hated riding him to school because he would balk and throw her off.

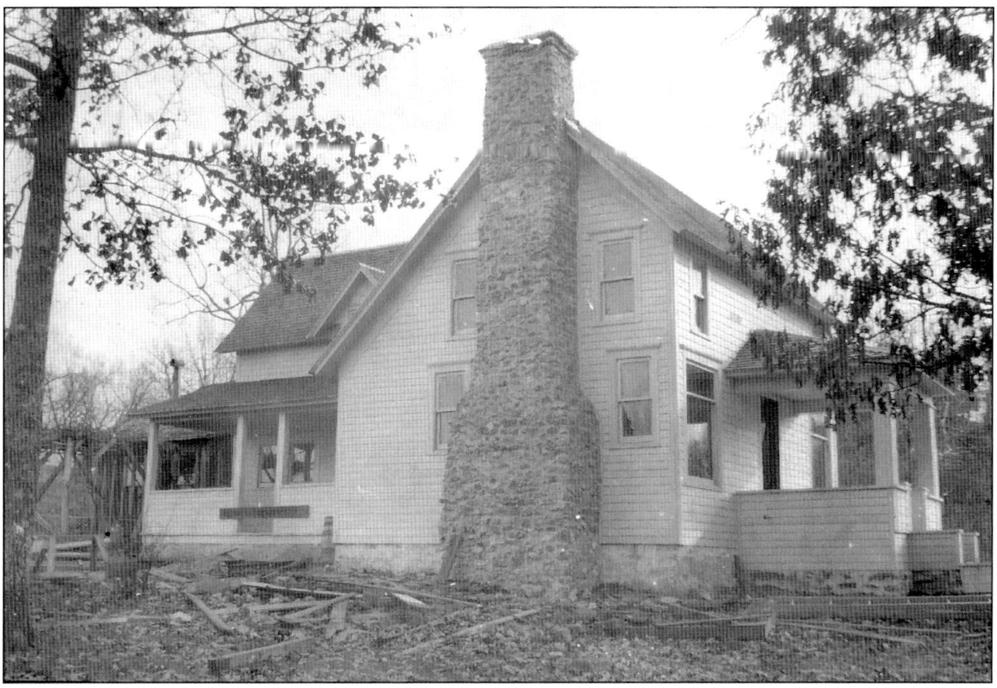

Needing more money, in 1898, the Wilders decided to rent a house in town for $5 a month. Almanzo worked as a drayman and later as a salesman for an oil company. Laura kept the books and sold lunches from their house. During a visit to Mansfield, Almanzo's parents bought the house in town and gave it to them. In 1911, they sold it and remodeled their two-room house at Rocky Ridge into the farmhouse pictured here.

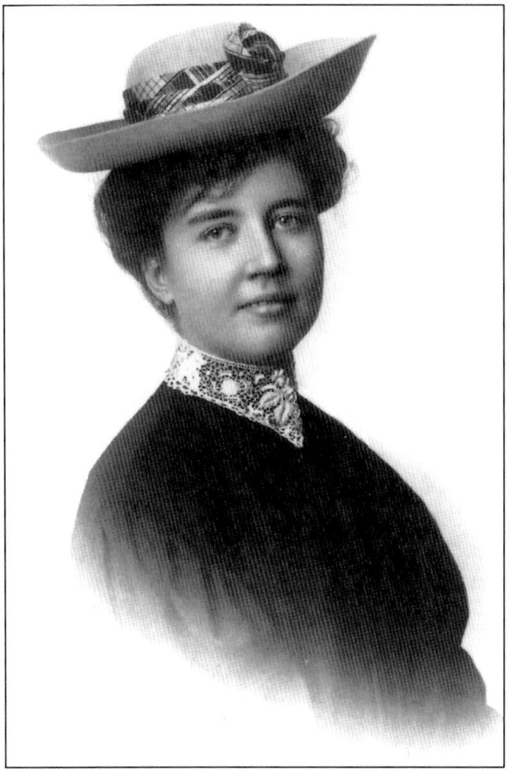

In 1903, Almanzo's sister Eliza Jane and her son Wilder visited them. Because Rose wanted to attend a high school that taught Latin, she returned with them to Crowley, Louisiana. After graduating, Rose, with no money for college, returned to Mansfield and became a telegraph operator. When she was 17, she acquired a telegraphing job in Kansas City that paid $2.50 per week. Rose shortened her hair and her skirts and became known as a bachelor girl, which made her a curiosity when visiting her parents. Western Union sent her to many places, including California, where she met and later married Gillette Lane. Rose's writing career began when she was hired by the *Kansas City Post*. On a trip to Kansas City to visit the Lanes, Laura posed for the studio portrait below. At the same time, Rose posed for the picture at left.

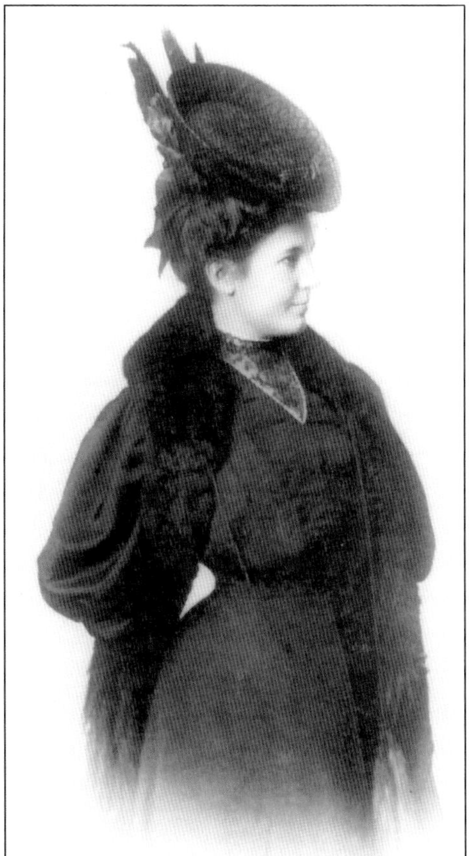

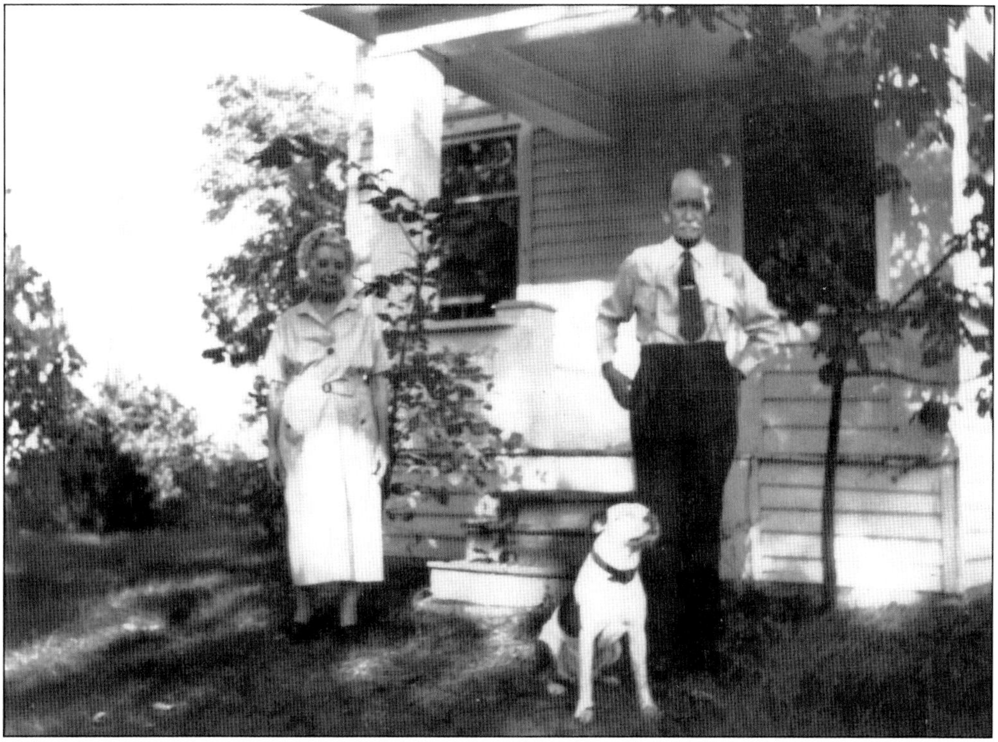

Rocky Ridge Farm flourished, producing bountiful fruit. Apples, pears, and peaches were shipped by train to Memphis and St. Louis. The milk from Almanzo's Jersey cows and the eggs from Laura's Leghorn hens brought prime prices in Mansfield. Gaining recognition as an expert on poultry, Laura served as a main speaker at farmers' meetings. The *Missouri Ruralist* asked her to submit articles, which eventually led to her writing her own column.

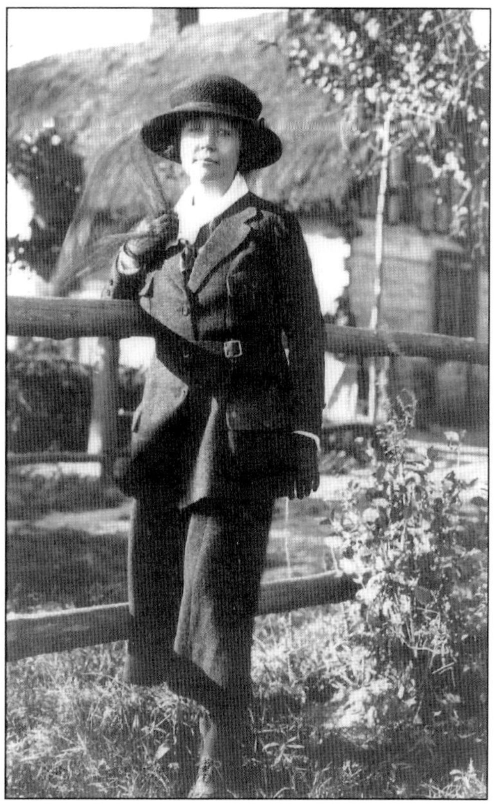

In California, Rose excelled in real estate, selling millions of acres until World War I began. She then became a journalist for the *San Francisco Bulletin*, interviewing celebrities of the day. Rose and Gillette Lane divorced in 1918. In 1920, Rose's freelance articles led to a job in the publicity department of the American Red Cross in Paris, France. Here, Rose is shown in Brittany, France, on one of her world travels.

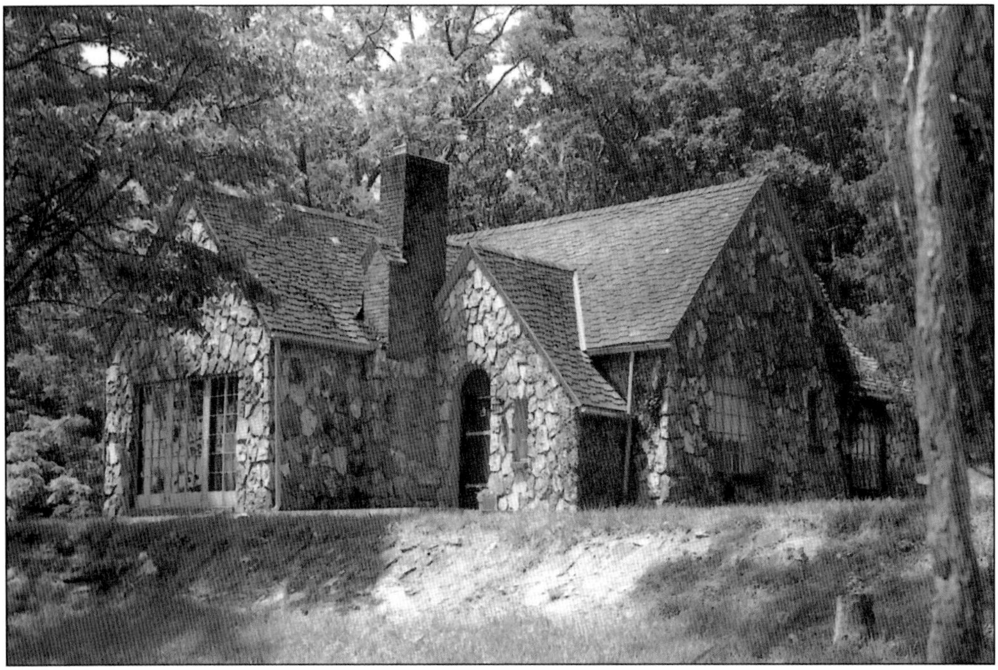

In 1923, Rose returned to Rocky Ridge. The sleeping porch on the second floor became her studio where she wrote books, in addition to the short stories and articles she wrote for nationally published magazines. She earned enough money to buy her parents "Isabelle," a 1923 Buick. In 1928, Rose began construction on an English-style, five-room stone cottage, pictured above, known as the Rock House. She gave her parents the key on Christmas day. Laura began to write her autobiography *Pioneer Girl.* No one was interested in publishing it until she rewrote it. In 1931, Harper & Brothers published *Little House in the Big Woods.* Laura wrote her first four books while living in the Rock House. In 1937, after Rose moved to New York, Laura and Almanzo moved back to the farmhouse, seen below. Laura finished the Little House series there.

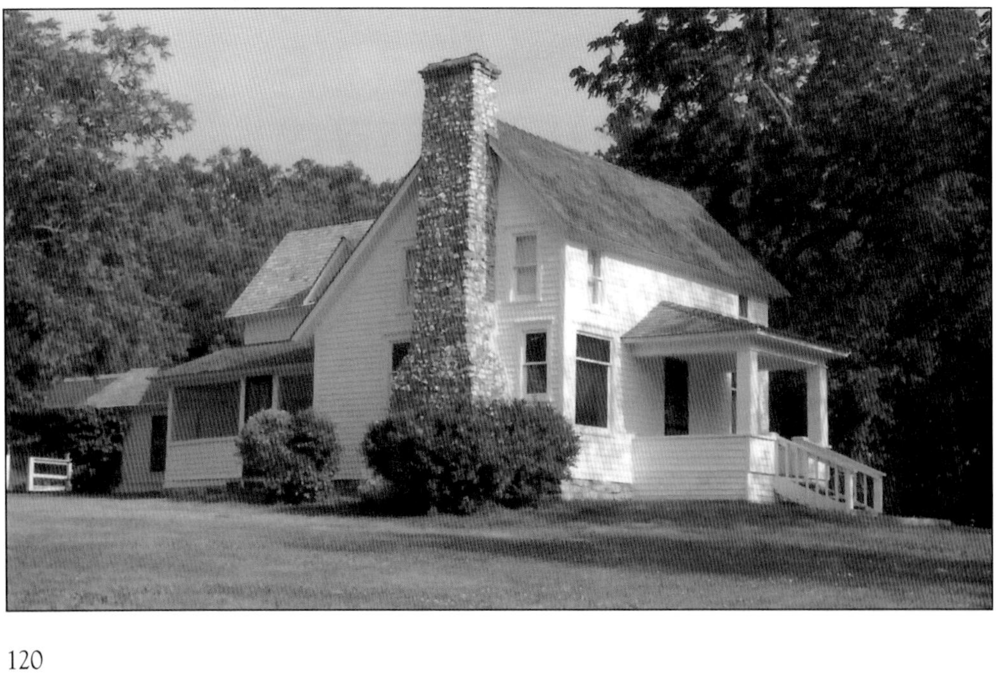

In 1938, Laura began her Dakota books and wanted to return to DeSmet for research. Since Silas Seals had to close his service station because Highway 60 was being paved, Almanzo asked him to drive them. The three of them, plus Silas's wife Neta, turned the trip into a long vacation through 12 states. From that point on, Laura and Almanzo, pictured here, considered Silas and Neta Seals their closest friends.

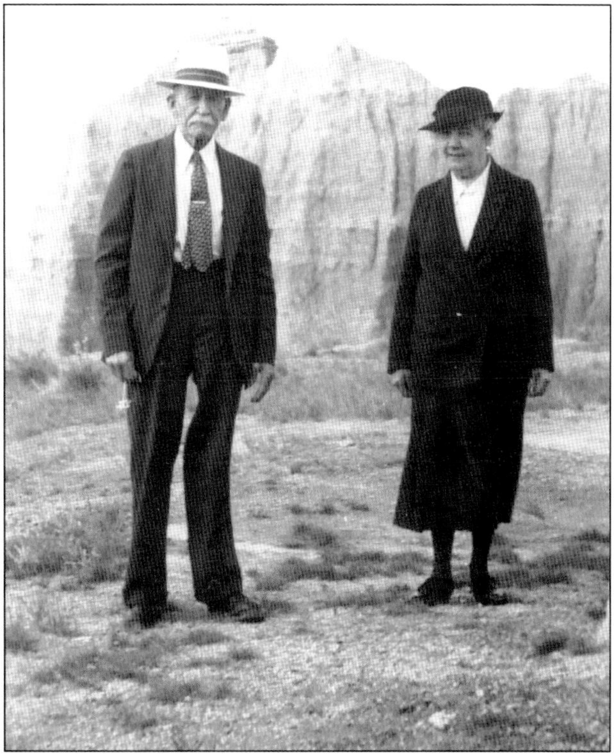

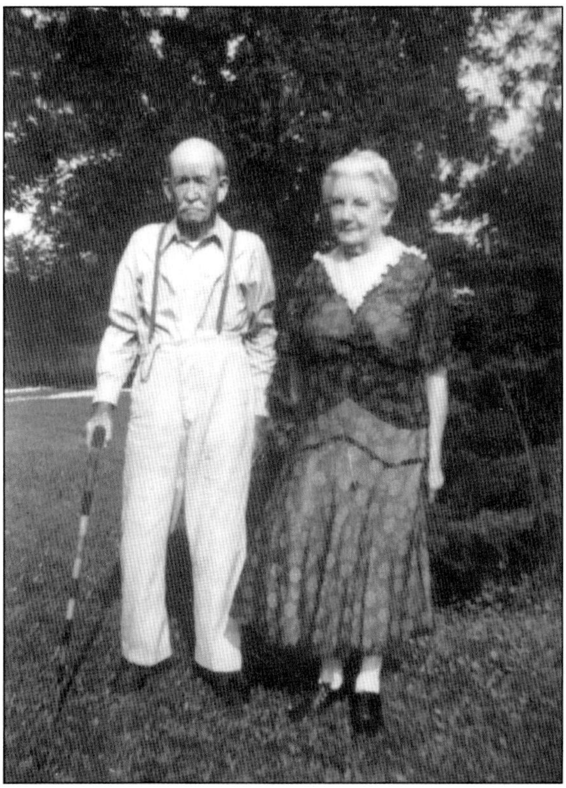

Laura and Almanzo continued living on Rocky Ridge. In this photograph, Almanzo is 91 years old, and Laura is 81. They loved playing cribbage, reading their magazines and newspapers, and working in the garden. The popularity of Laura's Little House books continued to grow, but Almanzo's health began to decline, leading to a heart attack. On October 23, 1949, a second heart attack resulted in his death. He was 92 years old.

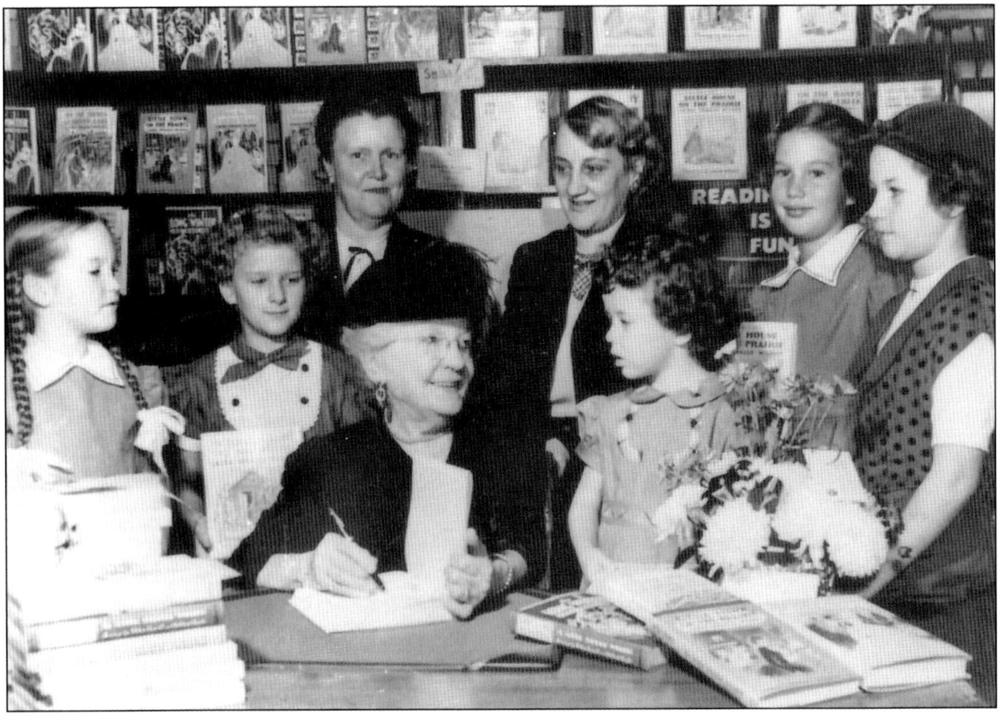

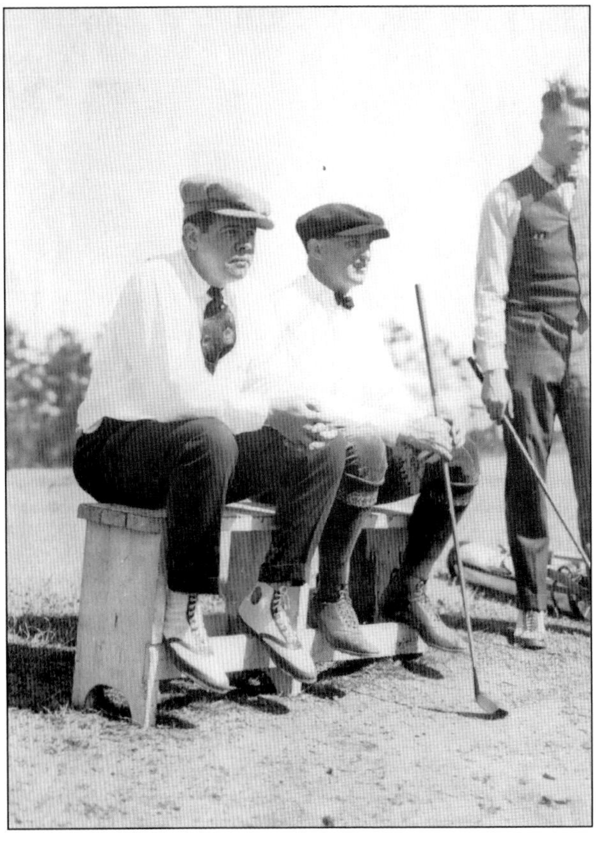

On September 28, 1951, Mansfield honored Laura by naming the town library after her. In the fall of 1952, she made a public appearance at Brown's Bookstore in Springfield, Missouri, to autograph books for her faithful fans, as pictured above. In 1954, the American Library Association announced the creation of the Laura Ingalls Wilder Award. On February 10, 1957, Laura died at her home. Laura, Almanzo, and Rose are buried in the Mansfield Cemetery.

Former Mansfield resident Carl William Mays played with and pitched against some of Major League Baseball's greatest players. Mays and his roommate Babe Ruth were called up the final week of the Red Sox 1914 regular season from the minor league team the Providence Grays. They had just pitched the Grays to the International League Pennant. Ruth debuted promptly as a pitcher; however, Mays did not join the roster until the following season.

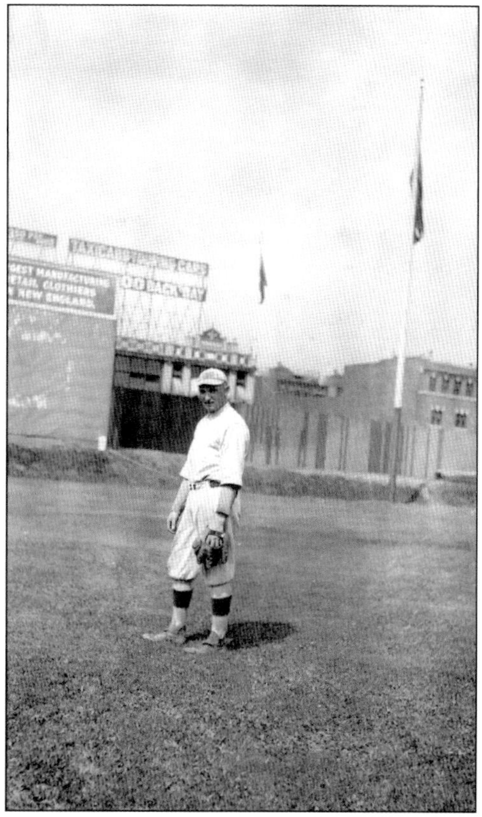

Carl William "Sub" Mays, Mansfield's native son, pitched for four major league teams: the Boston Red Sox, the New York Yankees, the Cincinnati Reds, and the New York Giants. During his career, he threw 29 shutouts and 862 strikeouts in 490 games, posted 208 wins against 126 losses, touted a 2.92 ERA, and became the first pitcher to achieve 20-win seasons in both the American and National Leagues. On August 30, 1918, he pitched two nine-inning victories on the same day against Philadelphia. He pitched three complete games in the 1921 World Series without walking a man and held the World Series record of thirty-one-and-two-thirds consecutive innings without a walk. Carl's lifetime batting average of .268 ranks him with the best-hitting pitchers of all time.

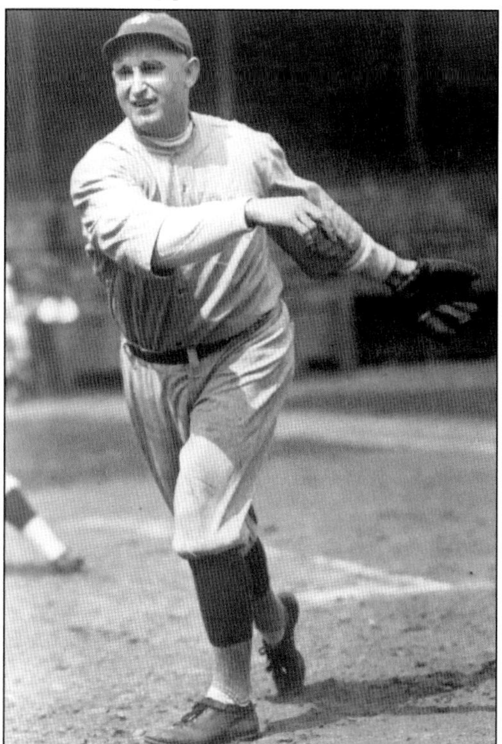

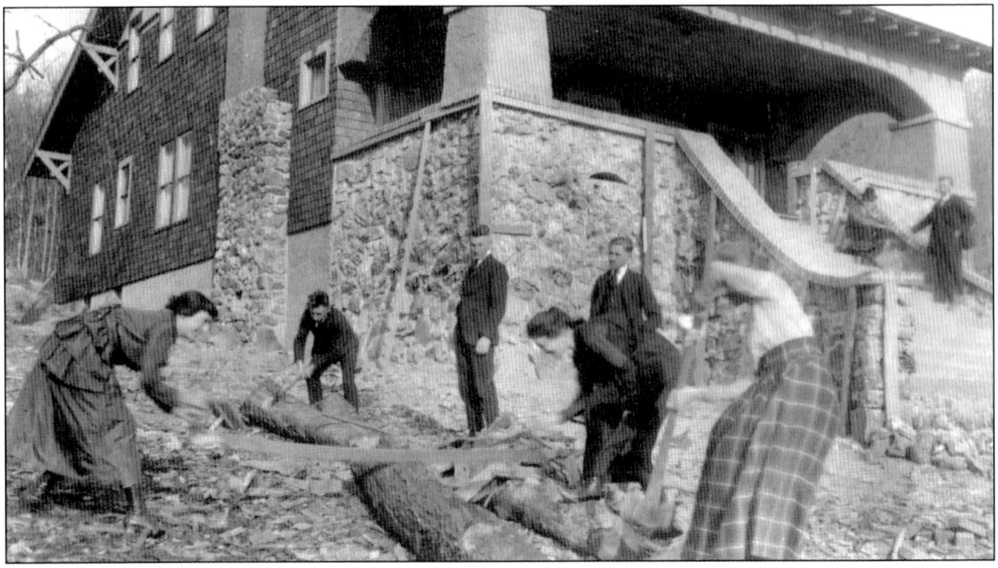

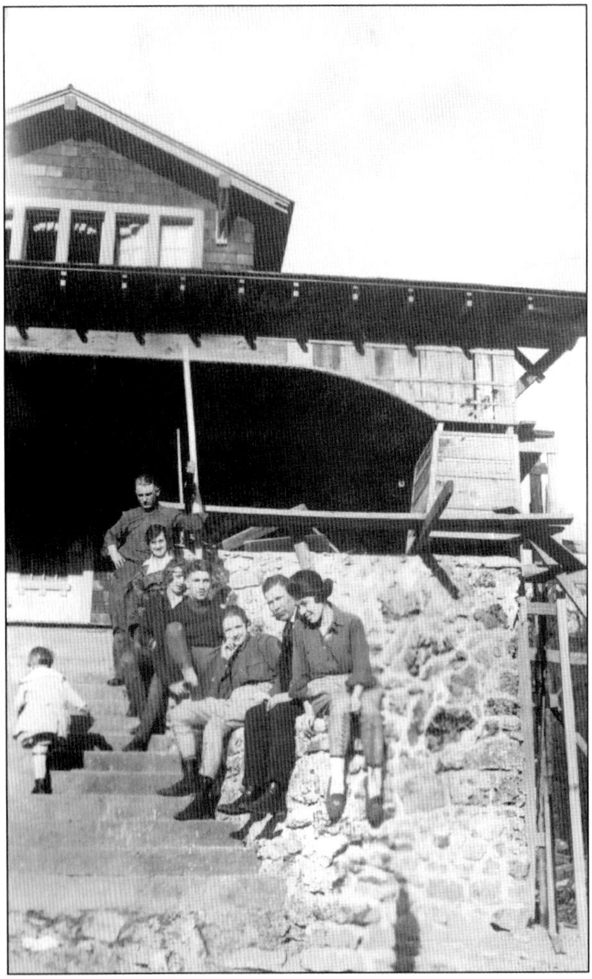

Carl Mays's first year in the majors was with the World Series–winning Boston Red Sox. He used a portion of his $4,000 cut, along with a bank loan from his friend Gorman "Pete" Freeman at the Bank of Mansfield, to finance the construction of a new house in Prairie Hollow for his mother, Callie. The Mays Mansion, as it was commonly known, had its own lighting system, bathroom, and sun porch where Callie Mays entertained her Sunday school class. On March 26, 1919, Mays received a call from Freeman that his mother's house had burned to the ground. While in Mansfield making arrangements for the rebuilding of the house, Carl pitched six innings each for both Mansfield High and rival team Mountain Grove. Carl's family and friends, both local and professional, aided in the reconstruction.

Mays's early years in Prairie Hollow were filled with farmwork, attending church, and going to school with his seven siblings. Following the death of their father, William H., a Methodist minister, Mays recalled how his older siblings had to leave school to help their mother. Hard work and baseball were core subjects with Mays. He had been a major leaguer four years when he and Marjorie Fredricka "Freddie" Madden, a student of the New England Conservatory of Music, married. They were blessed with a daughter, Betty, pictured at right with her parents. Their son, Carl Jr. ("Bill"), is seen below with his dad. Bill was born in Springfield, since, as he said, "Dad had to come home for bird season." Freddie died suddenly on February 22, 1934, at the age of 36, leaving a 12-year-old daughter, a seven-year-old son, and a grieving husband.

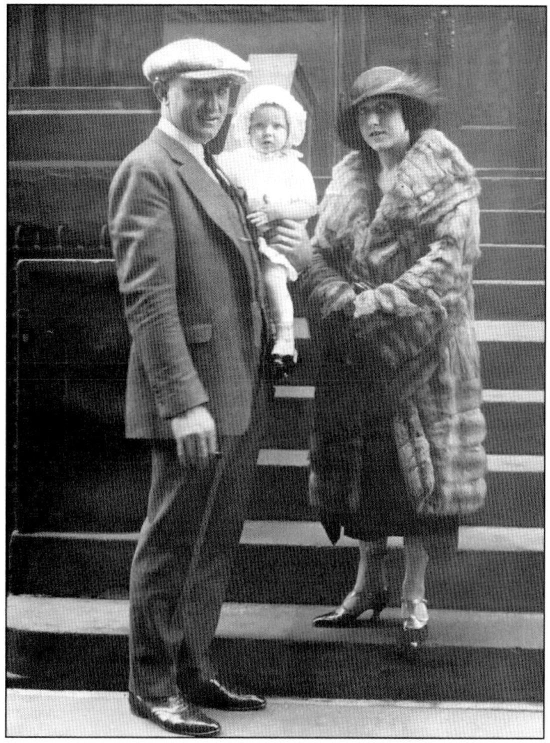

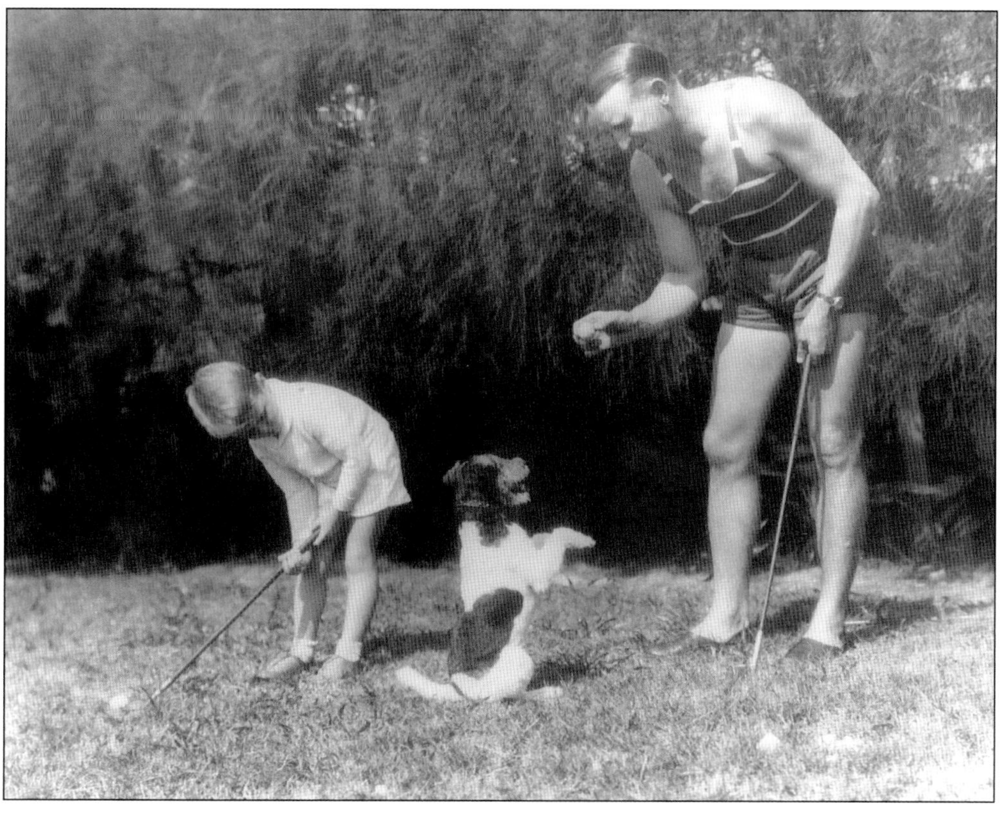

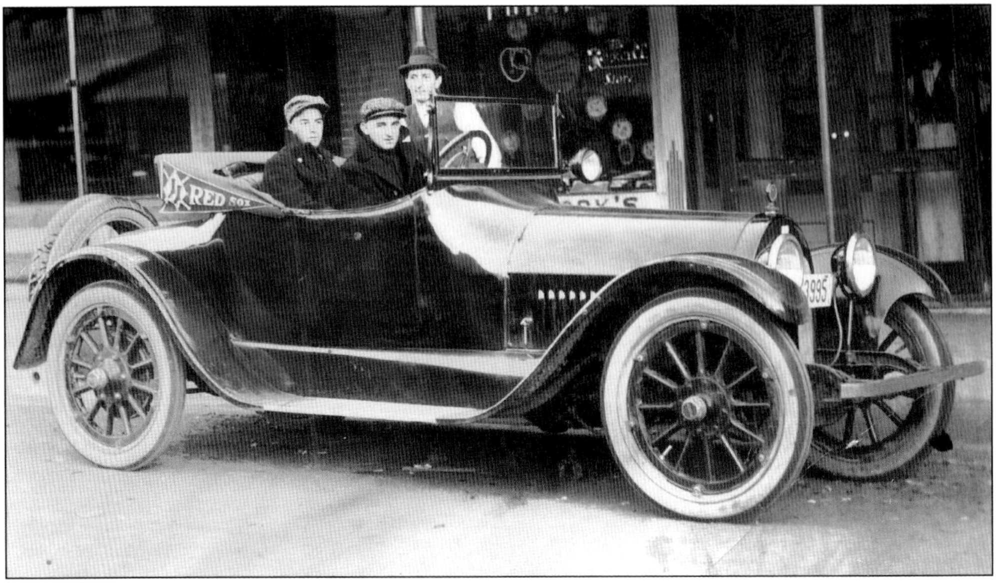

Second only to family and baseball was Mays's penchant for nice cars. For 15 years following his retirement in 1929, Mays conducted the Oregon Baseball School for Boys. For the next 15 years, he scouted for the Cleveland Indians, Kansas City Athletics, and Milwaukee Braves. Later, Mays and his wife, Esther, operated a hunting and fishing lodge near Dayville, Oregon.

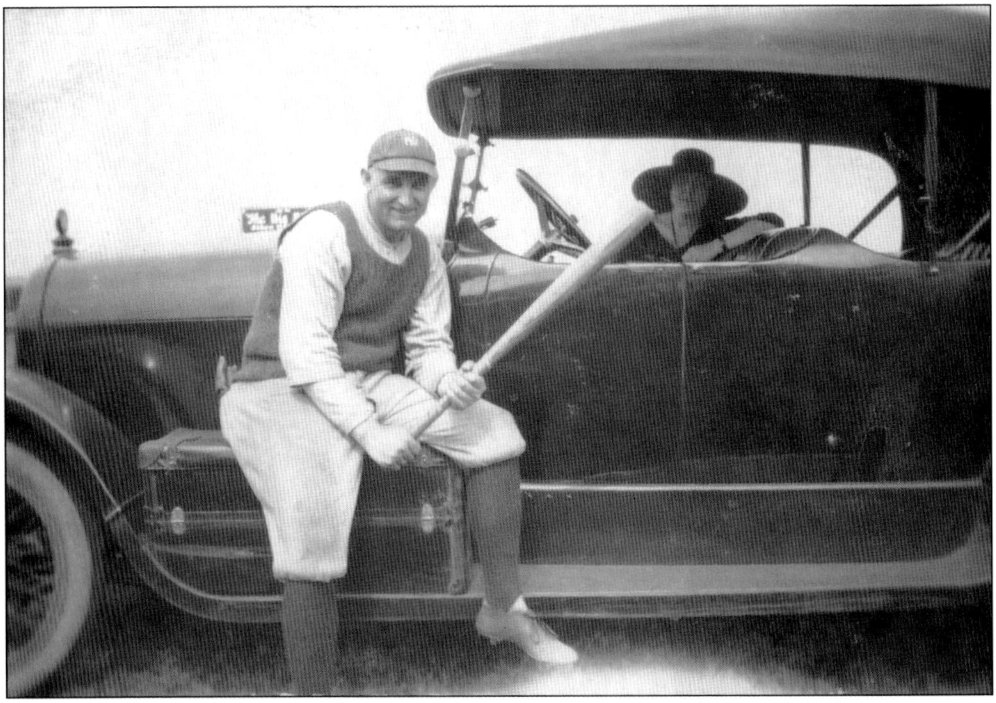

It was no accident that Carl William Mays became a major league pitcher. Hard work, commitment, and determination led the way, but most of all, it was his courage that sustained him through tragedy and heartache. His baseball glove, the only one he ever used, is housed at the National Baseball Hall of Fame in Cooperstown, New York. Mays was inducted into the Missouri Sports Hall of Fame in 2009.

About the Organization

The Mansfield Area Historical Society was formed in 2003. Since that time, the membership has continued to grow, incorporating younger members along the way. As a result, the museum, which relies primarily upon donations, has been blessed with enough volunteers to enable the building to be open Monday through Saturday. Additional displays are constantly added to the contents of the museum, so its appearance changes every few months. The museum strives to develop and maintain items of interest not only to local residents, but also to the many visitors who stop on their way to the Laura Ingalls Wilder Museum and Baker Creek Seeds. Laura Ingalls Wilder and Carl Mays, a Major League Baseball player from Mansfield, draw the attention of most visitors to the area. The Mansfield Area Historical Society is extremely proud to showcase not only these two residents, but also all the early settlers and their descendants who struggled to make ends meet in an area rich in farmland and water sources, even though the elements were sometimes unforgiving.

It is hoped that the publication of this book will enable the Mansfield Area Historical Society to continue its attempts to record the fascinating historical events of this area. Those interested in learning more about the organization can visit www.mansfieldhistorical.org.

Discover Thousands of Local History Books Featuring Millions of Vintage Images

Arcadia Publishing, the leading local history publisher in the United States, is committed to making history accessible and meaningful through publishing books that celebrate and preserve the heritage of America's people and places.

Find more books like this at
www.arcadiapublishing.com

Search for your hometown history, your old stomping grounds, and even your favorite sports team.

Consistent with our mission to preserve history on a local level, this book was printed in South Carolina on American-made paper and manufactured entirely in the United States. Products carrying the accredited Forest Stewardship Council (FSC) label are printed on 100 percent FSC-certified paper.

MADE IN THE USA